GW00535560

OUT OF AUSTRIA

OUT OF AUSTRIA

The Austrian Centre in London in World War II

MARIETTA BEARMAN
CHARMIAN BRINSON
RICHARD DOVE
ANTHONY GRENVILLE
JENNIFER TAYLOR

Tauris Academic Studies
LONDON • NEW YORK

Published in 2008 by Tauris Academic Studies,
An imprint of I.B.Tauris & Co Ltd
6 Salem Road, London W2 4BU
175 Fifth Avenue, New York NY 10010

In the United States of America and in Canada distributed by St Martins Press,
175 Fifth Avenue, New York NY 10010
www.ibtauris.com

Copyright © 2008 Marietta Bearman, Charmian Brinson, Richard Dove, Anthony Grenville
and Jennifer Taylor

The right of Marietta Bearman, Charmian Brinson, Richard Dove, Anthony Grenville
and Jennifer Taylor to be identified as the authors of this work has been asserted by the
authors in accordance with the copyright, Designs and Patent Act 1988

All rights reserved. Except for brief quotations in a review, this book, or any part
thereof, may not be reproduced, stored in or introduced into a retrieval system, or
transmitted, in any form or by any means, electronic, mechanical, photocopying,
recording or otherwise, without the prior written permission of the publisher.

International Library of Twentieth Century History 12

ISBN: 978 1 84511 475 6

A full CIP record for this book is available from the British Library
A full CIP record for this book is available from the Library of Congress

Library of Congress Catalog Card Number: available

Printed and bound in India by Thomson Press India Limited
camera-ready copy edited and supplied by the authors

CONTENTS

LIST OF ILLUSTRATIONS

ACKNOWLEDGEMENTS

First and foremost, the authors would like to acknowledge their indebtedness to Daniel Miller whose generous support has made the publication of this book possible. We are also grateful to the Austrian Cultural Forum, London, for their kind assistance as well as to the British Academy, London, for funding much of the research on which the present volume is based.

In addition, we should like to thank the following institutions for permitting us access to archive material and for their help and interest: the Alfred Klahr Gesellschaft, Vienna; the Anglo-Austrian Society/Anglo-Austrian Music Society; London; the Archiv für die Geschichte der Arbeiterbewegung, Vienna; the Archiv für die Geschichte der Soziologie in Österreich, University of Graz (and Reinhard Müller); the BBC Written Archives, Caversham; the British Library, London; the Deutsche Bücherei, Leipzig; the Dokumentationsarchiv des österreichischen Widerstandes, Vienna (and Dr Siegwart Ganglmair); the Hamburger Arbeitsgruppe Exilmusik, University of Hamburg; the Home Office, London (and Mr J.M. Lloyd); the Institute of Germanic & Romance Studies, School of Advanced Studies, University of London; Lambeth Palace Library, London; the National Museum of Labour History, Manchester; the Österreichische Nationalbibliothek (Musiksammlung), Vienna; the Österreichische Exilbibliothek im Literaturhaus, Vienna (and Dr Ursula Seeber); the National Archives, Kew; the Wiener Library, London; the Women's Library, London Metropolitan University; and the Workers' Music Association, London.

We particularly wish to acknowledge the assistance of: Otto Brichacek; Dr Hans Desser; Dr Lisbeth Dichter; Ernst Flesch; Walter J. Foster, OBE; Alice Graber; Dr Primavera Gruber; Dr Richard Grunberger; Schlomo and Franziska Kesten; Prof Dr Georg Knepler; Ruth Kolmer; Hanne Norbert-Miller; Hilde Nürnberger-Mareiner; Dr Rachel O'Higgins; Michael Roeder; Dr Walter Schmidt; Dr Anthony

Scholz; Wolf Suschitzky; Otto Tausig; Prof Dr Erwin Weiss; Prof Arthur West; Dr Heinz Zaslawski.

Finally we wish to thank the Czernin Verlag, Vienna, for their kind permission to reproduce the illustrations that appeared in the German-language version of this book, *Wien–London, hin und retour* (2004).

Austrian Centre, Westbourne Terrace, London W2

INTRODUCTION

RICHARD DOVE

This volume is the first full-length English-language study of the Austrian Centre, an organization set up by Austrian refugees in London shortly before the Second World War. The Centre is very much a paradigm of Austrian exile in Britain: founded as a self-help organization, intended to promote the welfare of Austrian refugees and to offer advice in their dealings with the British authorities, it became a wide-ranging social and cultural organization, which had branches in several parts of Britain and even, through its proxy, the Free Austrian Movement (FAM), aspired to influence British policy towards Austria.

During the early years of its existence, the Austrian Centre focused primarily on relief work, offering advice to Austrian refugees in their dealings with the British authorities and, in 1940, campaigning against the internment of 'enemy aliens'. When the Soviet Union entered the war in June 1941, the Centre was able to pursue a more overtly political role, playing an important part in establishing the Free Austrian Movement which campaigned for the post-war restoration of a democratic and independent Austria. Established in 1941, the FAM was an umbrella organization, to which the Austrian Centre was nominally affiliated: it was in fact the Centre's political mouthpiece, articulating and coordinating the political aspirations of Austrian refugees. The mandarins of the Foreign Office, minuting their mistrust in official memoranda, concluded that the Austrian Centre tail very much wagged the FAM dog.

By 1941, the Austrian Centre had three branches in London, as well as centres in Birmingham and Glasgow. The Centre at Westbourne Terrace in Paddington ran a restaurant, a library and a reading-room. It also promoted a wide range of cultural activities, both directly and through its youth organization Young Austria. It produced a weekly newspaper, *Zeitspiegel*, with a circulation of some 3000, and published a series of books and pamphlets under the imprint Free Austrian Books. It also sponsored a regular musical programme comprising concerts and choral performances, while its centre in Swiss Cottage housed a theatre, the Laterndl, which produced a regular programme of plays and revues, featuring well-known actors and directors. The political aim of this cultural programme was to establish a distinctive Austrian cultural identity, a conscious correlative to the political agenda pursued more overtly through the Free Austrian Movement.

Although the Austrian Centre was probably the most successful organization created by Austrian exiles in any country in the years from 1939 to 1945 – a success achieved despite the daunting material and political difficulties in wartime London – it has attracted very limited scholarly interest, even in Austria. Although there have been useful short accounts of its work in the standard historical studies of Austrian exile in Britain, such as Helene Maimann's *Politik im Wartesaal* and the documentary volume *Österreicher im Exil: Großbritannien*,[1] no work has focused in detail on the Centre and its activities, still less on its interaction with British society, on which its effectiveness and even its very existence depended. Most of the previous publications dealing with the Austrian Centre have been memoirs by former participants which, however indispensable as source material, do not pretend to provide the depth of analysis or the historical objectivity required of an academic study.

The reasons for this striking neglect in Austria are embedded in the country's post-war history, and the climate of academic research it induced. Research into German-speaking exile started much later in Austria than in Germany, beginning only in the 1980s and gathering momentum in the following decade. Austria's reluctance to confront its recent past was both the cause and the consequence of the 'Opferthese', the assertion that the country had been the first victim of Nazi aggression and occupation. This version of the country's recent history, first elaborated by Austrian exiles (not least those connected with the Austrian Centre), was subsequently endorsed by the wartime Allies in the Moscow Declaration of 1943 which stated that Austria had been the first independent country to fall victim to Nazi aggression and described the 1938 Anschluss as an 'occupation'. The Declaration also stated that Austria 'carries responsibility for its participation in the war on Hitler's side', a claim of which little more was heard.

The myth of Austria's victimhood was endorsed by the Western powers in the immediate post-war years; in the new alignments of the Cold War it became an important aspect of Austria's post-war identity. It was later enshrined in the State Treaty of 1955 which formally ended the occupation of Austria and restored full sovereignty to the new Austrian state. The historical construct of the 'Opfergesellschaft', or victim society, became an accepted part of the Austrian Republic, obscuring the historical truth that most Austrians had in fact welcomed the Anschluss, and some had been involved in Nazi crimes.

Only in 1986 did the Waldheim Affair finally precipitate a different reading of Austrian history. During the 1970s Kurt Waldheim had been a successful, if somewhat anonymous Secretary-General of the United Nations, but it was only during his campaign for the Austrian Presidency that questions began to emerge about his wartime role as a young army officer – and by association, about Austria's still unacknowledged involvement in Nazi genocide. In July 1991 Austrian Chancellor Franz Vranitzky made a statement acknowledging that many Austrians had supported the Third Reich and that some had participated in its crimes, calling for a reassessment of public attitudes.

The reverberations of the campaign against Waldheim gave belated impetus to exile research in Austria, legitimizing a field of study which had long been academically marginalized. Even today, exile research in Austria has not prospered in the academic mainstream, having been conducted almost entirely by organizations and associations outside the university system. The most notable of these pioneers was the Dokumentationsarchiv des österreichischen Widerstandes (Documentation Archive of Austrian Resistance), set up in 1963 by the former émigré Herbert Steiner, joined more recently, in 1984, by the Theodor Kramer Gesellschaft (whose name commemorates the lyric poet who found refuge in London), the Exilbibliothek im Literaturhaus (Exile Library of the Literature House), opened in 1993, and the Orpheus Trust, an association dedicated to the research of Austrian music in exile. However, for many years the only outpost of exile research within an academic institution was the University of Vienna's Institut für Zeitgeschichte (Institute for Contemporary History), where Erika Weinzierl was *Ordinaria*. Indeed, it was only in the 1980s that Austrian exile became a legitimate subject for academic research, resulting in a steady trickle of publications, such as those by Klaus Amann, Sylvia Patsch, Wolfgang Muchitsch, Friedrich Stadler and others.[2] More recently, other centres of exile research within university institutes have developed, such as the Institut für die Geschichte der Soziologie in Österreich (Institute for the History of Sociology in Austria) at the University of Graz, the University of Salzburg's Institut für Germanistik (Institute for German Studies), and the Institut für Theater- Film- und Medienwissenschaft (Institute for Theatre, Film and Media Studies) in Vienna. Despite such developments, it remains the case that there is not a single Chair of Exile Studies at an Austrian university.

While there is a body of academic opinion in Germany which regards exile studies as an area likely to yield diminishing returns, the consensus in Austria is that research into exile is still only at an early stage of development.[3] Perhaps the most striking confirmation of this is the establishment of an Österreichische Gesellschaft für Exilforschung (Austrian Society for Research into Exile) in March 2002 – virtually two decades after its equivalent was founded in Germany (1983).

There have also been other signs of a new-found readiness to come to terms with the past in Austria. In 1998, the government of the day appointed a Commission of Historians to investigate the ruthless expropriation of émigrés by the Nazis and post-war measures of restitution. The Commission's final report, submitted in February 2003, revealed a new openness, criticizing the Second Republic's half-hearted efforts to provide restitution for the victims of Nazi persecution.

Research into German-speaking exile in Great Britain has gathered pace significantly over the last two decades. The Research Centre for German and Austrian Exile Studies (originally formed in 1990 and finally finding a home in 1995 at the University of London's Institute of Germanic Studies), to which the five authors of this study belong, is itself an example of the blossoming interest. However, the distinctive experience of *Austrian* exile in Britain has received little attention from British academics, with the obvious consequence that the specific problems of Austrians in wartime London, and even more their aspirations and achievements, have remained largely hidden from history. The Research Centre's decision to undertake a major research project into the Austrian Centre was therefore an attempt to make good this deficit of historiography.

One of the commonplaces of exile research is the relative lack of documentary sources. This is certainly true of the Austrian Centre. No complete archive of the Centre has survived and such records as do exist have been widely dispersed. Eye-witness testimony is now increasingly rare. Most of the leading participants in the Austrian Centre have now died, or their memories have faded, so that research becomes increasingly an attempt to record an historical narrative before the traces disappear.

The Austrian Centre closed at the beginning of 1947, having been badly affected, both organizationally and financially, by the return of key members to Austria. Looking back, the Centre's last President, Jenö Desser, wrote: 'The activity and the achievements of the Austrian Centre during the wartime years in London were, in my opinion, truly unique,' adding, with an understatement perhaps learnt in British exile: 'It would be worthwhile to write the history of the Austrian Centre.'[4] For nearly sixty years this story has remained unwritten, an historic oversight which the present volume seeks finally to redress.

Notes

1   Helene Maimann, *Politik im Wartesaal: Österreichische Exilpolitik in Großbritannien 1938-1945*, Vienna/Cologne/Graz 1975; Wolfgang Muchitsch (ed.), *Österreicher im Exil: Großbritannien 1938-1945: Eine Dokumentation*, Vienna 1992.

2   Klaus Amann, *PEN: Politik, Emigration, Nationalsozialismus: Ein österreichischer Schriftstellerclub*, Vienna 1982; Sylvia Patsch, *Österreichische Schriftsteller im Exil*

in Großbritannien: Ein Kapitel vergessene österreichische Literatur, Vienna/Munich 1985; Friedrich Stadler (ed.), *Vertriebene Vernunft: Emigration und Exil der österreichischen Wissenschaft,* vols. I and II, Vienna/Munich 1987/1988; Wolfgang Muchitsch, *Mit Spaten, Waffen und Worten: Die Einbindung österreichicher Flüchtlinge in die britischen Kriegsanstrengungen 1939-1945,* Vienna/Zurich 1992.

3 Cf. *Mit der Ziehharmonika* (now *Zwischenwelt*), March 2000, p. 5: 'In Austrian academic discourse, the attention paid to exile has up to now been very patchy. Big names like Erich Fried, Elias Canetti, Hilde Spiel or Manès Sperber are frequently mentioned and discussed. But many less prominent names and fates remain unacknowledged and largely unresearched.'

4 Cf. Jenö Desser, 'Mein Lebenslauf. 8. März 1904 – 8. März 1984', p. 92, unpublished manuscript in the possession of Hans Desser, Vienna.

PART ONE

'A VERY AMBITIOUS PLAN'
THE EARLY DAYS OF THE
AUSTRIAN CENTRE

CHARMIAN BRINSON

Although precise figures are hard to come by, there were probably around 30,000 Austrian refugees from National Socialism in Britain by September 1939, of whom perhaps 90 per cent were Jewish and the remaining 10 per cent political or intellectual exiles (these groups cannot, of course, be seen as mutually exclusive).[1] The first found their way to Britain as early as 1933, others arrived in the wake of the brief Austrian Civil War of February 1934. However, it was the Anschluss, Hitler's annexation of Austria on 11 March 1938, that was the cause of really significant numbers of Austrian refugees seeking refuge in Britain, while the events of Reichskristallnacht or Crystal Night in November 1938 precipitated a further influx of refugees that continued up until the outbreak of war.

In April 1938, shortly after the Anschluss, the first official organization of Austrian refugees in Great Britain was established: Austrian Self-Aid was set up as a charitable and non-political organization to provide assistance and information to fellow countrymen by Austrians already resident in Britain. Among them was a group of exceptionally committed and active members of the Austrian Communist Party (KPÖ) – though for the most part they chose not to advertise their political affiliations – who included Hilde Mareiner, Eva Kolmer and Franz West, each of whom would soon also play an important role in the associated Austrian organizations, the Council of Austrians and the Austrian Centre. All three of these organizations were able to boast the support of powerful British patrons: in the case of Austrian Self-Aid, for instance, they included the Cardinal Archbishop of Westminster, the

Chief Rabbi, the Duchess of Atholl, the Liberal feminist Margery Corbett Ashby and the Socialist Catherine Marshall.

The scope of Austrian Self-Aid's activities was initially a wide one, comprising assistance to Austrians both in Britain and abroad. A pre-war report on the organization listed as its main tasks the obtaining of entry permits for Austrian children, and domestic and other permits for adults; the arranging of hospitality for refugees arriving in Britain; the provision of legal advice; as well as the assisting of Austrian interbrigadists interned in France after fighting in the Spanish Civil War and of Austrian prisoners in Nazi concentration camps.[2] Austrian Self-Aid's functions changed considerably after the outbreak of war when, in addition to offering employment advice, it was called upon to assist refugees facing the Alien Tribunals and those in internment camps in both Britain and France.[3]

In the autumn of 1938, prominent members of the Austrian exile community in Britain founded a second organization, the Ausschuss der Österreicher in Grossbritannien (originally rendered in English as the 'Committee', later as the 'Council of Austrians in Great Britain'). The organization was conceived as broad-based, initially bringing together Liberals, Christian Socials, Socialists, Monarchists and Communists. Its founding statutes defined the Council's task as being 'to represent the cultural, social and economic interests of all Austrians in Great Britain';[4] however the Council's mission also included a political dimension, for instance in the making of representations to the British authorities (formally distinguishing it from the later formation, the Austrian Centre, whose primary responsibility was to be for welfare). Once again, the project was supported by such prominent British patrons as the Archbishop of York and the Bishop of Chichester. The eminent Liberal, Professor Friedrich Otto Hertz, became the Chairman (he resigned from the position early in 1940, however, because of internal tensions within the Council), while the Communist Eva Kolmer assumed the role of Secretary.

It was Kolmer who also played an important part in setting up the Austrian Centre, a plan conceived at around New Year 1938/39 to provide a meeting-place for the often isolated Austrian refugees in London and also to secure the continuing work of Austrian Self-Aid, threatened by lack of funds (it was hoped that further income for its work could be raised by the foundation of an Austrian Canteen).[5] On 3 February 1939, a letter appeared in *The Spectator*, signed by Kolmer, requesting public help for a 'very ambitious plan – namely to build up an "Austrian Centre", to have a house where the many refugees, who live in dreary quarters or in shelters where they cannot stay during the day,

Austrian Centre Restaurant, 1940 (Suschitzky)

could come, read and write, have classes and retraining, music, and all sorts of artistic circles'.[6] That same month, the Council of Austrians called a meeting of Austrian refugees at Friends' House, Euston Road (London WC1), at which, after Austrian Self-Aid and the Council had reported on their activities to date, they announced their decision now to work for the establishment of the Austrian Centre.[7]

The Austrians were fortunate in being granted the use by the Paddington Estate of a vacant house near Paddington Station (124 Westbourne Terrace) that was awaiting demolition and, a few months later, of the house next door, no. 126. A third house, 132 Westbourne Terrace, was acquired in the same way later in the year. Work was begun immediately on renovation and furnishing, as Kolmer herself described:

The entire contents, library, musical instruments, furniture, kitchen equipment and the radio were the result of donations. All the work in the house was carried out by exiled Austrians. Carpenters, decorators, plumbers did their job. Doctors rubbed down the floors and washed the walls, and physicists had to test out their theoretical knowledge and instal electric circuits.[8]

In the event, everything must have been carried out at record speed as by 11 March 1939, the first anniversary of the Anschluss, invitations to a commemorative 'Meeting of Austrians' were able to announce that the Austrian Centre would open the following week.[9] The Centre was indeed inaugurated on 15 and 16 March 1939, the latter occasion being the official opening by Lord Hailey (Chairman of the Coordinating Committee for Refugees and a patron of the Council of Austrians) in the presence of around 150 British friends.

The Austrian Centre was set up as a charitable non-profitable organization under the Honorary Presidency of Sigmund Freud and, after Freud's death, of the former Austrian Ambassador to Britain, Sir George Franckenstein. It was run by a Committee that included representatives of a wide range of political affiliations (though, as in the sister organizations, the Communists played a particularly active role), and set itself equally wide-ranging aims, defined in 1939 as follows:

1. It should give Austrians the possibility of fostering their culture, their abilities and their talents within and on behalf of a community and of collectively preserving Austria's cultural inheritance and tradition.
2. It should serve as a bridge between the Austrians and the English in this, our host country. Equipped with the riches of our culture, we do not stand here empty handed, as beggars, expecting to receive charity; rather, we come as one people of culture to another and bring with us something that will enrich life in this country.
3. It will make possible the continuation and extension of our representational and welfare duties, our educational and cultural tasks, financed from income from our events and our work.[10]

The Centre, where in addition both Austrian Self-Aid and the Council of Austrians established their permanent base, proved successful from the very beginning, with several further branches being founded in London and the provinces. By June 1939 it already had 2000 members,[11] a figure that within five years was to increase to 3500,[12] and was the

Austrian Centre Reading Room, 1940 (Suschitzky)

largest and probably   the most effective organization   of Austrian refugees in Britain. Wilhelm Jerusalem, an habitual visitor to the Centre during the second half of 1939, fondly recalled the dispossessed yet resolute people he encountered there as well as the remarkable range of facilities on offer:

> I quickly grew to value and love the new type of people who came together here. There was not a single one among them whom the new barbarism had not robbed of a vital aspect of their life: their livelihood, their means, their family ties. Children without parents, parents without children. And yet with a will and a courage beyond compare, all were setting about establishing a new life [...]

And the Centre gatherered them all to its bosom. It offered them food and drink at the cheapest possible prices. – Newspapers and radio. –

Books, shoe repairs. – Lectures. For a paltry sum of money, one could experience the very best that art, science, music and literature have to offer.[13]

Certainly the Canteen (or Restaurant) proved to be as popular as the Austrian Centre's founders could have hoped, providing 'Genuine Austrian Cooking [...] at a price which is far cheaper than would be needed to purchase similar quantities elsewhere'[14] in an attractive setting (where friezes on the walls illustrated scenes from Austrian life). From early on, the kitchen was catering for between 500 and 600 customers each day and almost twice that number on Sundays.[15] There was also a library – where the young poet Erich Fried worked for a time – and a reading room for members' use; the Centre's *First Annual Report* recorded a library stock by 1940 of 1530 German and 1020 English-language books as well as some in other languages, to be lent out at 1*d.* per book each week, while the reading room took copies of a wide range of newspapers in both English and German.[16] As a further service to members, the Library Committee decided to issue a weekly German-language digest of the British press for refugees with poor English:[17] entitled *Zeitspiegel*, it would evolve into the main newspaper of the Austrian emigration (this too would retain the Austrian Centre as its base, as would the Centre's own later publishing enterprise, Free Austrian Books). In addition, from as early as November 1938, the Council of Austrians was producing a regular publication, *Österreichische Nachrichten*, containing 'notes and paragraphs about practical refugee questions and such news as was available and of interest to Austrian refugees'[18] that included, from the time of the Austrian Centre's foundation, the full programme of events, lectures and performances to be found there.

These were of course part and parcel of the Austrian Centre's cultural remit to the émigré population it served. In his *Five Years of the Austrian Centre* (1943), the musician Georg Knepler would report thus on the Centre's endeavours to foster Austrian cultural traditions in Britain:

> Most of our activities in this sphere have been devoted to music. The Austrian Centre was opened with a concert. The numbers of concerts we have arranged since must be several hundred and many famous musicians of many nationalities have performed in our club premises or in concerts arranged by the Austrian Centre in concert halls.[19]

An earlier report on culture at the Austrian Centre, from June 1939, also took music as its starting point, before passing on to other artistic activities:

For the benefit of AC members, the writers' group have put on, among other things, a Karl Kraus evening, and an Austrian authors' evening featuring Hilde Spiel and Richard Duschinsky. No fewer than 400 people took part in the 'Eternal Austria' evening. Our commitment to German antifascist literature resulted in an Ernst Toller evening [...] The establishment of a theatre for cabaret, that typical Viennese art form, completes the picture of our cultural activities.[20]

This theatre, the Laterndl, which was originally situated on the first floor at 124/126 Westbourne Terrace, opened in June 1939 and became an important focus of Austrian émigré life in North London.

In addition, the Austrian Centre set about putting on courses of various kinds for its membership to assist them in their new lives: English classes were organized from early on, for instance, backed up by a Debating Circle and an English shorthand course, and before long three rooms at 124 Westbourne Terrace were in continual use as class-rooms.[21] Retraining possibilities were offered, especially following the outbreak of war (when the existing employment restrictions for aliens began to be lifted): thus classes in welding and engineering were organized at the end of 1939,[22] while by March 1940 the Austrian Centre's 'Volks-Hochschule' or College would be advertising training in a further range of practical skills, listed as 'mural painting for advertising, handwork, carpentry, car mechanics, welding, painting and varnishing, lacquerwork, photography, electrical installation, cable laying, tailoring, machine-knitting, laundry work, decorating, machine-sewing'.[23] Other refugees already possessing skills of use to the membership were enabled to continue working in their own professions: workshops were opened at the Centre in August 1939 in which skilled tailors, dressmakers and cobblers could carry out repairs at reasonable cost on other members' clothes and shoes.[24] Moreover, in November 1939, the Austrian Studio for Arts and Crafts (ASTU) was established to enable refugee artists and craftsmen, too, to earn their living while carrying on 'the best traditions of Austrian Arts and Crafts as symbolised by "Wiener Werkstätte" and "Werkbund"'.[25]

Among the various professional and interest groups represented at the Austrian Centre, domestic workers were seen to warrant especial attention. Large numbers of Austrian women, frequently unpractised in domestic work, had arrived in Britain on domestic permits in 1938 and 1939 (there were, of course, few other employment options open to aliens at the time). The Association of Austrian Domestic Workers was

One of the Austrian Centre Workshops (Tailoring), 1940 (Suschitzky)

founded at around New Year 1939/40, soon moving its headquarters into the Austrian Centre premises, to cater for such women; as well as regular social events, the women were offered remedial classes in Englishand domestic skills, legal advice, and a monthly bulletin, *Die Österreicherin im Haushalt.* [26]

A further group encouraged to make its home within the Austrian Centre – and a particularly important one in the life of the Centre – was its lively youth group, Young Austria. Arising from a small circle of young refugees in North London, who had originally come together to commemorate the first anniversary of the Anschluss, Young Austria offered its members, aged 25 and under, a wide range of social and cultural activities aimed at organizing and educating young Austrians in exile, with the struggle against Nazism and the future of Austria very much in mind. It also produced its own periodicals and publications (the latter under the imprint 'Jugend voran'). A thriving organization, by December 1943 Young Austria had no fewer than 1000 members (of whom around half lived in London, 350 belonged to provincial groups and 100 were serving in the British armed forces).[27]

* * *

Mention has already been made of the internal disagreements within the Council of Austrians that finally led to the resignation of its Chairman, Friedrich Hertz, early in 1940. Indeed, political tensions set in almost from the beginning: the Social Democrats, for one, parted company with the Council shortly after its foundation in protest at its engagement in political activities.[28] The Monarchist Graf Strachwitz was excluded from the Council in October 1939 in acrimonious circumstances,[29] while a further dispute centred around Dr Paul Wiesner, another spokesman of the Right, who in January 1940 tried but failed to organize a takeover of the Council in the course of which 'it almost came to a fight'.[30]

This last episode had its origins in the most enduring problem that Hertz, as first Council Chairman, had to address, namely the relations between the very energetic Communist faction on the Council and the other members. It was rumoured in the Austrian exile community at large during 1939 that the Council of Austrians and the Austrian Centre were falling under Communist influence, a matter that Hertz felt necessary to investigate. Some of the accusations, certainly, he found to be totally without foundation: a room used at night at the Austrian Centre, for instance, allegedly by Communists printing leaflets, turned out to be occupied by the cooks while making apple strudel![31] Hertz was extremely concerned to quell any rumours of this kind, which he feared might damage the reputation of the refugees in Britain, as well as to ensure potential critics that, regardless of the personal political position of any of the Council's members, the work of the Council itself had at no time been influenced by Communist considerations.[32]

The matter came to a head, however, in October 1939 when Leopold Hornik, a Council member, made an openly pro-Communist speech; Hertz seized the opportunity to move that supporters of totalitarian systems, whether these be Communist or Fascist, should be barred from membership of the Council. His proposal was not accepted but an alternative position was agreed, namely that the Council should from then on operate as a politically neutral body.[33] Indeed, at the end of January 1940, after his resignation, Hertz would assure Franckenstein, still the Honorary President of the Austrian Centre, that 'since that time

Lounge of the Austrian Centre Hostel, 1940 (Suschitzky)

the Council has really discarded politics, and has devoted his [*sic*] activity to welfare work on behalf of the refugees'.[34] However, the old difficulties had begun to resurface: two groups affiliated to the Austrian Centre, the Association of Austrian Domestic Workers and Young Austria, had published 'tactless remarks about the Austrian monarchists' without any attempt at restraint being made by the Centre leadership. In addition, theCouncil of Austrians had taken up a hostile position towards the newly established Austria Office.[35]

Hertz resigned from the Council on 26 January 1940, officially in order to be able to devote more time to academic work. Others followed his example: by 13 February Hertz was informing Franckenstein that most of the Monarchists had by then left the Council, leaving behind them a preponderance of left-wing members.[36] To Baron Alexis de Vivenot, shortly before, he had reported of the Centre: 'According to my information the tension has greatly increased.'[37] Indeed to Vivenot and others he even raised the possibility of a 'collapse of the Centre', though he remained of the firm opinion, despite the problems, that such an outcome 'would be extremely regrettable since the Centre is really giving good service to many Austrians and could do much more besides'.[38]

In fact the Council of Austrians and the Austrian Centre not only succeeded in surviving this period but proceeded from strength to strength. Hertz and Franckenstein withdrew their support, certainly – they went on to hold leading positions at the Austria Office – but Hertz's post as Chairman of the Council was quickly filled by a well-known Socialist, Professor Walter Schiff. Other non-Communists, like Schiff, continued to play their part in Council and Centre, as well as in the later Free Austrian Movement with which, in terms of aims, policy and personnel, the Austrian Centre was intimately linked. It is true that from the time of Hertz's resignation, if not before, the Communists constituted the dominant influence within these bodies – the very state of affairs that Hertz and others, hopeful of achieving a truly broad-based platform for cooperation within the Austrian emigration, had hoped to avoid. Yet it should also be noted that the Communists achieved their ascendancy as a result of their superior organization and dedication, qualities that were put to excellent use in the service of the exiled Austrians in Britain during the years of emigration.

In a memorandum of mid-February 1940, in which Hertz considered, if belatedly, how the political balance might yet be redressed, he reiterated his belief that 'the ultimate aim should be to make the Centre a really efficient welfare institution which requires that it is kept aloof from political activities'.[39] As things turned out, Hertz would see his wish fulfilled, at least for a while: for, at the time of the Hitler-Stalin pact (a difficult period for all Communists in Britain, let alone for 'enemy aliens'), the Communists involved in the Council and Centre felt it expedient to maintain a low political profile. Such a stance was particularly prudent in the face of the large-scale internment of aliens in mid-1940.[40] Consequently, leading functionaries in the Council of Austrians and the Austrian Centre had little choice but to devote their considerable energies to welfare work, at least until June 1941, when the entry of the Soviet Union into the war transformed the political climate in Britain, leading, *inter alia*, to the foundation of the unashamedly political Free Austrian Movement a few months later.

* * *

Without doubt, the most urgent areas of welfare work for Austrian Self-Aid, the Council of Austrians and the Austrian Centre were matters relating to the tribunals, which categorized all aliens in terms of their perceived security risk, and problems of internment and deportation affecting their members. For tribunal purposes, 'full records of about 3000 Austrians were obtained to supplement those available at the various refugee committees',[41] while support and legal advice were made available to individual refugees. By the middle of 1940, at the height of the mass internment measures, the Austrian organizations found themselves under still greater pressure when, with ever increasing calls upon their services, they had to contend with a decreasing work force (as employees, too, were interned) as well as a drop in their income from membership fees and from the restaurant. Eva Kolmer has described how they endeavoured to rise to the situation:

> Our answer was to double our efforts. The Council became our headquarters; day and night, members of the Council took it in turns to deal with the swiftly changing situation, with the demands and the calls for help.[42]

Kolmer herself was permitted to visit some of the Austrians in internment, not only early in 1940,[43] that is before the introduction of alien internment on a mass scale, but also at the end of 1940 when she visited both men's and women's camps on the Isle of Man. Her report on the latter visit, while covering such general issues as food, books, clothes and visitation rights, also pinpointed current difficulties in maintaining contact with the internees, including the fact that *Zeitspiegel*, which was being dispatched from London on a weekly basis to all interned Austrian Centre members, was reaching them 'only sporadically in each camp', since the camp intelligence officers appeared to 'distribute the bulletin as it pleases them or retain it if the particular number does not fit their taste'.[44]

In addition to newspapers, however, books, clothes and food parcels were also being sent to the camps, financed by a fund for internees set up in May 1940, and youth work was being organized in the camps under the Young Austria umbrella. At Christmas 1940, in collaboration with German, Czech and other Austrian refugee organizations, the Austrian Centre was instrumental in setting up a special Christmas action fund for internees, raising £800 for parcels to internees in Britain as well as in the camps in Canada and Australia (to which a number of male internees had been deported).[45]

Nor did the welfare work stop there: support often had to be offered to the wives and children of interned men while, for internees who had been released, an Association of Ex-Internees was established, with Kolmer as its Secretary. Indeed, in February 1941, as increasing numbers were released, the War Emergency Fund for Austrian Refugees was established to help Austrians still interned, but also to assist those just released and especially those intending to join the Pioneer Corps.[46]

Moreover, from its earliest days, the Austrian Centre had set out to provide accommodation for Austrians in need (these latter changing in character as time went on, in line with changing circumstances). When the Austrian Centre was founded, two rooms were set aside as emergency quarters for refugees arriving without accommodation, for instance, or for domestics in search of a post. Then, when the third house, 132 Westbourne Terrace, was made available to the Austrian Centre, a full-scale hostel was opened that was quickly made use of by Austrians displaced in one way or another by the war: women dismissed from their domestic jobs on the outbreak of war, for example, others arriving homeless in London after having left the prohibited coastal areas. As the war progressed, hostel accommodation was provided for young Austrians engaged in war work and finally for those in HM Forces, the 'Soldiers' Hostel' constituting part of an extensive support programme for serving Austrians, organized by the Austrian Centre and the Free Austrian Movement.[47]

In addition, a 'Coordinating Committee of Austrian Women' was established in November 1941 to cater for the special needs of women members. In 1942, under its aegis, a Cooperative of Austrian Needlewomen was set up at the Austrian Centre whose task, as a contribution to the British war effort, was to repair clothes and linen for war workers. Later in the year, in October 1942, an Austrian Day Nursery was opened in order to relieve women of childcare responsibilities and thereby free them, too, for war work.[48]

Alongside this comprehensive welfare provision, of course, the Austrian Centre continued to organize its rich programme of cultural, educational and social events as well as to provide a much needed – and appreciated – meeting place for Austrian refugees. Moreover, from the beginning, the Centre enjoyed an atmosphere all of its own: 'It will be a long time before I stop yearning for the Austrian Centre and its wobbly chairs and its enthusiastic young people,' Wilhelm Jerusalem would reflect nostalgically before his departure from Britain in 1940.[49] But, above and beyond that, the Austrian Centre aimed to offer exiled Austrians a vision of Austria – not the Austria then pertaining, of course, in the grip of National Socialism, but the vision of a free, independent and democratic Austria that had inspired the founders of the First Republic and that was now to give exiled Austrians some hope for the future. The 'very ambitious plan', in Kolmer's words, of establishing a base for the Austrian emigration in Britain was achieved on a scale and with a dedication that must surely have exceeded even the highest aspirations of the Austrian Centre's founders.

Notes

1   See Wolfgang Muchitsch, ed., *Österreicher im Exil: Großbritannien 1938-1945: Eine Dokumentation*, Vienna 1992, p. 8.
2   'Generalversammlung des Klubs Austrian Centre, London, 26. Juni 1939', Friedrich Otto Hertz Papers, Archive for the History of Sociology in Austria [AGSÖ], Graz, p. 4, 28/5.15.
3   *First Annual Report of the Austrian Centre*, London 1940, p. 24.
4   'Statut des Ausschusses der Österreicher in Groß Britannien [sic]', Friedrich Otto Hertz Papers, AGSÖ, 28/5.15.
5   *First Annual Report*, p. 9.
6   Eva Kolmer, 'Austrians in England', *The Spectator*, 3 February 1939, p. 181.
7   *First Annual Report*, p. 21.
8   Speech given at the opening ceremony on 16 March 1939, as reported in 'Österreichisches Emigrantenheim in London', *Pariser Tageszeitung*, 24 March 1939, p. 3.
9   'Einladung zur Versammlung der Österreicher zum 11. März, Queen Mary Hall, Y.M.C.A., Great Russell Street, W.C.1', Friedrich Otto Hertz Papers, AGSÖ, 28/5.15.
10   'Generalversammlung des Klubs Austrian Centre', p. 3.
11   *Ibid.*, p. 6.
12   See Georg Knepler, *Five years of the Austrian Centre*, London 1944, p. 9.
13   Wilhelm Jerusalem to the Clubvorstand des Austrian Centre, n. d. [18 January 1940], Documentation Archive of Austrian Resistance [DÖW], Vienna, DÖW 18.924.
14   *First Annual Report*, p. 14.
15   *Ibid.*
16   *Ibid.*, p. 11.
17   *Ibid.*
18   *Ibid.*, pp. 13-14.
19   Knepler, p. 6.
20   'Generalversammlung des Klubs Austrian Centre', p. 7.
21   *First Annual Report*, p. 12.
22   *Ibid.*, p. 22.
23   See flyer advertising 'Austrian Centre Volks-Hochschule', n. d. [March 1940], Friedrich Otto Hertz Papers, AGSÖ, 28/5.15.

24 Eva Kolmer, *Das Austrian Centre: 7 Jahre österreichische Gemeinschaftsarbeit*, London [1946], p. 3.

25 *First Annual Report*, p. 28.

26 *Ibid.*, p. 24.

27 See, for example, Reinhard Müller, ed., *Fluchtpunkt England: Spuren der österreichischen Emigration in Großbritannien 1938 bis 1945*, Graz 1996, p. 77.

28 Untitled Memorandum, enclosed in Friedrich Hertz to Sir George Franckenstein, 13 February 1940, Friedrich Otto Hertz Papers, AGSÖ, 28/1.1.

29 On this, see, for example, Friedrich Hertz, 'Rundschreiben an die Mitglieder des Ausschusses der Österreicher in England', 14 October 1939, Friedrich Otto Hertz Papers, AGSÖ, 28/5.15.

30 See Friedrich Hertz to Martin Fuchs, 3 February 1940, Friedrich Otto Hertz Papers, AGSÖ, 28/1.1.

31 'Council of Austrians in Great Britain – Austrian Centre: Memorandum submitted to Sir George Franckenstein by Professor Friedrich Hertz', n. d. [February 1940], Friedrich Otto Hertz Papers, AGSÖ, 28/5.15.

32 *Ibid.*

33 See, for example, Friedrich Hertz, 'Rundschreiben an die Mitglieder des Ausschusses der Österreicher in England', 14 October 1939.

34 'Council of Austrians in Great Britain – Austrian Centre: Memorandum submitted to Sir George Franckenstein by Professor Friedrich Hertz', n. d. [February 1940].

35 *Ibid.* The Austria Office was an exile organization bringing together representatives of the Centre and the Right. It was spurned by the Communists and Socialists, however, with the exception of Heinrich Allina and his group of Social Democrats.

36 Untitled Memorandum, enclosed in Friedrich Hertz to Sir George Franckenstein, 13 February 1940.

37 Friedrich Hertz to Alexis de Vivenot, 3 February 1940, Friedrich Otto Hertz Papers, AGSÖ, 28/1.1.

38 *Ibid.*

39 Untitled Memorandum, enclosed in Friedrich Hertz to Sir George Franckenstein, 13 February 1940.

40 Although officials in the refugee organizations could in general claim exemption from internment, known Communists among them were nonetheless often interned.

41 *First Annual Report*, p. 21.

42 Kolmer, *Das Austrian Centre*, p. 7.

43 As indicated by an entry in the Austrian Centre's 'Budgetzusammenstellung Jänner 1940', Friedrich Otto Hertz Papers, AGSÖ, 28/5.15.

44 See Eva Kolmer, 'Problems of the Internment Camps: Impressions from a visit to the Isle of Man', n. d. [late 1940?], Bishop Bell Papers, vol. 31, Lambeth Palace Library, London.

45 Kolmer, *Das Austrian Centre*, p. 11.

46 *Ibid.*, p. 12.

47 Knepler, pp. 13-14.

48 On the achievements of the Coordinating Committee, see, for example, Kolmer, *Das Austrian Centre*, pp. 18-19.

49 Jerusalem to Austrian Centre Committee members, n. d. [18 January 1940], DÖW 18.92.

THE POLITICS OF THE AUSTRIAN CENTRE

ANTHONY GRENVILLE□

I. Time of Trial: March 1938–June 1941

The political situation facing the small group of activists who provided the driving force behind the Austrian Centre was by no means promising when they arrived in Britain in the months after the Anschluss. They were predominantly Communists, young and inexperienced, and with few resources on which to draw. The Austrian Communist Party (KPÖ) had, unlike its German sister party, never developed into a mass organization attracting votes by the million, since the Austrian Social Democrats had retained the loyalty of the great majority of the Austrian working class, marginalizing their Communist rivals. The failure of the Social Democrats to resist the onslaught of the authoritarian Dollfuss regime in February 1934 effectively and the subsequent banning of their organization had allowed the Communists to gain some support from disillusioned Social Democrats, but the conditions of illegality under which the KPÖ had to operate after February 1934 were not conducive to a large growth in membership.

Like all other anti-Nazi organizations, the Communists were unable to mount any significant resistance to the Nazi incorporation of Austria into the Reich in March 1938. With the relaxation of British immigration policy during 1938/39, many Austrians, including some Communists, fled to Britain; the large majority, however, were Jews, drawn in the main from the assimilated, well-to-do Viennese Jewish middle class and politically far removed from left-wing radicalism. They were also too preoccupied with the problems of gaining a foothold in a foreign country and earning a living to have time or energy for politics. Many were women working as domestic servants, many were children who had come unaccompanied on specially designated trains (Kindertransports), while many of the men were housed in temporary camps (like Kitchener Camp in Richborough) or were simply unable to work for want of work permits; the Austrian refugees in Britain would be hard to reach and difficult to organize in any political organization, especially a radical left-wing party. The leading Communists were themselves mostly Jewish, but their allegiance to Marxist ideology had led them largely to reject their religious, racial and social origins.

The Communists who were the prime movers behind the Austrian Centre were, however, at an advantage in that they faced no strong and effective rival group when it came to creating an organization within which the isolated and struggling refugees might be united, since the other Austrian political parties represented in Britain proved poor competitors for the allegiance of the refugees. For obvious reasons, the Austrian Nazis and the supporters of the incorporation of Austria into Hitler's Reich had no constituency among the refugees in Britain. Of the other right-wing parties, the Christian Socials, the largest party in Austria before 1938, had no significant presence in Britain, nor would their traditional anti-Semitism have allowed them much support amongst a largely Jewish group of refugees; the supporters of the deposed Schuschnigg government were likewise scarcely a major factor in émigré politics in Britain, though the former ambassador, Sir George Franckenstein, sometimes performed the useful role of ceremonial figurehead, for example as Honorary President of the Austrian Centre from October 1939, in succession to Sigmund Freud, to May 1940.

More substantial were the Monarchists, organized in the Austria Office in London, who looked to a restoration of the Habsburg monarchy under Otto von Habsburg. They were a potentially influential political force, with a network of organizations that aspired to reach out to the refugees, and it was the success of the Communists in building a working alliance with them that was to be the cornerstone of the unitary organizations created under the auspices of the Austrian Centre. But there were limitations on the following among the refugees that the Monarchists could attract: relations between Austrian Jews and the camp followers of the high-born aristocracy were at best distant, while a political platform based on a return to the pre-1918 status quo appealed to few refugees. The accession to the Austria Office of a breakaway group of Social Democrats, the Association of Austrian Social Democrats in Great Britain, led by the dissident right-wing Socialist Heinrich Allina, made little difference in that respect. Nor was the principal bourgeois group, the Austrian Democratic Union, a sizeable rival; created in 1941 by former members of the Austria Office, led by Julius Meinl, Emil Müller-Sturmheim and Professor Friedrich Hertz, head of the Council of Austrians, it remained small in numbers.

The most likely principal rivals to the Communists for the loyalty of the Austrian refugees were those of the Social Democrats who had renamed themselves Revolutionary Socialists; they, however, embarked on a strategy that might almost have been designed to squander their opportunities. Thrown into disarray by its defeat and humiliation in 1934, the great Social Democratic Party of Victor Adler and Otto Bauer, formerly the proud champions of Austro-Marxism and the Austrian working class, failed signally to develop effective and successful policies in exile. The party leadership had had its seat in Paris at the outbreak of war, moving hastily to New York when France collapsed in 1940, and the leader of the Socialists in London, Karl Czernetz, barely attempted to recruit new members from among the refugees.

Instead, the Socialists formed themselves into the Austrian Labour Club, limiting themselves to political discussions and other activities proper to a club. As a result of this self-imposed isolation, the Austrian Socialists could count only on the support of their own club members, who numbered little more than a hundred. The arrival of Oscar Pollak in Britain in autumn 1940 ushered in a more active line, and in April 1941 the Socialists founded the London Bureau of the Austrian Socialists in Great Britain. Even so, much of the Socialists' activity consisted in bitter sectarian attacks on the Communists; any organizational or political initiatives they undertook were almost always taken in response to Communist successes, such as the creation of the Free Austrian Movement in December 1941, as a united front of Austrians against Hitler, encompassing Monarchists, bourgeois groups and Communists, but leaving the Socialists excluded of their own volition. The Socialists were also handicapped by their ambivalent attitude to the Anschluss, deriving from their earlier support of a German state including Austria, which left them open to the charge of following a policy not dissimilar in this respect from that of the Nazis.

The Socialists' acute suspicion of the Communists, self-defeating though it arguably was, must be understood in the context of the relations between the two parties during the decade that preceded the war, for these set the broad parameters within which those relations continued to evolve in wartime exile. In the late 1920s most European Communist Parties, following the line laid down by Moscow, had switched to a radical left-wing strategy, seeking to promote class war and revolution and, especially in Germany, denouncing the moderate Social Democrats as 'Social Fascists' and targeting them as the principal foe, as traitors to the working class. With Hitler's accession to power and the emergence of Nazi Germany as a serious threat to the Soviet Union, the hard left line was dropped in favour of the Popular Front policy, the attempt to build an anti-Nazi front comprising both working-class parties and also liberal and moderate bourgeois groups (and thereby threatening to outflank and envelop the Social Democrats). The Communists became adept at creating Popular Front organizations over which they exercised a considerable degree of control from behind the scenes, and in which members of all political parties within the Front, anti-Nazi intellectuals, liberal opinion-formers, artists, academics and proponents of progressive humanism generally, could be marshalled.

This was the model on which the Austrian Communists in Britain were to build with great success, once they were able to become politically active after Hitler's invasion of the Soviet Union in 1941. The Popular Front concept proved readily adaptable to the creation of a national united front of all Austrians opposing Hitler and supporting the war effort; it proved possible to subordinate differences of politics and ideology to the overarching cause of fighting National Socialism and prosecuting the war. However, historical events did not permit a smooth transition from the Popular Front strategy of the mid-1930s to the grand anti-Nazi alliance after 1941. For the signing of the pact between Nazi Germany and the Soviet Union in August 1939 signified another dramatic strategic about-face: it meant that when war broke out between Hitler and the Western Allies the following month, Communist parties loyal to Moscow were bound by the pact to view Britain and France, rather than Germany, as hostile powers. The Austrian Socialists' mistrust of Communist professions of eternal loyalty to the united front of Austrians after June 1941 was thus not wholly unjustified.

The outbreak of war between Britain and Germany in September 1939 caught the activists behind the Austrian Centre in an unenviable position. Having been in Britain as refugees only for a relatively short time, they had not been able to build up a strong and established organizational structure for their political work; the Centre itself was only a few months old. They had to contend with the problems of refugee status, which deteriorated into 'enemy alien' status once war broke out and further restricted their activities; they had no easy means of communicating with their potential membership, a situation which was to worsen drastically when the British government embarked on the mass internment of 'enemy aliens' in early summer 1940; and they had to exercise great caution in their political work, since the British authorities would have looked with disfavour on any radical left-wing politics.

The signing of the pact between Nazi Germany and the Soviet Union greatly added to these difficulties. As Communists loyal to Moscow, the Austrian Centre activists were now open to the charge of being associates of an ally of the enemy. This meant in effect that they were banned from any significant political activity (as were all refugees) and they had to exercise considerable care not to incur the displeasure of the British authorities, who had not been slow to detain the few supporters of Nazism (and others) resident in Britain. The sudden outbreak of official friendship between Berlin and Moscow also created an acute political dilemma for the Austrian Communists, as it did for Communists in all countries at war with Germany and eager to support the national war effort against Hitler. The Austrians would have experienced this conflict of loyalties particularly acutely: their country had been overrun by the Germans – at the outbreak of war they and the Czechs were as yet the only peoples to have experienced Nazi territorial expansionism – and they had been forced to flee their homeland for their lives, both as Communists and as Jews. For them, given the horrors that the Nazis were perpetrating in Austria, the pact must have seemed like a pact with the devil. Nevertheless, the Austrian Centre activists appear to have accepted the pact, if only as a necessary evil, and there is no evidence of any dissension in their ranks over it.

Indeed, the publications of the Austrian Centre reveal so little about its politics during the period before Hitler's invasion of the Soviet Union, when it was practising an enforced abstinence from politics under the watchful eye of the British authorities, that it is hard to speak of a political line at all at this time. Before September 1939 publications like *Young Austria* (from its first issue in May 1939 entitled in German *Österreichische Jugend*, then from July 1939 *Junges Österreich*) had energetically supported the cause of the liberation of Austria from the Nazi invader and had, with an eye to British public opinion, given over considerable column space to resistance activities within Austria and to the prospect of unity among Austrians in the fight for an independent Austria and against Fascism. On the outbreak of war, a brief spurt of enthusiasm for the war and of support for the Allied war effort against the hated Nazis dominated the issue of September 1939:

> We, the young Austrians in England, solemnly declare: In this hour, when Great Britain and France are giving their help to the Polish nation, which has become the object of another attack of Hitlerism, we are ready fully and unanimously to support Great Britain's fight against aggression [...] Great Britain's enemy is our enemy. We are bound by the bonds of sincerest friendship and gratitude to the British people and the British Youth who have offered to us, the victims of a previous aggression, a sanctuary asylum in England.[1]

The young Austrians offered to support the British war effort by joining the A.R.P. and by filling sandbags.

But the pact between Hitler and Stalin forbade any such overt approval of the Allied war against Germany, and the requirements of party policy, emanating from Moscow, ensured that for the duration of the pact no such pro-British excesses appeared in *Young Austria* after the issue of September 1939. The pact presented the Communist anti-Fascists with the most agonising of choices: whether to abandon the fight against Hitler, the embodiment of evil, or to betray their duty of unconditional loyalty to their party and its leadership in Moscow. The Communist line during the life of the pact was that the war was an imperialist war between contending capitalist powers, from which the international Communist movement should stand aloof in a position of neutrality. In practice, given the Soviet Union's intense concern not to cause a breach with Hitler, the sharing of the spoils in Poland and the Baltic states between the two signatories to the pact, and Stalin's abiding suspicion of the British, this neutrality had a pro-Axis bias. It was of course impossible for the Austrian Centre to propound this line in its publications in wartime Britain; doing so would have invited the closure of the publications concerned, and worse.

Instead, the publications of the Austrian Centre reverted to a left-wing line, stressing the antagonism between classes, rather than the conflict between nations, and playing up the opportunities offered by the war for a revolutionary reordering of existing society in Austria and Germany. The war between Britain and Germany was mostly conspicuous by its absence, until 22 June 1941. This was the compromise position adopted by the activists in order to comply with the political demands of the line from Moscow, but without incurring the wrath of the British authorities. The left-wing line was evident in the association of the liberation of Austria with a clear exposition of the class divide that separated the Reich's ruling classes from its oppressed masses; the right-wing line of the unity of the Austrian people in a national war against German occupation still lay in the future.

Thus *Young Austria* was careful to differentiate in class war terms between rulers and ruled in both Austria and Germany, setting the revolutionary endeavours of the German people alongside the fight of the Austrian people for liberation:

> Never has it been possible to treat enslaved peoples as equivalent to their oppressors. And above all not when these peoples have defended themselves as have the Austrian and the German people with their hundreds of thousands of brave anti-Fascists, who for their struggle must languish in concentration camps and prisons. Without a free democratic Germany – no independent Austria.[2]

This emphasis on the revolutionary class struggle, rather than national liberation, and on the common cause of the proletarian masses in Austria and Germany, rather than Austrian independence from German rule, contrasts markedly with the later Austrian Centre line, after the pact of August 1939 had been smashed by the tanks of the Wehrmacht. Then the struggle for the re-establishment of a free, independent and democratic Austria against the foreign rule of the Nazis, and the consequent depiction of Austria as occupied and enslaved against the will of its people and as mounting determined resistance to the Germans, came once more to the fore.

Banned from political activity, the Austrian Centre activists made a virtue of necessity by concentrating instead on the areas where they were arguably to achieve their greatest successes: the provision of welfare, cultural, educational and social facilities for the refugees from Austria, and the representation of their interests with the British authorities. By attracting large numbers of refugees to the events and facilities it provided, the Austrian Centre was also able to expose them to its politics. Its weekly, *Zeitspiegel*, and its many brochures, pamphlets and other publications greatly helped to disseminate its viewpoint on a wide range of issues. The dedicated work which the Austrian Centre performed for the benefit of the refugees, particularly during the dark days of mass internment in 1940, made it by far the largest and most successful of the Austrian refugee organizations, earning it the loyalty of thousands of refugees to a degree that extended far beyond their affinity with its politics.

The Austrian Centre thus presented the façade of a largely non-political organization, but this concealed the complexity of its true relationship to other Austrian refugee organizations and other political groups. We have already seen how the Council of Austrians was founded in September 1938, and how the Austrian Centre, established in February 1939, became the object of a power struggle between the original leaders of the Council and a group of energetic and determined young Communists, who effectively took over the running of the Centre. As already stated, the Centre engaged in a great number of welfare activities that were largely non-political and set up a number of groups, of which its youth organization, Young Austria, was the most obviously politicized. Even Young Austria, however, was by no means a mere creature of the Communist activists, but was designed to appeal to a far wider spectrum of youthful Austrian refugees. The model of the Popular Front organization emerges in the way in which the Communists were able to exercise a measure of control from behind the scenes over the Austrian Centre and Young Austria, and also over the organizations that included other political parties, like the Free Austrian Movement (FAM) and the Free Austrian World Movement (FAWM) that were founded later in the war.

The Austrian Centre did also act as a cover for Communist activity. The attempt to attract mass support from among the refugees by propagating broad anti-Fascist slogans and democratic-patriotic policies, in accordance with the Popular Front line, while at the same time converting sympathizers into Communist activists, is particularly clear in the case of Young Austria, which sought to recruit them into more disciplined and exclusive Party cadre organizations like the

'Kommunistischer Jugendverband' (Communist Youth Organization); this was a covert, conspiratorial body that functioned away from the public gaze. But the policies of the KPÖ in exile, which in Britain called itself the Group of Austrian Communists and was led by Hans Winterberg, were so moderate, and its aims, the creation of a national front uniting all Austrians in the fight against Hitler and ultimately the re-establishment of a free, independent and democratic Austria, so widely acceptable that political differences could mostly be easily smoothed over. For the duration of the Nazi-Soviet pact, in any case, the Communists were constrained by their uneasy situation from indulging in overt political activity, and the adoption of a non-political stance suited them well.

II. Time of Hope and Achievement: June 1941–November 1943

Hitler's invasion of the Soviet Union on 22 June 1941 transformed the political situation and consequently the political strategy of those who directed the Austrian Centre. Churchill's determined promotion of the alliance between Britain and the Soviet Union against Hitler, their common enemy, meant that the leaders of the Austrian Centre, no longer suspect as indirect allies of the Nazis through the Hitler-Stalin Pact, could discard their enforced concentration on non-political work and once more pursue overt political activity. The Austrian Centre's new-found enthusiasm for the British war effort allowed its members both to support Britain's Soviet ally and to align themselves wholeheartedly with the British people in its struggle against Hitler; the reservations of the Pact period about the 'imperialist war' were gratefully consigned to oblivion, along with every vestige of opposition to the war. The acute dilemma caused by Stalin's ultimately disastrous policy of reaching an accommodation with Hitler was resolved in favour of a renewed and decisive battle against Nazism.

The Soviet line of the people united in defence of the fatherland against the Fascist invader, encapsulated in the concept of the 'Great Patriotic War', was remarkably well suited to the position of the Austrian Communists; they were able to revert to the Popular Front slogan of unity against Fascism, now transmuted into an anti-Fascist 'nationale Einheitsfront' (national united front) of all true Austrians that transcended every barrier of party and class, and they were also able to promote as their overriding priority the re-establishment of an independent Austria. Above all, this new national, patriotic line, with its pronounced rejection of class-based politics in favour of national unity against Fascism, gave the Communists the ideological foundation on which could be built a movement capable of uniting all the Austrian groups in exile. Thereby they could create a mass base over which, in accordance with the tactics of the Popular Front, they could exercise a large measure of control, while maintaining good collaborative relations with Monarchists, Liberal bourgeois groups and Socialists.

The change in line emerged officially on 29 July 1941, when a statement in the name of the Council of Austrians called for unity against Hitler and signalled the new line of total mobilization of all resources for the war. Pacifism and anti-war sentiments were replaced by a new militancy. Preparation for battle ('Zum Kampf antreten!') became the watchword.[3] The rhetoric now deployed by *Young Austria/Junges Österreich*, the journal of the Austrian youth organization of the same name, emphasized the titanic nature of the conflict in which Nazi tyranny would be bloodily overthrown by a people's war uncompromisingly prosecuted by a coalition of the free Allied nations and those fighting for their freedom, Austria included: 'One day, in a future that is no longer distant, the bloodstained spectre of Nazism will be wiped from the face of the earth under the hammer blows of the armies of freedom and amidst the storm of peoples in revolt.'[4] The values underpinning this anti-Fascist struggle were derived from the Popular Front: the war was presented as the rising up of the peoples of the world in defence of liberty, culture, civilization and humanity against Nazi barbarism.

In its efforts to assist the anti-Fascist cause, the Austrian Centre gave pride of place to a determined campaign to maximize the contribution of its members to the British war effort. It exhorted them constantly to subordinate all other considerations to this end, urging them at every opportunity to seek employment in the munitions factories, in agriculture, in civil defence or in other sectors vital to the war effort. This in turn furthered the Centre's aim of persuading the authorities to reduce or remove the special regulations imposed on 'enemy aliens', such as the curfew and the restrictions on their movements and residence rights, and in this it met with success. The Centre did everything in its power to ensure that Austrians were actively involved in the war against Nazism, by encouraging those of military age to join up. It was particularly proud of those of its members who joined the British armed services, and campaigned forcefully for the right of Austrian refugees, both men and women, to join all branches of His Majesty's Forces. However, the ultimate goal of setting up a separate Austrian fighting unit, a symbol of sovereign autonomy like that of the Poles or Czechs, remained unachieved. The Centre presented the image of the refugees as communally committed to securing victory over Fascism, by fighting and, if necessary, dying in battle, by serving loyally in the Pioneer Corps, and by bearing their share of the burden on the home front, as fire-watchers or munitions workers.

Young Austrians volunteer for the British Army

The Austrian Centre also made every effort to contribute to the defence of the embattled USSR against the Fascist onslaught. The policy of the Pact period was completely reversed in favour of maximum commitment to the war effort, as many other considerations were subordinated to supporting the Soviet Union in its life-or-death struggle to defeat Hitler. This included the abrupt dropping of all class-based slogans, reflecting Stalin's fear that any continuation of revolutionary rhetoric might make the Western Allies less committed to assisting the Bolshevik state. The publications of the Austrian Centre brim with articles lauding the heroic struggle of the Red Army and the Soviet people, and also with unconditional praise of Stalin and the Soviet system, presented as a model form of popular, Socialist democracy. The new popularity of 'Uncle Joe' in Britain provided the Communists with a weapon against the London Bureau of the Austrian Social Democrats, who remained openly critical of the totalitarian and anti-democratic aspects of the Stalinist regime, and could therefore be accused of undermining the Anglo-Soviet alliance and the common war effort. The Austrian Centre, by contrast, worked hard in the cause of providing material, moral and propaganda support for the USSR, as exemplified in such campaigns as its 'Russian Aid Week' and the Austrian-Soviet Friendship Week of June 1942. Its publications also kept up a drumbeat of demands for the opening of a Second Front by the Western Allies, to reduce the military pressure on the USSR.

The Austrian Centre placed the highest hopes on the Anglo-Soviet alliance, later to include the USA. It was seen as the basis for the defeat of Fascism and for the establishment of a regime of common security, similar to that espoused by the Soviet Union in the period of the Popular Front, which would prevent any recurrence of German aggression and would usher in an era of peace and international cooperation. This was reflected precisely, at the national level, by the Austrian Centre's efforts to create a united organization of the Austrians in exile, in which political and ideological differences could be more or less harmoniously resolved, in the interests of defeating Hitler, the common foe, and of rebuilding a free, independent and democratic Austria. The alliance came to be seen as the cornerstone of the efforts of all free peoples to throw off the yoke of Fascism and as the guarantor of the sovereign right of all nations, especially the small Central and South-Eastern European states, to determine their own affairs free from the threat of German expansionism.

After June 1941 the Austrian Centre accorded absolute primacy to the goal of victory over Nazism, as *Zeitspiegel* declared unambiguously: 'Fascism must be eradicated at its roots – everything else must be subordinated to this end.'[5] This was to be achieved by creating the maximum unity and solidarity among all those Austrians devoted to the anti-Fascist cause of expelling the German invader and re-establishing an independent Austria. The war against Nazism thus became virtually synonymous with the patriotic struggle of all nationally-minded Austrians to liberate their homeland from alien occupation and reassert Austrian sovereignty and liberty: 'This war is in its essence and origin a war of peoples for their national existence, for their right to live in a state of their own.'[6] The Austrian Centre aimed particularly to enrol the energies and idealism of youth in the battle for a free Austria; with the vigorous youth movement Young Austria at its side, it appeared well equipped to win over the mass of the younger émigrés to the twin tasks of national liberation in war and national reconstruction thereafter.

The priority accorded to unity among all groups of exiled Austrians in the struggle for national liberation and reconstruction meant that the Communists and the Austrian Centre could propound only a fairly limited political agenda. They were reluctant to enter publicly into detailed blueprints for the political and constitutional organization of the future Austria, at least until the war was won. Although in other spheres, such as education, they did work out plans in detail, these were very much secondary to the grand aim of the defeat of Hitler and the creation of a free and independent Austria, which would enjoy full popular democracy, the total elimination of Fascism from its national life and good relations with its neighbours, especially Czechoslovakia. Broadly, the Austrian Centre preferred to keep its detailed plans for post-war Austria a matter for internal debate; public discussion was on the whole avoided, at least until later on in the war, when the Free Austrian Movement began to publish a considerable volume of documents on the future of Austria.

The Communists, more moderate than the Social Democrats, refused even to state that the future Austria would be a republic, for fear of alienating the Monarchists, with whom they were to work closely in the Free Austrian Movement. This question was to be left open until after the war; in the meantime, political debate and dissension, which might lead to the fracturing of the Austrian 'national front' if carried on publicly, was discouraged. This was graphically articulated by Marie Köstler, leader of the League of Austrian Socialists in Great Britain, a small splinter group that sided with the Communists against the Social Democrats: 'When a house is on fire, everyone comes running to help put it out. One talks about the causes of the fire later. What matters here is the common struggle against Hitler, we can discuss the future form of the Austrian state once we have beaten him.'[7]

The publicly propounded aim of re-establishing a democratic Austria did not define what democracy meant in practice, which was to be left until after the war; the powerful emphasis on wartime unity also relegated to the post-war future the difficult task of reconciling the divergent views of democracy held by the various Austrian groups in exile. The Austrian Centre argued that those fighting Hitler knew very well what democracy was, as did the victims of Nazism at home in Austria, both of whom were defending democracy by the very act of resisting Hitler's dictatorship. It went on to argue that the more national unity there was in a country, the more democracy there was, and the more resolve to defend its freedom and independence.

This stance was dictated by the pronouncedly national character of the Austrian Centre's policies and statements, which centred overwhelmingly on the re-establishment of a free and independent Austria, as demonstrated by such of its publications as *The Case of Austria* (1942), *This Is Austria* (1942) and *The Austrian Ally* (1942). All that counted politically was the division between the Nazis and their Austrian adherents on the one side and the anti-Fascist forces of resistance and national liberation on the other; the unity of the latter was paramount, whether within Austria or in exile, and it embraced Monarchists and Communists, peasants and workers, bourgeois and intellectuals. The propaganda of the Austrian Centre was designed to appeal to Catholics, with the aim of sealing the national pact between 'Black' (Catholic) and 'Red' (Socialist) adherents.

To create and preserve this all-important unity in the fight for an independent Austria, the Austrian Centre and, later, the Free Austrian Movement had first to reinterpret the turbulent events leading up to the incorporation of Austria into the Third Reich. The influence of Alfred Klahr's ideas on Austria's separate national identity and consciousness and its independence from Germany is very significant here. To establish the ideological basis for the struggle for national liberation against the German aggressor, it was necessary to rewrite recent Austrian history from the perspective of popular unity against Fascism and resistance to Hitler, and this is a recurrent theme in the Austrian Centre's publications. To avoid damaging relations with the right-wing Monarchists and adherents of the Dollfuss-Schuschnigg regime, the abolition of democracy and the forcible repression of the Left under the 'Ständestaat' (corporate state) were largely stripped of their connotations of class conflict and generally downplayed – though the Social Democrats, who remained outside the Austrian Centre and the Free Austrian Movement, could be lambasted with impunity for their failure to resist Dollfuss's forces effectively in February 1934.

The Austrian Centre usually limited itself to expressing regret at these events for creating the divisions and demoralization that enabled the agents of Nazism in Austria to undermine the alleged unity of the people and its will to resist the Anschluss four years later. The image of the Anschluss itself was also tailored to fit the demands of the ideology of national liberation. Far from welcoming Hitler, the Austrian people was presented as submitting under duress to a combination of military might, propagandistic manipulation and the manoeuvres of a handful of highly placed traitors. Austria was effectively placed on the same footing as the other small, peace-loving countries overrun by Hitler, thus giving rise to the crucial concept of Austria as the 'first victim' of Nazi aggression, a concept that sat somewhat uneasily with the evident enthusiasm with which Hitler had been received in Vienna in March 1938 and with the willing integration of a sizeable number of Austrians into the Reich and its activities. The revocation of Britain's *de facto* recognition of the Anschluss was a central objective of the Austrian Centre.

Writing on the occasion of the fourth anniversary of the Anschluss in March 1942, F.C. West, President of the Austrian Centre, gave a classic exposition of the Centre's view of the Anschluss as a brutal act of conquest inflicted on a predominantly resentful and hostile population, a line that the Centre had constantly reiterated ever since 1938. West claimed that already in the last weeks of Austrian independence a 'national resistance front' against Hitler had sprung into being; this was the basis on which a widespread and growing movement of resistance to German occupation could be predicated. The existence of a significant resistance movement within Austria, later to be dignified with the title

'Austrian Freedom Front', was crucial to the image of Austria as an occupied nation, not as a loyal part of the Third Reich. For only by contributing to its own liberation could Austria claim its place among the oppressed nations struggling for their freedom against Nazi tyranny. As West put it: 'When the free peoples of the world, when the oppressed peoples declare today that after their victory over Hitler each nation will be valued according to its contribution to the struggle against Hitler, we are convinced that the Austrian people will be among those peoples that have contributed their share in the struggle against the common enemy.'[8]

Proponents of this view of Austria had been much encouraged by Churchill's speech of 19 February 1942, when he promised that Britain would never forget that Austria had been the first victim of Nazi aggression, that Britain would stand loyally by Austria in her struggle for liberation from the 'Prussian yoke', and that on the day of an Allied victory Austria would take her place of honour among the free nations. Foreign Office disapproval of the speech meant that it was still far from becoming government policy, but leaders of the Austrian Centre like Eva Kolmer seized on it eagerly, though she knew the reservations of British policy-makers towards Austria full well from her Foreign Office contacts.

When writing for public consumption, Kolmer interpreted the speech firstly as a declaration by the Prime Minister that it was a British war aim to reverse the Anschluss, as an illegal act of violence that was *de facto* null and void, and that the British Government now recognized Austria to be an independent state that had been overrun by the Nazi armies; and secondly as a statement by the British government that the Austrian people could only earn its place of honour among the nations by actively participating in resistance to German rule and by mounting a national liberation movement.[9] The leaders of the Austrian Centre were gratified by official British policy statements that they could interpret as moving towards the fulfilment of that crucial aim: the re-establishment of a free and independent Austria, on the condition that Austria played an active part in its own liberation. They welcomed Eden's declaration regarding Austria in the Commons in September 1942 and Lord Cranborne's statement in the Lords in May 1942, pointers towards the eventual acceptance of Austrian independence as an Allied war aim in the Moscow Declaration in November 1943. The Foreign Office was again dismayed by Cranborne's speech, which was indeed close to the policy propagated by the Austrian Centre.

The greatest success of the Austrian Centre in creating a united front of the Austrian groups in exile came with the founding of the Free Austrian Movement (FAM) on 3 December 1941. Ideologically, it fulfilled the Centre's overriding requirement for national unity in the fight against Hitler; politically, it brought into being an umbrella organization effectively controlled by the Centre, but which reached out further to enable the Centre to mobilize for its aims most sections of the Austrian emigration. It had thus created the conditions for a mass base, to match the united mass base of resistance within Austria that was, according to the Centre and its publications, being built with heroic effort by the Austrian Freedom Front.

The Free Austrian Movement consisted initially of the Austrian Centre, the Council of Austrians, the Monarchists organized in the Austrian League, the Austrian Democratic Union (a small bourgeois group led by Emil Müller-Sturmheim and Julius Meinl), the Association of Austrian Social Democrats (a breakaway group led by Heinrich Allina), Marie Köstler's League of Austrian Socialists in Great Britain, the Austrian Communists in Great Britain, and a number of youth, professional and regional organizations, fifteen member organizations in all. The Communists had by far the greatest number of adherents, especially given their influence in the Austrian Centre, and could effectively dominate the FAM; only the Monarchists and their allies in the Austrian Office provided something of a counterweight.

In time more Austrian groups joined the FAM. Its success was such that it expanded to embrace Austrian organizations abroad, principally in Palestine, in the Mediterranean area and the Middle East where Austrians were serving with the British forces, and also in Latin America; this led to the founding of the yet more grandiosely named Free Austrian World Movement. But the underlying problem of creating a politically coherent movement, whose strategy and ideology would unite the Austrian exiles and which could then play a decisive part in the rebuilding of a new post-war Austria, was not fully resolved. The Austrian Democratic Union left the FAM in July 1943, followed by the Monarchists and the Association of Austrian Social Democrats two months later, but the effect of these withdrawals on the FAM's activities was in practice small.

Central to the activities of the Austrian Centre and the FAM was their support for the British war effort, with Young Austria playing a particularly energetic part. The Austrian Centre was tireless in exhorting its civilian members to do essential war work, in the munitions factories and other sites of war production, in agriculture and forestry, and to participate in such vital tasks of civil defence as fire-watching. The refugees from Austria were still subject after the end of mass internment to considerable restrictions on their activities, classed as they were as 'enemy aliens', and the determined struggle waged by the Austrian Centre against those restrictions was aimed in no small measure at removing the barriers that prevented the civilian refugees from making their full contribution to the war effort. In this the Centre was largely successful, as more and more areas were opened up to the refugees and irksome, discriminatory regulations made less burdensome or removed entirely.

The refugees encountered even more formidable obstacles when they sought to participate in the war effort in a military capacity. At first, 'enemy aliens' were only permitted to join the non-combatant Pioneer Corps, but gradually they gained access to almost all branches of the British forces. The publications of the Austrian Centre registered with evident satisfaction the contribution made by its members, both men and women, in the armed services, detailing some of the exploits of those on active service, and recording with pride the names of those fallen in action. However, the Austrian Centre failed in one of its key aims, the creation of a separate Austrian Fighting Unit. Its repeated and insistent efforts towards this end met with no positive response from the British authorities; this represented a limitation on the acceptance in practice by the British government of Austria as an equal member of the coalition of allied nations fighting Nazi Germany. This was reflected at the highest political level in the failure of the Austrian Centre to establish an Austrian government in exile, like that of the Czechs or Poles.

The Austrian Centre saw the contribution made by Austrians in exile to the British war effort as the counterpart abroad of the struggle against Nazi rule being waged by the forces of resistance inside Austria. Contributing to the war effort would prove that the Austrians were ready to make sacrifices for the liberation of their country, that they were dedicated to the British cause, and that they were thereby earning themselves and their country their deserved status as one of the Allied nations. The great war effort campaign launched by the FAM with a mass meeting in Porchester Hall, London, on 24 January 1942 and culminating in the 'Austrians for Britain' campaign in September 1942 was designed to secure the legitimation of Austria's claim to independent self-determination in the eyes of the free peoples, by virtue of its contribution to the common battle against Hitler.

For this reason the Austrian Centre was eager to emphasize its achievements in publications like *The Austrian Ally* (1942), which highlighted the five War Effort Committees it had set up, as well as the War Production Conference held by the FAM in February 1942. The publicity given by the Austrian Centre to its mobilization of its members for the war effort was also aimed, very successfully, at influencing British public opinion. By systematically targeting opinion-formers and sympathizers in prominent positions, the Austrian Centre built up for itself a public profile surprisingly favourable for a group of largely Jewish 'enemy aliens'. But the British government again proved less amenable in the sphere of propaganda and publicity; the FAM made only a limited independent input into British broadcasting to Austria, despite its repeated efforts and despite the evident sympathy of Patrick Smith, who ran the BBC's Austrian Section, with the FAM line on Austria (though not always with the FAM itself).

The key absentees from the FAM, whose refusal to join condemned it to fall short of fully representing the Austrians in exile, were the Socialists. Under the leadership of Karl Czernetz, they had organized themselves in the Austrian Labour Club and had exercised a surprising abstention from political activity, until Oscar Pollak introduced a more energetic and proactive strategy, partly in response to the success of the Communists in establishing the FAM. As explained previously, the Social Democrats remained thoroughly suspicious of the Communists, recognising that one of the abiding goals of the latter's Popular Front strategy was to gain control of the mass of the working class and to replace the Social Democrats as the principal political party of that class. The London Bureau of the Social Democrats pursued a sectarian and isolationist campaign aimed at maintaining its own political programme and its undiluted ascendancy over what it considered as its political constituency. It was determined not to be drawn into the FAM; indeed, it was later to create its rival to the FAM, the proposed Austrian Representative Body, which merely cut it off from the groups of Austrians organized in the FAM.

That the clash between the Austrian Centre-led FAM and the Social Democrats was to a considerable extent one for political control, rather than one of principle, is demonstrated by the very moderate and widely acceptable aims of the FAM, as stated in its founding declaration. Asserting their conviction that a free, democratic Austria with the right of self-determination was the wish of every Austrian, the member organizations urged all their fellow-countrymen in Britain to strain every sinew to support the Allied war effort, in parallel to the struggle for national liberation taking place inside Austria. Their aims were: to induce the British Government to withdraw its recognition of the forcible annexation of Austria; to work for the securing of the right of self-determination for the Austrian people; and to mobilize the Austrians in Britain for the Allied war effort, in a separate Austrian military unit, in civil defence and in war production, thereby achieving the removal of 'enemy alien' status from Austrians in Britain, as well as encouraging and strengthening resistance to Nazism inside Austria by means of propaganda.[10] These were hardly radical aims.

There were nevertheless heated exchanges between the Austrian Centre and the Social Democrats, often degenerating into political abuse. The Social Democrats, languishing ingloriously in self-imposed political isolation, were reduced to using the weapons of sectarian rhetoric and straightforward mudslinging against their more successful Communist rivals. The principal issue dividing them was the refusal of the Social Democrats to come out unambiguously in favour of an independent Austria, as the party still held to some vestiges of its post-1918 stance favouring a union of Austria with Germany. This enabled the publications of the Austrian Centre repeatedly to label the Social Democrats as defenders of the Anschluss, and hence as Pan-Germans whose policy was identical with Hitler's – though it was, in fairness, clear that a Greater Germany in which Social Democrats played a leading part would have differed hugely and fundamentally from the Third Reich. The Austrian Centre also did not shrink from criticizing its Monarchist partners when they went beyond the FAM's line, as when Otto von Habsburg attempted independently to create an Austrian battalion in the USA in late 1942, or whenever the Habsburg hankering after a Danubian confederation, denying Austria independent statehood, showed through.

The leaders of the Austrian Centre took particular issue with the Social Democrats' questioning of the viability of Austria as an independent economic and political entity, seizing every opportunity to emphasize the autonomy of Austria's culture and statehood and its economic self-sufficiency. They reserved particular wrath for the doubts expressed by the Social Democrats as to the extent of the resistance movement inside Austria. This was a point on which the Centre could make no concessions whatsoever, since the entire legitimation of all its activities in support of the war effort derived from its self-endowed status as the partner in exile of a strong and widespread patriotic liberation movement at home. Writing in *Zeitspiegel* on 21 August 1943, Willi Scholz made this point in the clearest terms: 'The only legitimation that the emigrant Austrians possess and can ever possess in appearing and acting as representatives of their country is their clear, programmatic alignment with the aims of the freedom fighters in the homeland itself' (p. 8). The FAM's programme, he wrote, accorded entirely with that of the Austrian Freedom Front, which was fighting for a free and independent Austria, governed according to the wishes of its own people and cleansed of all traces of the Nazis and their collaborators.

The Austrian Centre's stance was founded on the assumption of bitter and widespread hostility within Austria towards the German occupier and seething resentment of German rule (reflected in the titles of such brochures as *Restive Austria*). Reports in its publications on events under Nazi rule breathed a spirit of nationalistic enmity towards the Germans, who were referred to by the derogatory term 'Piefkes' and as 'Preußen', playing on the historic animosity between Austrians and militaristic, expansionist Prussians to demonstrate that Nazi ideology had had to be imposed on a reluctant Austria under the terroristic 'Fremdherrschaft' (foreign rule) of the hated 'Nazipreußen' (Nazi Prussians). Taking a line similar to that of BBC propaganda beamed at Austria, at least after 1942/43, the Austrian Centre depicted the Austrian population as loathing the locust swarm of 'alien' officials and carpetbaggers who had descended on them to take the best jobs and live off the fat of the land, a situation exacerbated by the evacuees escaping the Allied bombing by moving from Germany to Austria and by the deportation of Austrians as forced labour in the reverse direction. No opportunity was missed to detail graphically the miserable conditions endured by Austrians under German rule.

In every sphere of life, the Austrian Centre's publications played up the resistance to German occupation: strikes and sabotage of production in the factories; the illegal hoarding of agricultural produce on the land; mutinies, mass desertions and disaffection among Austrians in the Wehrmacht on account of their use as cannon-fodder on the most exposed parts of the battlefield; public demonstrations of sympathy for prisoners of war and foreign workers doing forced labour in Austria, and even for Jews about to be deported to the death camps; Austrian patriots executed in large numbers for anti-Nazi activities; a rising tide of organized resistance, especially once the activities of Tito's partisans on Austria's Southern borders inspired their Austrian counterparts to action, including the derailment of trains, the ambushing of army and SS convoys, and the steady growth of a national network of resistance groups. A critical point was reached in October 1942, with the founding conference of the underground Austrian Freedom Front. This was hailed as a patriotic organization which, declaring itself at war with Germany, could coordinate resistance groups nationwide and give expression to the national desire for liberation, by virtue of its ability to represent all strata of the Austrian population and all anti-Fascist political forces and to conduct a real campaign of popular resistance.

The Social Democrats dismissed most of this as existing only in the columns of the Austrian Centre's press and suspected (correctly) that the radio station 'Free Austria', the mouthpiece of the internal resistance, was in reality based in Moscow, a suspicion confirmed by the fact that the transmitter remained mysteriously immune to Gestapo detector vans, even though *Zeitspiegel* obligingly published details of its transmissions and wavelengths. It is only fair to say that the Moscow Declaration, which classed Austria as the first victim of Nazi aggression, gave the imprimatur of the three great Allied powers to the image of Austria as a small, oppressed nation struggling valiantly against Nazi rule. Nevertheless, this exaggeration of resistance to Nazi rule, aimed at bringing Austria into line with occupied countries like France or Yugoslavia, was later to have serious consequences: the leaders of the Austrian Centre fell victim to their own propaganda and, basing their strategy on a mistaken estimate of the support for their actively anti-Fascist line among the Austrian population, returned to Austria after the war with unrealistic policies and expectations. (In this, it must be said, they were encouraged by the Foreign Office, which was for a while receptive to this view of the situation inside Austria and approved the sending of British help to strengthen partisan groups, until a change of policy supervened.)

Nor would the emphasis on Austrian anti-Fascism and on the steadfast rejection of Nazism by the mass of the population have impressed the Austrian Jewish exiles favourably: too many of them had witnessed at first hand the exultation with which many Austrians had welcomed the Anschluss, and too many had suffered at first hand from the zeal with which some Austrians had implemented the new regime's anti-Semitic measures. The fact was that the great majority of the Austrian refugees in Britain were non-political Jews, whom it was difficult to rally to the Austrian Centre by means of appeals to Austrian nationalism and patriotism. Nationalism in Austria had become tarred with the explosion of pro-German enthusiasm that followed the Anschluss and spelt suffering and death to many thousands of Jews.

It was hard for Austrian Jews to square the image of Austria as the first victim of Nazi aggression with their own experience of the level of Austrian support for Hitler and for Nazi anti-Semitism after the Anschluss. Jewish readers would also have felt uncomfortable with the depiction of the systematic elimination of Austrian Jewry under National Socialism by the publications of the Austrian Centre, which tended to treat the persecution of the Jews as but one instance among many cases of Nazi oppression of occupied nations; the special dimension of Hitler's 'Final Solution' of the 'Jewish question' was often understated. This was the case even though most of the Austrian Centre activists were themselves Jewish and could not be insensitive to the fate of the Jews. However, they had made a very conscious decision to give their primary loyalty to Marxist ideology and the Communist Party, which inevitably meant renouncing the greater part of their Jewishness, in terms of religion, the Jewish way of life and personal identity.

In the middle years of the war, brochures like Wilhelm Scholz's *Ein Weg ins Leben: Das neue Österreich und die Judenfrage* (*The Road to Life: The New Austria and the Jewish Question*) (1943) concentrated on persuading as many Jewish refugees as possible to return home and on attacking Zionism, which was seen as the principal ideological competitor to Austrian patriotism for their loyalty. The Austrian Centre was keen to emphasize the image of the Jews as fighters, not as passive victims, thereby enlisting them in the anti-Fascist struggle which, it argued, would end with the defeat of Nazism and thus with the elimination of anti-Semitism, in parallel with the liberation of all oppressed groups from Nazi tyranny. It repeatedly asserted that it was entirely possible to be both a good Jew and a loyal Austrian patriot: 'The Jews of Austria can best resolve their problems within the overall framework of Austria's struggle for freedom, as the Jews of England resolve theirs as soldiers in the English army and in other sectors of England's battlefront'.[11] This difficult area was, however, a problem that lay largely in the future. In late 1943, the Austrian Centre and the FAM could concentrate on their greatest triumph, the recognition of the reestablishment of an independent Austria in the Moscow Declaration.

III. Time of Triumph and Illusion: November 1943–May 1945

On 30 October 1943 the Allied Powers signed the Moscow Declaration, which stated their intention of restoring a free and independent Austria, the goal for which the Austrian Centre and the FAM had long striven. The Moscow Declaration was a crucial event in the politics of the exiled Austrians, for it marked the unambiguous commitment of the Allies to the re-emergence of Austria as a sovereign state once it had been freed from German rule. It also spelled the end for any plans to create a multinational Central European block, such as a Danubian federation of states or a reconstituted Habsburg Empire; since these had been in part conceived of as a *cordon sanitaire* against the westward advance of Soviet Communism, they had always been anathema to the Austrian Centre activists.

The Declaration stated that Austria had been the first free nation to fall victim to Nazi aggression and that the Allies consequently regarded the Anschluss of March 1938 as null and void. The liberation of Austria from German rule and its re-establishment as a free nation now became enshrined as Allied war aims. The Moscow Declaration came very close to enunciating the central doctrines of the Austrian Centre and the FAM. They were able to claim that the Allies shared their view that the Anschluss had been an act of violence and coercion inflicted on a largely unwilling populace and that Austria was an occupied and oppressed nation struggling alongside its European sister nations for liberation from Nazi tyranny. In denominating Austria as one of the countries suffering under foreign occupation, the Moscow Declaration fulfilled one of the dearest wishes of the Austrian Centre, by drawing the sharpest distinction between Austria and Germany as national entities, by recognising the legitimacy of Austria's struggle for independence and thus elevating its fight for freedom to the status of a war of national liberation.

The Austrian Centre's publications could justifiably claim that the battle against German rule was now inseparably linked to the restoration of Austrian independence. By declaring that the liberation of Austria from German rule must take the political form of the re-establishment of a free and independent Austria, the Allies had provided the Austrian Centre with a handy weapon against any group that did not take its stance unambiguously on the central principle of Austrian independence; the Socialists, reluctant to commit themselves on this issue, could be accused of opposing Allied policy and working against the Grand Alliance itself. Another welcome point in the Moscow Declaration was the statement that the restoration of national sovereignty would provide Austria and its

Central European neighbours with the means to achieve the political and economic security that would guarantee peace; this chimed with the thinking of the Austrian Centre, both in its implicit recognition of Austria as a viable economic unit and in its advocacy of close cooperation between Austria and states like Czechoslovakia and Yugoslavia. The collaboration between the FAM and the Czech government in exile could be seen as validated by the Moscow Declaration.

To its credit, the Austrian Centre did not shy away from the second part of the Moscow Declaration, which stated that Austrians could not evade their responsibility for participating in the war on the side of Nazi Germany and that any final settlement must take account of the part that Austria played in bringing about its own liberation. This made Austria responsible for atoning for its earlier involvement with Hitler's criminal activities by contributing actively to his defeat and its freedom. For the Austrian Centre that responsibility was the determining factor behind all policy for Austria:

> It imposes on all Austrians, at home and abroad, the obligation of intensifying Austria's resistance to the point of a people's war, of ensuring the total commitment of every Austrian to that cause, of holding the traitors to Austria, the lackeys of foreign German rule, to account in the most rigorous fashion, and of subordinating everything else to the task of winning our independence ourselves by our common commitment to the Austrian Freedom Front.[12]

Here, however, lay the weakness that was to undermine the political position of the Austrian Centre activists. For while the Moscow Declaration represented their greatest success, in that it formally adopted as Allied war aims their cardinal points of policy, it also foreshadowed their failure to realise their post-war vision, in which a nationwide resistance movement was to have forged in the crucible of the people's liberation struggle a new Austria purged of the impurities that had led to its association with Nazi Germany.

The paramount necessity for Austrians to demonstrate that they had contributed significantly to their own liberation obliged the Austrian Centre to lay the greatest emphasis on the magnitude of resistance within Austria. Above all, it portrayed the Austrian Freedom Front as the key body within which the resistance movement was organized and which would play a vital part in determining the shape of post-war Austria, after successfully concluding its struggle for national liberation. The activities of the Austrian Freedom Front were adduced as evidence of Austria's status as an occupied country fighting for its freedom; the alleged dimensions of internal resistance within Austria became the means whereby Austria earned parity with other oppressed nations in the Allied ranks; and the image of a people rising up against the German oppressor became the basis on which Austria's claim to independence could be justified in the eyes of the world. The result of this was a tendency to overstate the levels of resistance within Austria on a grand scale, whether it was the intensity of hostility of the populace to the German intruders, the numbers supporting the Freedom Front, or the prevalence of acts of overt resistance like the sabotaging of industrial production, attacks on German and SS forces or the formation of active partisan units.

It was vital for the Austrian Centre and the FAM to be able to claim that their entire activities were orientated towards supporting the Freedom Front, which was struggling heroically inside Austria for the paramount goal of national liberation. Within days of the Moscow Declaration, the FAM announced that it was constituting itself as the committee charged with preparing the way for an Austrian National Committee; this, the nearest it managed to come to a government in exile, was intended to become the parallel body in Britain to the Freedom Front at home, as the organization embodying the will to unity and victory among the Austrians in exile. Unity was indeed the cardinal watchword: unity among the exiled Austrians in the new National Committee; and unity among all patriots inside Austria within the Freedom Front, which stood above political parties as the supreme directing body of the resistance movement, appealing to Austrians across all ideological and religious differences, all social and occupational divides like that between peasants, workers and intellectuals, all divisions of age and class, of traditional orientation and institutional allegiance.

However, that unity was to remain a dream. Reacting to the Moscow Declaration, the Socialists embraced a new activism and announced the creation of their own Austrian Representative Body ('österreichische Vertretungskörperschaft'), which was also intended to gather the exiled Austrians together politically under its pennant. The FAM was not slow to reject this alternative body, and it was joined by the Communists, whose line on the Moscow Declaration, the Austrian Freedom Front and the Austrian National Committee was identical to that of the FAM, in their shared enthusiasm for national patriotism and unity. The predictable result was a stand-off between the two bodies, each of which could block its rival's claim to represent the totality of the Austrians in exile, but neither of which could overcome its rival's opposition or bring itself to reach a compromise.

There ensued a continuing exchange of insults and accusations, creating a situation of institutionalized stalemate between the warring parties, gratifying only to the British authorities, who were anxious to avoid taking decisions about the post-war government of Austria. The position inside Austria remained obscure: the Austrian Centre and the FAM claimed legitimacy by virtue of their link to the Freedom Front, which, they said, was fulfilling through its active and widespread resistance to Nazi rule the Allies' demand that Austria must contribute to its own liberation. They attacked the Socialists for allegedly casting doubt on the reliability of reports of the Freedom Front's achievements and declared that questioning the extent of Austrian resistance to Nazism served only to undermine the will to fight and to weaken and divide the anti-Fascist forces.

As will be shown in a later chapter, the Moscow Declaration represented the high-water mark of the Austrian Centre's political achievements. From late 1943 until the end of the war, the Centre's publications continued to reiterate, with increasing intensity and urgency, the same concepts of national unity, patriotism and popular liberation, with variations but with no essential advances. The Centre had pinned its faith on that political line, and it could now do little more than wait for the course of the war to prove it right or wrong in its strategy. With the advance of the Red Army into Eastern Europe in early 1944 and the invasion of France by the Western Allies in the summer, the leaders of the exiled Austrians could mostly only react to events, as the tide of war approached the borders of Austria, and political slogans and positions had their validity tested by the realities of events on the battlefield.

The statement of the tasks facing the Austrian people for 1944, as set out in *Zeitspiegel* on the front page of its final issue of 1943, is a typical summary of the position of the Austrian Centre and the FAM in this last phase of the war. It was that people's duty

> To fight its way out of German slavery and into the ranks of the freedom-loving nations, to rise in open war against the German intruders, and in the struggle against German imperialism to take up its future position: to be a link in a secure bulwark against the German drive to the East, and thereby to establish once and for all its independence, its stability and economic prosperity in cooperation with its Slav neighbours and with the Allies in the East and the West.

Nationalism had become a key value, for at a time when German capitalism had degenerated into the worst kind of imperialistic Fascism, the concept of the nation had gained fresh power and significance, as the solid bastion that could repel the aggressor and invader. Austrians had to become conscious of their independent national identity, as distinct from their German oppressors. In this war, when all progressive forces were ranged against Hitler in a struggle for national freedom, the most urgent need for the Austrian people was to liberate itself from Nazi bondage. As the Austrian Centre repeated ceaselessly, Austria would be admitted to the ranks of the freedom-loving peoples only insofar as it contributed towards its own liberation and, recognising its duty as a nation, fought its way over to the Allied camp.

Increasingly, the events of the war overshadowed the formulations of the Austrian Centre and the FAM. *Zeitspiegel* of 25 March 1944 carried both a ringing appeal by Jenö Kostmann to Austrians to assert their right to national self-determination by rising up against German tyranny and the news of the first Allied bombing raid on Vienna; the war was being brought home to the people of Austria directly, and it would not necessarily impel them towards the Allied side as anti-Nazi militants. Even the news of the internationalization of the FAM through the creation of the Free Austrian World Movement in March 1944, in parallel to the earlier creation of an Austrian World Youth Movement from Young Austria, carried less weight than it would have done earlier in the war.

For the integration of Austrians worldwide into a single organization, however impressive a feat, remained on the sidelines of the conflict, unlikely to impact more than marginally on the attitudes and actions of Austrians at home in the Reich. Ultimately, the realization of the familiar aims of the new FAWM – the restoration of an independent Austria, support for the Freedom Front, cooperation with nations which approved the Moscow Declaration and the creation of a National Committee recognized by the Allies as the external trustee of the interests of the Freedom Front – was now dependent on the actions of others.

As the Allied armies approached Austria, the Austrian Centre focused its attention ever more closely on the resistance movement inside Austria, without which its political goals and aspirations could not be achieved. Reports of activities by Tito's partisans close to the Austro-Yugoslav border aroused hopes of a reordering of Austrian society in the wake of a successful war of national liberation, modelled on the national, ethnic and social reconciliation that the Austrian Centre activists claimed to detect in the new Yugoslavia. They also inspired the vision of Austrian partisan units operating in the mountains of the Southern provinces and acting as a focal point around which national resistance might crystallize, a phantom army waiting in the shadows for its moment to strike.

But the eagerness with which the publications of the Austrian Centre greeted every reported manifestation of anti-German activity betrayed some anxiety at the evident failure of a genuine national resistance movement to emerge. The urgency with which they exhorted Austrians to support the struggle for national liberation, as defeat loomed for the Nazis, served increasingly to highlight the absence of any such struggle in Austria. The unspoken fear could be read between the lines that the Allies would sweep into Austria and win the war without decisive action by Austrians to throw off the Nazi yoke and to earn their liberation as free Austrian patriots.[13]

Nevertheless, the Austrian Centre activists vehemently rejected any wait and see policy of inactivity. The Socialists, more cautious in their estimation of the fighting power of the Austrian resistance, advised against precipitate action; any attempt at a national uprising would, they believed, be suicidal. A resolution passed by the executive committee of the FAM in April 1944 branded such passivity as a betrayal of the Austrian people and the Allies and as providing assistance to the German oppressor. The FAM clearly hoped that by uniting the Catholic peasantry with the industrial workers in the struggle for liberation, it could marginalize the Socialists and create a Catholic-Communist national front that would exercise political control in Austria after the war. But the FAM could not escape the reality of the present situation: it recognized that despite the progress made in broadening and intensifying the resistance movement in Austria, the Germans were still able to use Austria as an operational base without encountering any serious armed opposition or any mass campaign of sabotage. The awareness that Austria was continuing to supply soldiers for Hitler's war and that its factories were continuing to provide munitions and supplies largely unopposed was a constant nagging problem for the proponents of a people's war against Nazism.

Brushing these considerations aside, the FAM argued that active resistance was the best means of defence against the German terror and that every day by which German rule was shortened would save thousands of lives, on the battlefields and in prisons and camps. The FAM was painfully aware of the responsibility that rested on Austrian shoulders for capitulating to Hitler without a fight in 1938, for participating in his criminal activities and supporting his war of aggression. Desperate to put an end to this intolerable situation, it explicitly advocated an armed war of popular liberation against German rule and exhorted Austrians openly to take up arms, to create a partisan movement and to launch a national liberation struggle against the occupying tyrant, so that the day of freedom would be brought nearer; it thus appeared to envisage the liberation struggle commencing before the final liberation of Austria by the Allies. Whether this was a realistic stance to adopt was to be demonstrated by events in the last year of the war. The FAM demanded a thorough purge of traitors, collaborators and Nazis at all levels of Austrian society; it evidently believed that the experiences of the Austrian people in the years since March 1938 could lead to an active and fundamental rejection of Nazism, its ideology and adherents on the part of the majority of Austrians.

The coordination of Allied military actions in France after the Normandy landings with well planned and widespread activities on the part of the Resistance was for the Austrian Centre an inspirational example to Austrians. Here an armed national uprising, amounting to a war of popular liberation, was transforming a conquered, inert people into a strong fighting ally against Hitler. The Austrian exiles should help in the task of preparing and organising an armed uprising in Austria, never doubting that the Austrian people were equally capable, under the leadership of the Freedom Front, of a great act of national regeneration. The formation in August 1944 of an Inter-Allied Commission to administer Austria after the war indicated that the Allies were less sanguine about the prospects for the emergence of a strong anti-Fascist movement with the potential to govern the country. Increasingly, the publications of the Austrian Centre resorted to the argument, also deployed on BBC broadcasts to Austria, that taking up the armed struggle was for Austria the only way of saving their country from the Nazis bent on dragging it down to destruction with them; this looked suspiciously like a counsel of despair.

The key question at this stage was indeed the level of resistance inside Austria and the degree to which it was coordinated within an organization nationwide. As occupied countries from Italy to Poland and from France to Slovakia burst into open resistance, the contrast with Austria could no longer be overlooked. The tendency systematically to exaggerate anti-German sentiment and activity inside Austria became ever harder to maintain. In August 1944 a long and thoughtful article by Hilde Mareiner compared the resistance in Austria with that in other countries awaiting liberation. While still advancing the familiar line that the Austrian people hated the Germans, felt alien rule to be intolerable and longed to be free of the burden of occupation, Mareiner acknowledged that the dimensions of Austrian resistance remained limited: the number of partisans and deserters was small compared with the number of soldiers fighting in Hitler's armies, as the incidence of disruption of production in the factories was not sufficient seriously to damage Austria's role as an arsenal for the Reich.

Austria, Mareiner wrote, lacked an organized mass resistance, the gathering together of all resistance forces, which was the precondition for the creation of a people's army that would mount a significant threat to the German occupation. She concluded that the task of the Freedom Front at this crucial juncture was to exploit the situation where the Germans were weakening, where their forces in Austria were being reduced and where the Austrian people was no longer in thrall to German propaganda and the myth of German invincibility. On that would depend the Allies' attitude to Austria.[14]

The collapse of the pro-Nazi governments in Romania and Bulgaria and the advance of Soviet forces into Poland, Hungary and Slovakia raised the prospect of the invasion of Austria by the Red Army. The Austrian Centre, like the BBC, was quick to move to dispel fears of the Red Army and the bogey of Bolshevism by citing Stalin's repeated declarations promising to respect the sovereignty of small nations and to abide by the principle of non-intervention in their affairs. The Red Army, it added, was universally recognized as an exemplary model of correct behaviour. As the war drew to a close, the Austrian Centre elaborated its vision of post-war Europe, which was inspired by the hope of a lasting peace. This would be guaranteed by continuing collaboration between the wartime Allies to prevent any recurrence of German aggression. Within a security system built by the Great Powers, the smaller Central European nations would play their part in deterring German expansionism both by asserting their national autonomy as sovereign states and by cooperating with neighbours who shared their foreign policy interests.

In Austria's case, this meant especially cooperation with Czechoslovakia, which had been a lone bastion of popular democracy in pre-war Central Europe and which was eager to develop close relations with the Soviet Union, the sole major European power not to have signed the betrayal of Czechoslovakia at Munich. During the war, the Czech government in exile espoused both the policies of a 'people's democracy', with the prospect of development in a Socialist direction, and a close alliance with the Soviet Union. The pact between the two countries served for the Austrian Centre as a demonstration of the role of the Soviet Union as the benevolent guarantor of peace and security from German expansionism in Central Europe. The FAM set great store by the 'Arbeitsgemeinschaft' (working group) that it had set up with sympathetic Czechs close to their government in exile, as a forum where joint plans for the post-war era could be worked out and coordinated; it saw Czechoslovakia as a model for post-war Austria. The vision of cooperation between the Great Powers had its logical counterpart in that between the smaller nations of Central Europe, and also between the progressive anti-Nazi forces, right- and left-wing, in Austrian internal politics.

In late March 1945 the Red Army crossed the border from Hungary and advanced into Austria, taking Vienna on 13 April. The Austrian Centre greeted the liberation of Vienna by Soviet forces with unrestrained enthusiasm, for it represented the culmination of all that it had struggled for over the wartime years. Reports in *Zeitspiegel* stressed the warmth with which Vienna welcomed the Red Army, painting a picture in which a city decked with Austrian and Soviet flags formed the backdrop to a friendly encounter between the Russian soldiers and the predominantly anti-Nazi population, which had helped to drive out the hated German occupier.[15] The Red Army, it was emphasized, would abide by the Moscow Declaration, respecting both the independence of Austria and the rights and property of its inhabitants.[16] Above all, the leading role of the Austrian Freedom Front was highlighted, in that it had ensured that Austria had fought for and earned its freedom and had not just received it as a present from the liberating armies.[17] The Austrian Centre vigorously contested the role played by the resistance group '05', which, though real enough, did not fit into its political scenario: the group functioned independently of the Freedom Front, and the Socialists had established contact with it, claiming it as their own.

The gap between reality and the politically inspired vision of the Austrian Centre was too evident to be concealed for long. Events in Austria at the war's end were to be a painful lesson for the Centre's activists. Initially, developments seemed to favour their cause. *Zeitspiegel* was able to hail the formation of the provisional government on 28 April 1945, with Karl Renner as Chancellor, as the rebirth of the Austrian state. The Communists were well represented in Renner's ministry, which was designed to give a measure of parity to the Social Democrats, the Christian Socials (now ÖVP) and the Communists. The Communists Ernst Fischer and Franz Honner became Secretary of State for Culture and Education and Secretary of State for the Interior respectively; the three Secretaries of State without portfolio and members of the Chancellor's political council were Adolf Schärf (Social Democrat), Leopold Kunschak (Christian Social) and Johann Koplenig (Communist); each Secretary of State had three Under-Secretaries, one from each party, thus maintaining the principle of three-way parity.

The Communists would have been encouraged by the inclusion of Koplenig, the leader of the KPÖ, who had returned from Moscow. But the fact that he sat alongside Kunschak, a notorious anti-Semite, did not bode well for the Austrian Centre's efforts to persuade its Jewish adherents in Britain to return to Austria. The weakness of the support for the Communists among Austrian voters became very clear in the poor performance of the KPÖ in the elections of November 1945. The Communists were never again to play more than a marginal role in Austrian national politics. This may have been due to the continuing effects of Nazi anti-Communist propaganda, or to the association of the Communists by voters with the Red Army, whose record of looting and rapine during the fighting of 1945 caused it to be seen as anything but an army of liberation, and with the much feared and highly unpopular Soviet occupying forces. Communist ideology was in any case not likely to achieve easy popularity with a predominantly Catholic population containing a relatively low proportion of industrial workers.

Another major disappointment was the failure of more than a tiny proportion of the Jewish refugees in Britain to return to Austria. Probably because their Marxist convictions had accustomed them to analyse social problems in terms of class, not race, the Austrian Centre activists had never addressed the Jewish question adequately and had consequently failed to address also the special nature of Nazi persecution of the Jews. The propaganda that they aimed at the Jewish refugees in England was ideological in nature: it sought to convince the Austrian Jews that they were part of the patriotic national front that united all Austrians against Nazism, and it combated the rival national appeal of Zionism.

But the reaction of the Jewish refugees was determined far more by the loss of their families and friends in the genocide and by their awareness of the part that many Austrians had played, actively or passively, in perpetrating, colluding in or supporting the despoliation and murder of the Jews; the Austrian Centre was quite unable to demonstrate that the bulk of the population at home had undergone any significant change of heart in its attitude to the Jews. The leading activists were able to return to Austria, often by resorting to subterfuges to get there earlier than the British authorities wished, but they were followed only by a small number of their erstwhile supporters. While some members of Young Austria returned, sometimes in groups, the vast majority of the Austrian exiles chose to remain in Britain. Politically, the Austrian Centre and the FAM vanished from the British scene once their leading spirits had returned to Austria; but back in Austria they were never able to establish themselves as a force of any real weight. In truth, their abiding legacy rests in their work for their members in Britain during the war.

Notes

1   *Young Austria*, September 1939, p. 2. Corrections have been made to the English of the original.

2   *Young Austria*, end October 1939, p. 2. The writer was a member of the Free German Youth (FDJ).

3   See Helene Maimann, *Politik im Wartesaal: Österreichische Exilpolitik in Großbritannien 1938-1945* , Vienna/Cologne/Graz, 1975, p. 82.

4   *Young Austria*, mid-July 1941, p. 6.

5   *Zeitspiegel*, 14 February 1942, p. 1.

6   *Zeitspiegel*, 23 May 1942, p. 2, in an article entitled 'Das Lebensrecht der Völker'.

7   *Zeitspiegel*, 25 October 1941, p. 5.

8   F.C. West, 'Die Stellung des österreichischen Volkes', *Zeitspiegel*, 7 March 1942, p. 3.

9   Eva Kolmer, 'Österreichs Sache', *Zeitspiegel*, 28 February 1942, p. 1. The front page of this issue is dominated by eager reactions to Churchill's speech.

10   The declaration appears under the heading 'Dokument der Einheit', *Zeitspiegel*, 13 December 1941, p. 5. See also the restatement of the FAM's aims in nine points in *Zeitspiegel*, 19 June 1943, p. 1.

11   *Zeitspiegel*, 17 October 1942, p. 2.

12   *Zeitspiegel*, 13 November 1943, p. 2.

13 As late as 17 March 1945, *Zeitspiegel* could present an impressive list of the alleged achievements of the Austrian resistance, but ended on the depressing note: 'Nevertheless it remains a fact [...] that we Austrians, seen as a community, lag so far behind the freedom-loving peoples in the struggle for freedom that they address us as an oppressed, but not yet as a freedom-loving people [...] In the very next weeks or never, Austria has the chance to win an honourable place for itself among the freedom-loving nations by its contribution to its liberation' (p. 3).

14 Hilde Mareiner, 'Die Chance des österreichischen Freiheitskampfes', *Zeitspiegel*, 19 August 1943, p. 3.

15 The headline on the front page of *Zeitspiegel* on 14 April 1945 ran: 'Österreichische Fahnen und Sowjetflaggen grüßen die Rote Armee im befreiten Wien' ('Austrian and Soviet Flags Greet the Red Army in Liberated Vienna').

16 'Eine Erklärung der Sowjetregierung über Österreich', *Zeitspiegel*, 14 April 1945, p. 1.

17 See 'Die erste Bewährung', *Zeitspiegel*, 14 April 1945, p. 1, which claims that only the ceaseless efforts of the Austrian Freedom Front made it possible for the Austrian people to 'pass the first test' of the liberation by participating in the expulsion of the Nazis.

PART TWO

KULTURPOLITIK IN EXILE

RICHARD DOVE

The interrelation of politics and culture, a central tenet of Communist ideology, gained particular importance in exile. The overriding political goal of the Austrian Centre, articulated after 1941 through the mouthpiece of the Free Austrian Movement, was the re-establishment of an independent and democratic Austria. The formulation of this policy owed much to the ideas of the Communist journalist and theoretician Alfred Klahr, whose seminal essay 'Zur nationalen Frage in Österreich' ('Concerning the National Question in Austria') decisively influenced the policy of the KPÖ after 1937.[1] Klahr emphasized the development of national consciousness as a precondition of nationhood. Rejecting the 'bourgeois' conception of 'nation' as a 'linguistic and cultural community', he argued that Austrian identity had been formed by a separate historical (and therefore cultural) development from Germany. Since the movement for national independence was 'indissolubly linked' to the struggle for democratic freedoms, it would be led by the working-class movement in Austria. In 1937, the KPÖ declared that the Party's prime task was the defence of national independence against attempts at annexation by the German Reich, a policy later adapted to the exigencies of exile. Strong echoes of Klahr's ideas can be heard in the pronouncements of leading functionaries of the Austrian Centre, such as its secretary Albert Fuchs and the journalist Jenö Kostmann.

Constraints on political activity in Britain, particularly in the early years of the war, left the Austrian Centre only limited scope for direct political propaganda. In the circumstances it became all the more important to affirm Austria's specific cultural identity, from which the corollary of political independence could be derived. Cultural events therefore became political activity by proxy, a fact helping to explain the extraordinary flourishing of Austrian cultural activity in wartime London. As we shall see, the Austrian Centre ran a full programme of cultural events – ranging from books and pamphlets, published under the imprint Free Austrian books, and the weekly newspaper *Zeitspiegel*, to theatre and cabaret, and above all music.

The aspect of the Austrian Centre's cultural programme which is best remembered by exiles is probably the small theatre, the Laterndl. Opening in June 1939 as a cabaret theatre, designed to foster a specifically Austrian tradition of political cabaret, the Laterndl became home to a theatre ensemble performing plays from the European and (later) Austrian repertoire. During the last year of its existence, the Laterndl staged a programme of exclusively Austrian plays, intended to demonstrate the distinctive nature of the Austrian theatre repertoire.

While theatre had a central place in Austrian national consciousness, it was music which was widely considered as the epitome of Austrian cultural achievement. The opening of the Austrian Centre concluded with a concert and music became a crucial accompaniment to many of its events thereafter. Music had a dual role to play in the cultural framework of emigration. On the one hand, it proved to be the ideal medium to rally Austrians in exile. On the other, as an art form which transcended language, it could provide a valuable contact with their British hosts and therefore help to heighten awareness of Austria's situation amongst the British public. In fact, as we shall see, music was the basis of various collaborative ventures with the British and with representatives of other Allied nations, thus constituting a particularly effective means of cultural propaganda.

The political dimension is most evident in the case of *Zeitspiegel*, whose successive reincarnations mark the shifting political fortunes of the Austrian emigration. Originally sub-titled 'Eine Wochenschau' or 'Weekly Review', it was rebranded early in 1942 as an 'Anti-Nazi Weekly' (a change coinciding with the establishment of the Free Austrian Movement), before becoming, in September 1942, an 'Austrian Weekly', changes which mark its transition from simple news digest to weekly newspaper with a distinct editorial policy.

Many of the articles in the cultural pages of *Zeitspiegel* reveal the tendency to use cultural criticism as a surrogate for political argument, an early example being the article by the paper's editor-in-chief, Jenö Kostmann, entitled 'The Fight for Austrian Culture'. Kostmann argued that one of the major tasks for Austrian exiles was 'to preserve, defend and propagate Austria's cultural heritage', for it was precisely this heritage which could nourish national consciousness and hence the spirit of resistance to foreign domination. The tone is didactic, the political precept unmistakeable.[2]

Earlier in 1942, *Zeitspiegel* had instigated a debate as to the real purpose of exile theatre, and more specifically of the Laterndl, inquiring whether it should simply seek to preserve the best traditions of Austrian theatre, or should pursue expressly political objectives, a debate involving such leading representatives of Austrian culture as the writer Robert Neumann and the artist Oskar Kokoschka.

The key role assigned to culture in the political discourse of Austrian exiles, and the shifting focus of the political and cultural agenda, are also evident in the proceedings of the two 'Kulturkonferenzen' (Cultural Conferences) held in 1942 and 1944. The first of these conferences was an attempt to mobilize a broad front of opinion behind a specific (if modest) political programme, inviting comparison with the conferences 'In Defence of Culture' organized by the Communist movement during the Popular Front period in the 1930s.

The first Cultural Conference, held on 29/30 August 1942 under the auspices of the Austrian PEN, and chaired by its President Robert Neumann, was attended by some 250 writers and artists, including the music critic David Bach, the musicologists Otto Erich Deutsch and Hermann Ullrich, and Ernst Buschbeck, the former curator of the Kunsthistorisches Museum. In convening the conference, Robert Neumann had outlined its aims as being:

1 to affirm Austrian culture, and its national and international recognition

2 to define the cultural tasks facing Austrian émigrés, namely international cooperation and the fight against Fascism.[3]

In short, it was designed to create a united front of Austrian culture – and to project that unity to both Austrian émigrés and to the British authorities.[4]

The keynote speech was delivered by Albert Fuchs, who since arriving in London at the beginning of 1939 had become the Austrian Centre's most articulate spokesman in cultural matters.[5] In his address, Fuchs spoke of Germany's political and *cultural* annexation of Austria. He stressed the distinctive nature of Austrian culture: cultural autonomy from Germany being a prerequisite of political independence. In reviewing the course of Austria's history, Fuchs noted that, at crucial moments, it had diverged from Germany's. He was quick to link cultural achievement with political emancipation, particularly stressing the importance of music. If the new spirit of the Enlightenment had been slow to develop in Austria, there was one area in which 'the New breaks through: music. Throughout the work of Mozart and Beethoven blows the great wind of history – the breath of freedom, progress and humanity'. In turning to Austria's wars of liberation, he drew a contemporary moral, portraying Andreas Hofer as a leader of resistance to French – *and German* occupation.

In discussing 'Vormärz' (Pre-March Era, leading up to the failed March 1848 revolution), Fuchs cited the theatre repertoire as the medium of expression of an emerging middle class: 'Raimund, Nestroy and even

Grillparzer have their roots in the suburbs.' There was an interesting parallel in a speech on Austrian coffee-houses by Walter Hollitscher, who suggested that their reputation for apolitical 'Gemütlichkeit' was misplaced, since they had provided the stage for the political discussions which had adumbrated the 1848 revolution.[6]

While stressing the distinctive nature of Austrian culture, Fuchs disclaimed any nationalistic intent: 'We want to illustrate, to ourselves and to others, the particular nature of the Austrian spirit. Nothing else' (p. 6). The importance attached to this speech by the Austrian Centre is confirmed by the decision to issue the text as a pamphlet under the imprint Free Austrian Books.

The distinctiveness of Austrian culture and its international significance were both demonstrated in the pageant 'Immortal Austria', staged at the Kingsway Hall on 13 March 1943 'to mark the fifth anniversary of the occupation of Austria'. The text of the pageant was written by the journalist Eva Priester (one of the editorial triumvirate of *Zeitspiegel*) and the young Erich Fried, already a rising star on the exile literary scene. The music for the pageant was written by Hans Gál; this was one of a number of occasions on which the composer collaborated with the Austrian Centre or the Free Austrian Movement. The scenes ranged from a short depiction of the legendary Viennese figure 'der liebe Augustin' to 'A Concert in Bath 1795' in which young English ladies asked each other: 'How is it? Are all composers Austrians? Or all Austrians composers?', to a scene in which an Austrian patriot from the time of the Seven Years War confronted Frederick the Great of Prussia, eliciting from Albert Fuchs the comment: 'It was an original historical concept, which was revealed here.'[7] Both themes were reiterated in Hermann Ullrich's essay 'Austria's Culture – a European necessity', published in *Austrian News*.[8] Ullrich became the FAM's leading cultural spokesman, editing the *Kulturelle Schriftenreihe des Free Austrian Movement* from 1944 to 1946, which compressed into its pages a dazzling kaleidoscope of Austrian cultural achievement. Ullrich is also credited with the idea of the second Cultural Conference, which was organized by the FAM on 21/22 October 1944.

The progress of the war, and particularly the Moscow Declaration of November 1943, had set a new political and cultural agenda. The second Cultural Conference therefore took place in an entirely different context to the first. The new imperative was to establish a programme for cultural reconstruction in a liberated post-war Austria, in which many of the conference participants aspired to play a leading role. Among the numerous distinguished figures who attended both conferences, one of the few who were internationally known was Egon Wellesz. The composer and musicologist had come to England with a considerable reputation and had been appointed to a Research Fellowship in Oxford – only to be interned in 1940. In a keynote speech, Wellesz proposed a role for Austrian music in a post-war Europe. Austrians could not dream nostalgically of a past to which there was no return: 'We must try to imagine the musical life of a country which, being situated between the great powers in the West and the East, but also on the road from North to South, can become a new centre in the heart of Europe.'[9] According to Wellesz, the historical tradition of Austrian music was international in character, an argument also espoused by the FAM. It was only by welcoming the widest range of international artists in the post-war years that Austria could re-assert its own musical identity.

Also amongst the speakers at the second Cultural Conference was Albert Fuchs, whose speech 'Literature in the new Austria' contained a fourteen-point plan, which listed detailed measures for an independent Austria.[10] Among Fuchs's proposals was the idea of an 'Academy of Literature', which by analogy with the Académie française should be 'in the hands of outstanding cultural and political figures from all schools of thought'. Permeating all his fourteen points was the conviction that Austrian literature had a crucial role to play in shaping national identity (and therefore Austrian political independence) in the post-war period.[11]

Little was heard of any of these ambitious plans in the cold-war climate of post-war Austria, where many of the cultural cohorts of Nazism continued or soon resumed their careers. The ideas so carefully conceived in exile were largely stillborn, part of a wider failure by returning émigrés to set the cultural (and political) agenda in the early post-war years.

Notes

1   Klahr's essay 'Zur nationalen Frage in Österreich', which appeared under the pseudonym 'Rudolf', was published in two parts in *Weg und Ziel*, March/April 1937. The essay – copies of the journal were published in Czechoslovakia and smuggled into Austria for clandestine distribution – was the subject of lively discussion in Communist circles. It has been republished in Alfred Klahr, *Zur österreichischen Nation*, Vienna 1997.

2   *Zeitspiegel*, 30 May 1942, p. 8.

3   Circular from Robert Neumann, 20 May 1942, Neumann Papers, Austrian National Library, Vienna, Ser. n. 21.495c.

4   The success of the aim can be confirmed from the fact that a report on the conference was broadcast by the Austrian Programme of the BBC. Cf. J.K. [= Jenö Kostmann], 'Österreichische Kulturkonferenz', *Zeitspiegel*, 5 September 1942, p. 7.

5   See Albert Fuchs, *Über österreichische Kultur. Vortrag gehalten auf der Kulturkonferenz des PEN*, London 1942.

6   See Hollitscher, 'Vom Kaffeehaus, der Gemütlichkeit und ihren Grenzen', *Zeitspiegel*, 28 November 1942, p. 6.

7   Albert Fuchs, 'Immortal Austria' in *Zeitspiegel*, 20 March 1943, p. 7.

8   *Austrian News*, special edition marking the fifth anniversary of the Anschluss, March 1943, p. 5.

9   Egon Wellesz, 'Zum Wiederaufbau des Musiklebens in Österreich', *Zeitspiegel*, 4 November 1944, pp. 6-7.

10   See Willi Weinert, 'Zum Leben von Albert Fuchs', *Die Alfred Klahr Gesellschaft und ihr Archiv. Beiträge zur österreichischen Geschichte des 20. Jahrhunderts*, Vienna 2000, pp. 259-76.

11   Many of Fuchs's ideas were first drafted in his contributions to *Zeitspiegel*, some of them being subsequently integrated into his book *Geistige Strömungen in Österreich*, Vienna 1949.

THE PRESS OF THE AUSTRIAN CENTRE

JENNIFER TAYLOR

In July 1939, as war loomed ever closer, the library committee of the Austrian Centre held one of its regular meetings, making a decision which had far-reaching consequences. In the interests of keeping its membership informed, it was decided to compile a weekly digest of the British press for members who were unable to read English. Such were the modest beginnings of *Zeitspiegel* which developed from an internal news digest into a weekly newspaper that, at its height, achieved a circulation of 3,000 and was able to claim world-wide distribution. 'At last we can buy *Zeitspiegel* here,' wrote Louis Fürnberg from Jerusalem in 1942.[1] Not the least of the newspaper's achievements was to maintain regular publication throughout the war years in the face of prevailing paper shortages. As Anthony Eden informed Lord Vansittart in September 1942, the Communists had been 'able to pick up independently enough paper [...] to enable them to carry on [...] with publication'.[2]

As a German-language publication, *Zeitspiegel* played only a minor part in the campaign by the Austrian Centre to inform and influence British public opinion: its target audience were the Austrian refugees who were – or who might be persuaded to become – members of the Austrian Centre. Issued as a weekly newspaper from September 1941 to 1946, *Zeitspiegel* existed both to report the news and to interpret it. It sought to inform its readership on public events, not least the initiatives and campaigns mounted by the Austrian Centre and the FAM, but also to place those events in the perspective of its own political agenda.

While *Zeitspiegel* was certainly the most notable of the journals associated with the Austrian Centre, it was not the first. This distinction belongs to *Österreichische Nachrichten*, the bulletin of the Council of Austrians. First issued in September 1938, this newspaper abruptly ceased publication after the outbreak of war.[3] In September 1939, it was replaced by *Austrian Bulletin*, an English-language publication, which thereafter appeared irregularly. At this stage, *Zeitspiegel* was far inferior in terms of printing, layout and circulation for, while *Österreichische Nachrichten* had been printed, and had claimed a circulation of 3,500, *Zeitspiegel* was still cyclostyled and selling less than one thousand copies. After *Österreichische Nachrichten* had ceased publication, its function as a direct mouthpiece of the Council of Austrians was gradually assumed by *Zeitspiegel*, at that time under the editorship of the Czech Communist Ludwig Freund.

In the late summer of 1941, once the German invasion of the Soviet Union had radically altered the political landscape, and preliminary negotiations for the formation of the Free Austrian Movement (FAM) were under way, there was another abrupt upheaval in the affairs of the press of the Austrian Centre. Freund was replaced by an editorial triumvirate. Jenö Kostmann, an experienced journalist and veteran of the Austrian Communist Party (KPÖ) who had worked illegally in Austria became editor-in-chief, assisted by Hilde Mareiner, who had had similar political experience in Austria and who had worked for Austrian Self-Aid in London, and Eva Priester, a former member of the German Communist Party (KPD) who had worked on the *Berliner Tageblatt* and who had played an influential role on *Zeitspiegel* under Freund's editorship. Now that the Soviet Union was Britain's ally in the fight against Hitler, the focus of the newspaper shifted away from internal matters such as the anniversaries of the Austrian Centre itself[4] to a wider and more confident coverage of the course of the war, a development enhanced by the fact that from 28 September 1941 *Zeitspiegel* appeared as a proper printed newspaper.

This change of emphasis in *Zeitspiegel*'s coverage left a need for in-house reporting, and from 1941 the Austrian Centre issued a monthly bulletin for its members, publicizing the activities of the Centre itself and of various ancillary groups.[5] The later issues, under the title *Austrian Centre*, contained reports of aspects of the Centre's organization, such as the election of Committee members, the work of the Council of Austrians, the Annual Conference of the Austrian Centre, and potted biographies of officials such as Dr. Walter Hollitscher[6] and Dr. Walter Schiff.[7]

Like other exile organizations the Austrian Centre appreciated the importance of youth work: as soon as the premises in Paddington opened, existing youth groups were amalgamated and transferred to the Centre. This was the genesis of the youth organization Young Austria. Two months later the first issue of their periodical appeared. As there were several versions of the German title,[8] it will here be referred to by the English version. *Young Austria* had to appeal to young adults as well as readers of school age – in 1943 the average age of the members of the organization was twenty-two – and was run by an editorial committee acutely conscious of the need to steer between the Scylla of childishness and the Charybdis of incomprehensibility, matters hotly debated at the

Young Austria National Conference in December 1941.[9] Unlike *Zeitspiegel* the periodical was not edited by professional journalists, and the emphasis of the publication shifted to reflect the changing circumstances of the readers and contributors as their position in the workforce became more assured. The editorial team of Young Austria included Eva Brill, Fritz Walter and above all Georg Breuer, editor-in chief for most of the newspaper's lifetime.[10]

The inception of the Free Austrian Movement in December 1941 brought a further change to communicative strategy. *Austrian News,* issued as a cyclostyled news-sheet, began to appear at irregular intervals. In contrast to *Zeitspiegel* it was directed at English sympathizers and opinion formers: it was published throughout in English. The note appended to the top of the first page, 'All material for reprint – may be quoted without acknowledgement', indicated the sheet was intended primarily as a press release.[11] A digest of news about Austria with particular reference to resistance inside Austria, *Austrian News* also included the press of the Austrian Centre, *Zeitspiegel* and *Young Austria,* among its sources. Furthermore, it relied on substantially the same sources as these publications, that is, the British, German and Austrian press as well as the press of Scandinavia (particularly that of neutral Sweden) and Radio Moscow.

Under the aegis of the Austrian Centre these publications covered the milestones in the history of Austrian emigration in Great Britain: internment, the activities of the Free Austrian Movement, the Moscow Declaration, and reported on key aspects of the war from an Austrian perspective: the attack on the Soviet Union, resistance inside Austria and developments on her eastern borders in the final months of the war. A constant theme running throughout this chronicle of Austria's struggle was the affirmation of her historical and cultural identity as a nation in her own right, distinct from Germany.

Internment

In the spring and early summer of 1940 the work of the Council of Austrians was forcibly re-focused by the decision of the newly-appointed Prime Minister, Winston Churchill, to intern all enemy aliens, regardless of the recommendations of the tribunals which had been set up to determine the extent of their loyalty to their host country. This sudden and arbitrary measure provided a campaigning issue which united all shades of political opinion among the refugees. The periodicals of the Austrian Centre show that this agency of émigré self-help was equal to the challenge, delivering aid on a legal, political, economic and moral level. Care had to be taken to moderate the political tone – shrill protests at the injustice of the measures were not welcome, particularly in the early months of the process before release procedures had been put in train, as those attempting to publish in the internment camps themselves were swiftly made aware.[12]

At this time *Zeitspiegel* was still under Freund's editorship and functioning as a news-sheet of the Council of Austrians. One of the main focuses of the reporting was to act as a channel for official information – an approach, in fact, consistent with the original purpose of the periodical. Examples of the dissemination of such information were the special edition of *Zeitspiegel* of 2 August 1940 which contained a summary of the recent White Paper setting out the categories for the release of civil internees, and the *Young Austria* editions of August and September 1940 which incorporated similar information, while a special edition of the latter periodical, issued the following month, contained legal advice from the Youth Relief and Refugee Council. Subsequently, on 7 December, *Zeitspiegel* led with the parliamentary debate on the issue, concluding: 'This whole debate has brought the problem of the 19,500 internees to the attention of the English public.' The first anniversary of internment was marked by *Zeitspiegel* on 11 May and by *Young Austria* at the end of May: both periodicals led with the heading 'Ein Jahr Internierung' ('One Year of Internment') and both published Erich Fried's eponymous poem.

The periodicals followed the prudent course of basing reports on British official sources. This permitted the exiles to introduce a burning issue which affected all their readers without fear of adverse reaction from the censor, an ever-present figure in wartime. A similar tactic is evident even at a much later stage in the internment process after release procedures had been implemented: 'Ein Interview über die Lage der Internierten in Australien' ('An Interview about the Position of Internees in Australia') which appeared in *Zeitspiegel* on 21 Sept 1941 and which argued for a regulated release procedure and the integration of refugees into war work was based on the report from an aid worker employed by the Society of Friends.

'The provision of support for the internees makes up a substantial part of the Austrian Centre's work, besides the campaign for their release,' wrote Willi Scholz.[13] The furnishing of practical aid to the internees was a task which the Centre could support without fear of offending the host country, and no better means of raising the morale of the detainees could be devised. A fund was established which provided the internees with material comforts and pocket money, as well as financing the release campaign. The amounts collected were regularly and meticulously reported, down to the nearest penny. No doubt such reports encouraged further donations, and this aspect of the content of the press of the Austrian Centre reflected the practice of many other charitable organizations in the host country at that time.

As correspondence with the internees was permitted, news from the camps appeared in the form of letters and eye-witness accounts. This

Office of *Zeitspiegel* (from l. to r., Hilde Mareiner, Axi Bleier-Brody, Eva Priester)

aspect of reporting was given particular prominence in *Young Austria*. The special edition of October 1940 contained three pages of letters and reports from the camps in Huyton and on the Isle of Man, while Hans Probst, the Secretary of Young Austria, provided a detailed account of his activities in Central Promenade Camp in Douglas for the first anniversary issue.[14] Subsequent issues devoted several pages to letters from detainees, some composed in English in order to pass the censor more rapidly.[15] The distribution of *Zeitspiegel* and *Young Austria* in the internment camps as part of the support programme enabled the internees to read about their situation. The letters of thanks that were published provide evidence that corresponding with the exile press and reading the results of this correspondence provided the internees with moral support and also contributed to the intellectual life of the camps.

Mindful of the extent of the Austrian diaspora, the editors were also concerned with the fate of their countrymen overseas. The Fall of France exacerbated the situation for those held in that country, and in its edition no. 9, dated the beginning of July 1940, *Young Austria* published a telegram to Mrs Roosevelt, signed by various aid agencies, requesting help for those trapped in France – namely transit through Spain and Portugal and visas for the USA. Later, there were reports from 'Die Konzentrationslager in Frankreich' ('Concentration Camps in France') (*Zeitspiegel*, 20 April 1941) and from Le Vernet, Gurs, Argeles and Rivealtes (*Zeitspiegel*, 4 May 1941).

The deportation programme to the British dominions increased the disorientation of the internees and their sense of isolation. 'Our main complaint is the difficulty of communicating with the outside world,' wrote one internee from Australia.[16] As readers of *Young Austria* were informed, the internment camp at Hay was twenty-two hours from Sydney and letters from Europe took three months to arrive.[17] The fate of the deportees to the dominions was closely followed in the press of the Austrian Centre, starting with an unprecedented Stop Press report of the torpedoing of the *Arandora Star* in *Young Austria* in early July 1940. On 14 September 1940 *Zeitspiegel* reported the arrival of the *Dunera* in Sydney, 'Internierten-Schiff in Austalien angekommen' ('Internee Ship Arrives in Australia'), while a later issue carried details of the court martial of the military escort who had so harassed the refugees on the outward voyage, '*Dunera*-Verurteilung' ('*Dunera* Verdict') (29 June 1941). Official information on a variety of matters pertaining to deportation was printed. Details from the Home Office about the emigration of married people and material from Bloomsbury House about the location of camps in Australia appeared in *Zeitspiegel* on 21 September 1940 under the heading 'Informationen über Emigrationsfragen' ('Information on Emigration Questions'), while a list of those released from internment in Australia, compiled by the Council of Austrians, was published in the issue of 29 June 1941. Further releases were announced at the beginning of December.[18] Additionally, eye-witness reports, such as 'Zur Rückkehr internierter Flüchtlinge aus Kanada' ('Concerning the Return of Internees from Canada') (*Young Austria,* end January 1941) and 'Ich war auf der *Arandora Star* – Ich war auf der *Dunera*. Von einem Rückkehrer aus Australien' ('I was on the *Arandora Star* – I was on the *Dunera*. By a Returnee from Australia') (*Zeitspiegel*, 22 December 1941) kept readers up to date with the release process.

The reports of these disturbing experiences in the columns of *Zeitspiegel* are couched, in the main, in a measured tone. On the other hand, writers in *Young Austria* employ stylistic devices to emphasize their criticism of the internment policy, for example, heavy-handed irony:

> Czibi found it easier than other people to settle into camp life because he and his brother spent over a year in a Nazi concentration camp. Now he is in Australia, his brother in an internment camp in England and his sister in London.[19]

Or the plangent naiveté of the rhetorical question: 'Why was the treatment like that? Why did it have to make us remember the days and camps of a country we had all fled from?'[20]

The invasion of the Soviet Union

The attack on the Soviet Union in June 1941 released the editors from the embarrassment attendant on reporting the war while the Hitler-Stalin pact was in force. From August 1941, *Zeitspiegel* carried a regular survey of developments on the Eastern Front written by Hans Kahle, a Spanish Civil War veteran recently released from internment in Canada, who became the military correspondent of the *Daily Worker*. Kahle provided similar material for *Young Austria*, for example, 'Neue Formen des mechanisierten Krieges' ('New Forms of Mechanized Warfare') (mid-July 1941). The opportunity to publish pieces of all kinds in support of the Soviet war effort was eagerly seized by *Young Austria*. Two examples will suffice to give some indication of the nature of the material and its propagandistic slant. The first, 'Dreißig Stunden' ('Thirty Hours'), an account of the heroic efforts of an injured Soviet soldier who carried a wounded German to the Soviet lines, originally published in *Soviet War News* on 18 September, appeared in issue no. 20 at the beginning of October 1941, while the early November issue published 'Dnieprostroj', a poem by the Free German League of Culture (FGLC) member Alfred Becker lamenting the destruction of a hydro-electric dam on the Dnieper. The 25th anniversary of the Soviet Union in 1942 was marked by a special issue of *Young Austria*. This contained an extract from Henri Barbusse's book on Stalin and an article entitled 'Die Rote Armee und ihre Führer' ('The Red Army and its Leaders') by Major A. S. Hooper of the Wiltshire Regiment who had made several journeys to the Soviet Union. Additionally, both periodicals reported on the Anglo-Soviet Friendship Week held in conjunction with the FGLC in November 1941, and the Austro-Soviet Friendship Week in June 1942.[21] The attendant fundraising was publicized in much the same manner as the Internment Fund had been: 'Zwei österreichische Röntgenwagen werden verwundeten Rotarmisten helfen' ('Two Austrian X-Ray Vans to Help Red Army Casualties'), announced *Zeitspiegel* on 4 July 1942. Later in the war, as we shall see, the periodicals of the Austrian Centre relied heavily on Soviet sources such as TASS and Radio Moscow for their coverage of developments on Austria's south-eastern border: in particular, the activities of Tito's partisans and the depiction of resistance inside Austria.

The Free Austrian Movement

Among the most significant events in the political history of Austrian emigration was the foundation of the Free Austrian Movement in London on 3 December 1941. No mention of this key event was made in the 6 December issue, but the news appeared prominently on the front

Young Austria

PERIODICAL OF THE AUSTRIAN YOUTH IN GREAT BRITAIN

THIRD YEAR, NUMBER 21   PRICE 2 d   OCTOBER 11, 1941 .

GREETING YOU, WE SALUTE THE YOUTH OF THE WORLD!

INTERNATIONAL YOUTH RALLY FOR VICTORY 1941

By MARC SCHREIBER
of the Belgian Ministry of Foreign Affairs;
Chairman, Initiative Committee of the Rally.

On October 11th,1941, the Albert Hall,
which, in the course of its long history,has
held enthusiastic crowds of all kinds, which
has resounded to so many passionate words,
will witness a manifestation destined to take
its place in the annals of this war.

Here in London, at this moment of capi-
tal importance in the progress of humanity,
the youth of the whole world will meet to
declare its desire to conquer the forces of
evil and to build a new and better world.

The delegates of all the British youth
organisations will represent the country
which, by its firm resolution taken in the
summer of last year,has saved humanity from
an irremediable disaster. Boys and girls who
have found their way to England from countries
occupied by Germany, will be there to represent the nations which were successively in-
vaded, and which are now suffering under
German oppression and which, by their resistance, are paving the way for resurrection
of a Europe at present in chains.The Russians
will represent the Soviet forces which at
this very moment are bearing the brunt of the
attack of Hitler's army. The Chinese delegates
will be welcomed as the representatives of
a country which has held out against the
aggressor for four years. The Americans, together with the young people of all the other
countries, adversaries of Nazism and Fascism,

page of *Zeitspiegel* on 13 December, 'Free Austrian Movement geschaffen. Österreichische Einigung' ('Free Austrian Movement Founded. Austrians United'). The Movement's policy declaration was printed in full on an inside page. This approach was commensurate with Kostmann's editorial policy in two respects: there were no special issues under his editorship, and, as we have seen, he sedulously avoided giving the newspaper the outward appearance of a news-sheet. However, key events in the development of the FAM were reported – by the indefatigable Eva Kolmer in her 'Ein Jahr Free Austrian Movement' ('Free Austrian Movement One Year Old') (23 December 1942) and in 'Nachkriegsprobleme in der Tätigkeit des FAM' ('FAM Working on Post-War Problems') (9 October 1943) and by F.C. West, writing in *Young Austria*, who reported on the second year of the Movement's activities on 23 December 1943. Ever mindful of retaining good relations with the host country, on 28 February 1942 the editors printed the telegram thanking Prime Minister Winston Churchill for his support in Parliament.

The way in which *Zeitspiegel's* reporting can be used to illustrate the political programme of the FAM has been amply demonstrated by Helene Maimann.[22] Maimann does, however, remark on a certain reticence regarding the question of post-war independence.[23] She accounts for this by stating that the Communists were unsure of the amount of support they could muster. Reticence is also evident in the way in which the FAM conferences were reported in *Zeitspiegel*, and it is tempting to postulate a similar reason. For example, the first FAM Conference at Porchester Hall on 24 January 1942 featured in two inside pages of the issue of 31 January. To attract the reader's attention, photographs of prominent delegates were used: the functionaries Eva Kolmer and Marie Köstler appear but also, possibly of more interest to the general reader, so does the novelist Robert Neumann reading a message to Churchill. Neumann's conference address itself, however, did not appear until the following issue of 7 February. Later conferences received similarly fragmented reporting in the columns of *Zeitspiegel*.[24] One reason for this was that the conference proceedings were issued as separate pamphlets,[25] a procedure also followed by the German-speaking émigrés from Czechoslovakia, which did not, however, prevent the German-Bohemians from publishing extensive conference reports in their journal *Einheit*.[26] It must be supposed that Kostmann's refusal to let the affairs of the FAM take precedence over news reporting was in deference to the majority of his readers who were not Communists. Reticence, too, is evident in *Young Austria's* reports. Although this periodical did produce special issues, none was devoted in its entirety to the Movement. However, the FAM Teachers' Conference, a matter presumably considered to be of interest to young people, was featured in a short report by Hans Probst in the issue of 17 June 1944.

Coverage of the Free Austrian Movement for an English audience involved a difference of emphasis advancing some of the FAM's political aims, most notably the goal of political autonomy. *Austrian News* devoted much of its space to depicting Austria as a land under enemy occupation. Persuading the host country to establish an Austrian armed force to fight against this occupation was high on the agenda of publications in the English language. 'The loudest cheers [...] greeted all those speakers who spoke for the setting up of a Free Austrian Fighting Unit,' *Austrian News* claimed in its coverage of the FAM inaugural conference which appeared in the February 1942 issue. This point was mentioned more obliquely in *Zeitspiegel*'s coverage, where the sole reference was to be found in a caption under the photograph of a corporal in the Pioneer Corps, 'Ein Pioneer sagt: Wir wollen die Austrian Fighting Force' ('A Pioneer says: We want the Austrian Fighting Force') (31 January 1942). This demand was explained in some detail by Fritz Walter, the Young Austria Chairman, in another publication aimed at an English audience, the English-language issue of *Young Austria* of March 1942:

The Free Austrian Fighting Unit is one of the aims for which fifteen Austrian organizations have combined into the FAM as the common front of all Austrians in this country who eagerly look forward to the opportunity to play an active part in the ranks of the Allied nations thus helping their country too to regain freedom and independence from Nazi Germany.

Just over a year later, on 22 April 1943, it was announced in Parliament that Austrians would be able to join the British Armed Forces. It was not the independently commanded unit they had hoped for, but the development was nevertheless reported positively by *Zeitspiegel* on 8 May, where it featured on the front page with the announcement, 'Zu combattant [*sic*] units zugelassen' ('Admitted to Combatant Units'). Later that month, on 26 May, the FAM appeal to enlist, 'Österreichischer Aufschwung' ('Austrian Revival'), also appeared on the front page.[27] Then, on 3 July, one of *Zeitspiegel*'s rare photographs showed Austrians queuing to enlist, while on the same date *Young Austria* carried a similar photograph, a close-up of 'Vier Young-Austria-Mitglieder beim Rekrutierungsamt' ('Four Young Austria Members at the Recruiting Office'). Both photographs had previously appeared in the London *Evening News*, and both were placed on the front page. This development provided *Young Austria* with a new editorial objective; subsequently it devoted itself to representing the interests of Austrians serving in the British forces.

The Moscow Declaration

London Information, the newspaper of the Austrian Social Democrats, responded to the Moscow Declaration by issuing a special edition dated 5 December 1943.[28] The periodicals of the Austrian Centre and the Free Austrian Movement reacted more rapidly, however. The communiqué of 1 November was featured on *Zeitspiegel*'s front page on 6 November under the heading 'Freiheit und Unabhängigkeit für Österreich – die Erklärung der Großmächte' ('The Allied Declaration Means Freedom and Independence for Austria'), while *Austrian News* – at that time still cyclostyled and appearing at irregular intervals – published a two-page issue on 12 November. In foolscap instead of the customary quarto, this edition, no. 16, served the function of a special issue. Primarily a collation of material from official sources, it contained the 'Official Text of the Three-Power Moscow Conference' and a statement of the FAM Executive. To this extent the contents were substantially the same as the earlier *Zeitspiegel* issue. One difference – presumably attributable to the later press date – was the announcement of 'Preparation for a National Committee', an aspect of post-Moscow development which was covered by *Zeitspiegel* in the following issue.

By the time the next issues appeared – in the case of *Zeitspiegel* on 13 November and of *Austrian News* on 16 November – the leader writers had had time to polish their rhetoric. For example, *Austrian News* contained a four-page report headlined 'Clarion News' which proclaimed, in the introductory paragraph, 'The most powerful Alliance of nations ever known declares: "Austria shall be free again!"'. Significantly, both periodicals commented extensively on the clause requiring Austrians to be instrumental in their own liberation. *Zeitspiegel* spoke in terms of escalating resistance, commenting that civil war might be necessary to ensure that collaborators were punished, for they were regarded as traitors to Austria. It was considered a matter of paramount importance that independence should be achieved through the efforts of Austrians themselves, that is, through the Austrian Freedom Front. A similar point, shorn of declamatory rhetoric, was made by *Austrian News* which stated, with reference to the partisans on the Yugoslav border: 'In case of a crisis the forces, with the help of the Austrians, could carry partisan warfare right inside the German fortress.' As we shall see, reporting partisan warfare indeed became a priority in the final year of the war, but in these later issues the editors, possibly warned against incitement to armed insurrection, tended to avoid the sharp tones of the weeks immediately following the Moscow Declaration.

So important was the Moscow Declaration considered that for a short time FAM and its affairs featured on the front pages of *Zeitspiegel*. Moreover, the 13 November edition could almost be said to be a special

Meeting at Stoll Theatre, London, to mark Austrian-Soviet Friendship Week, 28 June 1942

issue, since it contained no fewer than four articles on the topic: 'Für die Bildung des österreichischen Nationalkomitees: Initiative und vorbereitende Schritte des FAM' ('FAM Initiative – Preparatory Steps in Forming the Austrian National Committee'); 'Zur österreichischen Erklärung der Moskauer Konferenz' ('Moscow Conference: the Austrian Declaration'); 'Sender Österreich: Jetzt ist es an uns' ('[Moscow-based] Radio Austria: Now It's Up To Us'; and, finally, an account of growing resistance under the heading of 'Wie Österreich die Deklaration von Moskau aufnahm' ('Austrian Reaction to the Moscow Declaration'). 'Österreichische Kommunisten in Moskau begrüßen Initiative des FAM' ('Austrian Communists in Moscow Welcome the FAM Initiative') it was asserted on the front page of the following issue on 20 November while, most unusually, the 4 December issue featured the Annual Conference of the FAM on its first two pages, headlined 'FAM ruft zur Einheit' ('FAM Calls for Unity').

This change in the political landscape was reflected much more obliquely in *Young Austria*. The 6 November issue made no mention of the Declaration, leading with 'Die französischen Partisanen schreiben uns' ('French partisans write to us'), recording thanks for Young Austria's financial support, while page three carried a report of the silver jubilee celebrations of the Young Communist League in Moscow. The following issue (20 November), at a time when *Zeitspiegel* was celebrating partisan activity, and when *Austrian News*, in its issue of 16 November, was publicizing the FAM proposal that an Austrian Fighting Force should include Austrian POWs 'who had been conscripted into the German Army', led with 'Neue Uniformen und neue Soldaten' ('New Uniforms and New Soldiers'), a conventional article couched in a chatty, friendly tone, encouraging young people to enlist in the British forces.

From December *Zeitspiegel*, too, devoted itself to domestic aspects of the matter. 'Die Umregistrierung der Österreicher' ('Re-registration of Austrians'), in the Christmas Day issue of 1943, reported the Home Secretary's decision, announced on 16 December, that those who had held Austrian nationality prior to 1938 could re-register as Austrians.[29] Subsequent coverage on 15 January and 22 January 1944 consisted of public service announcements of how this was to be done, and readers were referred to the Council of Austrians for advice. *Austrian News* briefly glossed this matter on 21 January, stating that the next step to be hoped for was reclassification as 'friendly' aliens, while *Zeitspiegel* found it necessary to ask Jenö Desser, the official responsible for repatriation, to counter fears that those who re-registered would be forcibly repatriated after the war. His article, entitled 'Ernstes und Heiteres von der Umregistrierung' ('Re-registration – the Serious Side and the Lighter Side'), appeared on 12 February.

Austrian resistance to German rule

The Moscow Declaration gave formal recognition to an argument that had informed the programme of the Free Austrian Movement. This programme, in turn, was based on a thesis expressed in the press of the Austrian Centre from the outset – namely, if Austria were to be perceived as a country occupied by the Germans, it must then follow that Austria was not part of Germany. Nor must the common language be allowed to obscure the political and cultural differences between the two nations.

The political aspect of this thesis demanded that the oppressed should be shown to be rising up against the oppressors. Resistance to the Germans was a leitmotif which ran through all the publications of the Austrian Centre, as the following representative examples show.

From the autumn of 1942 the names of persons imprisoned or executed for sedition and treason were made public.[30] Basing its information on official German sources, the press of the Austrian Centre published the names, dates and places of execution of those convicted, often enclosing this information in a black border to resemble an obituary notice, with the addition of an edifying editorial comment, as in the following examples from *Zeitspiegel*: 'Sechs Patrioten hingerichtet [...] Sie starben für die Freiheit Österreichs' ('Six patriots executed [...] they died for the freedom of Austria') (7 November 1942) and 'Ehrentafel der Märtyrer des österreichischen Freiheitskampfes [...] Das Volk Österreichs wird sie nie vergessen' ('Roll of honour of the martyrs for

Austrian freedom [...] The Austrian people will never forget them') (5 December 1942). Similar information was supplied by *Young Austria* whose mid-December issue carried a list of further executions, and by *Austrian News* the following year – 'The executioners at work – 17 die in a fortnight' (19 March 1943), 'The German executioners at work' (12 April 1943) – while, additionally, *Young Austria* reported on the repression of young people, 'Sechs österreichische Studenten von der Gestapo verhaftet' ('Six Austrian Students Arrested by Gestapo') (25 September 1943). Reports in the later years of the war reflected the intensified repression resulting from the increasingly desperate situation, 'Massenterrorprozesse gegen österreichische Patrioten – Die Hingerichteten werden wie Tiere am Zentralfriedhof verstaut' ('Mass Terror Trials of Austrian Patriots: Killed and Dumped like Animals in Vienna's Main Cemetery') (*Zeitspiegel*, 12 February 1944); '64 Hingerichtete in Wien' ('64 Executed in Vienna') (*Zeitspiegel*, 9 December 1944).

Mutiny and desertion among the Austrian members of the armed forces was another aspect of disaffection with German rule keenly emphasized by the periodicals. 'Österreichische Soldaten meutern' ('Austrian Soldiers Mutiny') was the headline of a composite account in *Zeitspiegel* on 21 February 1942, allegedly based on eyewitness reports, describing mutinies on the eastern front, in Greece and in France, while 'Desertionen in Norwegen, Afrika und Jugoslawien' ('Desertions in Norway, Africa and France'), a similar composite based on reports from the *News Chronicle* and TASS, appeared on the front page of *Zeitspiegel* on 10 April 1943 with the comment, 'Those deserting were almost exclusively Austrian'. A similar report was carried by *Austrian News* on 3 May 1943. Later, on 14 August, *Zeitspiegel* declared, 'Österreicher in der deutschen Armee wollen nicht mehr kämpfen' ('Austrians in the German Army Weary of Fighting'), and on 23 September *Young Austria* described an incident in Normandy in which 'Fünfzehn Österreicher töten Offizier, laufen über' ('Fifteen Austrians Kill Officer, Then Defect').

The final stages of the war

In the final years of the war significance was attached to guerrilla activity in the border regions. In the spring of 1943 Roland Freisler, the notorious President of the People's Court, presided over a trial of Austrian resistance fighters in Carinthia which ended in death sentences. This was the lead story in *Austrian News* on 3 May 1943, which announced, 'Trial Reveals Slovene and Austrian Guerrillas Fight Side by Side: Thirteen to Die', and in *Zeitspiegel* on 8 May.

As the war progressed, attention was focused on Austria's south-eastern borders, and so increased use was made of Soviet sources.

Information was also obtained from Tito's partisans. The recognition of these partisans as combatants in the Allied cause accorded by the Teheran Conference in May 1944 strengthened the argument for legitimization of armed resistance inside Austria. 'Die Voraussetzungen für österreichische Partisanen sind vorhanden: Titos Armee unterstützt Kärntner Partisanen,' ('Partisan Activity in Austria Now Possible - Tito's Army Supports Carinthian Partisans'), declared *Zeitspiegel* on 6 May in a report based on a Radio Moscow broadcast to Austria. 'Tito klopft an das Tor Österreichs' ('Tito Knocking on Austria's Door') wrote Willi Scholz in *Zeitspiegel* on 13 May 1944 in an article illustrated by a map of the border region, while the following month, on 3 June, *Young Austria* observed, '80% der jugoslawischen Partisanen sind Jugendliche' ('80% of the Yugoslavian Partisans are Juveniles'). Although the British Government officially pursued an even-handed policy towards the rival guerrilla groups of Tito and Mihailovic, after August 1944 Austrians serving in the British army could volunteer for transfer to Tito's army.[31] This development was reflected in many reports later that year, such as 'Österreicher schließen sich Tito an' ('Austrians Join Tito') (*Zeitspiegel*, 23 September 1944);[32] 'Verbindung zwischen Freiheitsfront und Tito-Armee hergestellt' ('Freedom Front Now in Contact with Tito's Army') (*Zeitspiegel*, 14 October 1944); and 'Austrian Fighting Unit with Yugoslav People's Army' (*Austrian News*, December 1944). The following year it could be reported that an Austrian battalion of the Slovene Liberation Army had been formed and had seen action, 'Feuertaufe des ersten österreichischen Bataillons' (Baptism of Fire for the First Austrian Battalion') (*Zeitspiegel*, 10 February 1945). The formation of a second battalion was announced by *Zeitspiegel* on 17 February and, on 31 March, the newspaper reported optimistically, 'Slowenische Zivilverwaltung in ständigem Kontakt mit ÖFF' ('Slovenian Civil Administration in Permanent Contact with AFF' [Austrian Freedom Front]).

The Red Army crossed the Austrian border on 29 March 1945. Vienna was liberated on 13 April, thus paving the way for the return of the exiles. In the immediate post-war period the periodicals of the Austrian Centre gave their full support to the Provisional Government whose writ was primarily confined to the Russian sector.

Economic Independence

The political independence promised by the Moscow Declaration, even given the favourable military solution which the Austrian exiles were aiming to achieve, would mean nothing unless economic independence could be guaranteed. For since the First World War Austria had been a small, landlocked country with little industry and few raw materials. Forward planning was essential if Austria were to survive as a small nation state in the harsh post-war economic climate. Czechoslovakia, an independent, democratic Socialist state, had provided a political model for the FAM's view of a post-war Austria, and the view was reflected in the press of the Austrian Centre. On 2 January 1942 a programmatic article by Hans Winterberg, 'Warum Österreich unabhängig sein muß' ('Why Austria Must Be Independent'), appeared in *Zeitspiegel*, rejecting the Pan-German aspirations of a post-war federation as advocated by the monarchists. Subsequently, on 23 January, the newspaper reported that Benes had welcomed this approach, 'FAM-Delegation bei Präsident Benes' ('FAM Delegation Visits President Benes'). There followed a series of articles by Benes himself and other members of the Czech Government-in-Exile in support of this policy: Edvard Benes, 'Gemeinsame Mission CSR-Österreich' ('Joint Mission – CSR-Austria') (20 March 1943); Jan Opocensky, 'Die Tschechoslowakei und Österreich' ('Czechoslovakia and Austria') (27 March 1943); Karl Kreibich, 'Deutschland weder groß noch größer' ('Germany Neither Great nor Greater') (17 July 1943); Hubert Ripka, 'Über Föderations- und Konföderationspläne' ('Federation and Confederation Plans') (21 August 1943); and 'Grundlagen der tschechoslowakisch-österreichischen Zusammenarbeit' ('Basis for Czech-Austrian Collaboration') (1 April 1944).

Good relations with Austria's immediate neighbours, the Czechs and Yugoslavs, would lessen the danger that Austria would be cut off from neighbouring markets by protectionist barriers. A sound economic base was regarded as an essential prerequisite for the return of the exiles. The planning documents issued by the FAM to this end, which will be discussed in greater detail in later chapters of this study, were complemented by reports in the press of the Austrian Centre. As early as 17 April 1943, *Zeitspiegel* announced 'Nachkriegsfragen im FAM' ('FAM Addresses Post-War Problems'), reporting that a FAM Committee had been founded to consider post-war developments, while the radical proposals for land reform appeared in the edition of 7 October 1944 under the heading 'Wiederaufbau der Land- und Forstwirtschaft' ('Regeneration of Agriculture and Forestry'). The importance of the FAM Economic Conference held from 9 to 10 December 1944 was endorsed by an article outlining the programme in the 2 December edition. A short report of the Conference was carried by *Austrian News* in its first issue of 1945.

Austria's viability as a small nation-state continued to be the subject of debate in the press. On 8 January 1944 *Zeitspiegel* reported the opening of the 'Austria Shall Be Free Exhibition' in Oxford by Sir William Beveridge, with the headline, 'Kleine Nationen ebenso lebensfähig wie große' ('Small Nations Just as Viable as Large Ones'), while on 11 March Theodor Prager of Young Austria addressed himself to the problem of how this could be achieved in a front-page article in *Zeitspiegel* entitled 'Can Austria live?'. He answered the question in the affirmative, citing Denmark as an analogy, adding that hydro-electric power would compensate for the lack of coal. The crucial importance attached to economic considerations can, finally, be illustrated by reference to a comparatively early publication, 'Five Years Hitler over Austria', the special issue of *Austrian News* in March 1943, where an essay by Viktor Bloch on the economy of Austria was illustrated by a photograph of nine large chimneys of a blast furnace with a steam locomotive belching smoke in the foreground. This contrast to the more numerous illustrations depicting the beautiful natural features which, for many British readers, were characteristic of Austria, made the point that such beauty could not, of itself, ensure post-war prosperity.

Culture

'Austria will never be part of Germany: her historical, cultural and ethnological background is different from that of Germany,' wrote the editors of *Austrian News* in response to the Moscow Declaration.[33] Only by the assertion of a distinctive national identity could the spectre of pan-Germanism be removed. The press of the Austrian Centre reflected the assumption that this distinction was evident in literature and music as well as history. Concomitantly, the publications encouraged continuity by publicizing contemporary literature – advertising and reviewing books and plays, and publishing excerpts of newly written works. *Young Austria* in particular made a decisive contribution to this process, fostering the careers of several young poets, including Erich Fried.

While *Young Austria* had featured cultural contributions from its inception, *Zeitspiegel* had not. By 1941 this omission had been rectified. The publication of Fried's internment poem in May of that year was followed, on 3 August, by an extract from Bruno Heilig's *Menschen am Kreuz*, an account of Buchenwald and Dachau recently published in English.[34] In the early years of its publication *Austrian News* focused on culture only occasionally – one example being Hermann Ullrich's essay 'Austrian Culture – a European Necessity' which appeared in March 1943 in the special anniversary edition. However, the journal did have the distinction of carrying one of the first appraisals of Austrian exile literature. This essay, published in the early months of 1945, was written with the cultural reconstruction of Austria in mind. Therefore the content is not confined to the works of writers exiled in Great Britain, but also refers to the resistance literature of Ferdinand Bruckner and the latest work of F.C. Csokor, the Austrian dramatist who had been liberated from internment on the Dalmatian island of Corcula by Yugoslav partisans and who, by the autumn of 1943, had managed to reach Bari, where he joined the FAM.[35]

In the earlier issues of *Young Austria*, an explicit attempt was made to inform young readers of key figures of Austrian cultural history. Typical

Table tennis in the Young Austrian Games Room, 132 Westbourne Terrace
(Erich Fried seated, in the middle)

examples from the first year of publication were short essays on Ludwig Anzengruber, Nikolaus Lenau and the pacifist novelist and Nobel Peace Laureate Bertha von Suttner which appeared under the rubrics 'Ein großer Österreicher' and 'Eine große Österreicherin' ('A Great Austrian').[36] The approach was overtly didactic, long on exposition and approbatory rhetoric – Anzengruber, for example, is described as 'deeply rooted in his Austrian homeland'[37] – and short on critical evaluation. A similar stance is evident in the obituary to the novelist Joseph Roth, who died in Parisian exile in May 1939.[38] Such an approach is understandable considering the circumstances of the readers, for not all had completed their schooling in Austria when they were forced to flee to Great Britain. Such articles stem from a didactic impulse similar to that which later led the editors to devise the 'Kennst du Österreich?' ('Do you know Austria?') competition, with its photographs of well-known landmarks.[39] The earlier issues of the periodical also included historical articles, on subjects such as Andreas Hofer, that icon of Austrian resistance to Napoleonic tyranny, and surveys of the 1848 revolution; and studies of selected non-Austrian writers such as the satirical dissident Heinrich Heine. However, as the war progressed, the combination of the pressure of political events, the urge to publish material from Young Austrians in the theatre of war and the drastic reduction in the number of pages after June 1943 meant that such articles were eventually phased out of *Young Austria*. However, as we shall see, the cultural essays which appeared in *Zeitspiegel* were written in very much the same vein.

The editors of *Young Austria* were also intent on fostering the work of contemporary writers. To this end Stefan Zweig, the best-known Austrian author in exile, was contacted in Bath in 1939. His letter in support of the organization was reproduced in the Second December issue, the last of that year, and the news of his death in Brazil on 23 February 1942 was reported promptly in early March, when he was described circumspectly as 'one of the most significant bourgeois authors of the present time'.[40] Examples of recent prose works which appeared in the periodical are 'Die drei Kühe' ('The Three Cows'), Egon Erwin Kisch's short story of the farmer who sold his stock in order to finance joining the International Brigade to fight in the Spanish Civil War, which appeared in translation on 21 June 1941 (the first of the three English-language editions issued that year), while a poem from Arnold Zweig's newly published anti-Nazi resistance novel *Das Beil von Wandsbek* (*The Axe from Wandsbek*) appeared on 25 September 1943.

However, *Young Austria's* greatest contribution to publicizing contemporary literature was in the field of poetry. The periodical did much to establish the reputation and preserve the memory of Jura Soyfer, the talented young Austrian Communist writer who, in February 1939 at the age of twenty-six, died of fever in Buchenwald before his friends could secure his release and arrange his transport to Great Britain, which had granted him a visa.[41] Soyfer's 'Dachauerlied' ('Song of Dachau') (written in that camp, where he had earlier been imprisoned) was printed prominently on the first page of the Second November issue 1939. A short biographical accolade was also included. This poem appeared as 'Song of the Austrians' in John Lehmann's translation in the final English-language issue of that year, on 11 October, while the mid-February issue had contained his 'Vagabundenlied' ('Vagabond Song') and a commemorative piece, 'Zu seinem Todestag am 16. Februar' ('On the Anniversary of his Death on 16 February'). Subsequent publications of work by Soyfer include, on 23 October 1943, 'Eisen hoch im Kurs' ('The High Price of Iron'), a prose piece about the gold rush which had previously appeared in the Viennese newspaper *Sonntag* in 1937, and, on 12 February 1944, 'Waffensuche' ('Searching for Weapons'), an extract from a first novel based on the February uprising, a work which perforce remains fragmentary since most of it had been confiscated by the Gestapo at the time of Soyfer's arrest.

When *Die Vertriebenen* (*The Exiles*), the first of the Austrian Centre publications to anthologize the work of Austrian poets living in England appeared in 1941,[42] *Young Austria* carried an advertisement, an unusual occurrence for a periodical which did not usually include advertising and an index of the importance attached to supporting the authors.[43] In 1941 and in subsequent years the works of the contributors to these volumes appeared, sporadically, in the columns of *Young Austria* and *Zeitspiegel*, as the following examples show: Eva Priester, 'Österreichische Klage' ('Austrian Lament') (which also appeared in *Die Vertriebenen*) (*Young Austria*, early July 1941) and 'Böhmische Polka' ('Bohemian Polka') (*Young Austria*, early October 1941); Eva Aschner, 'Weihnachten 1941' ('Christmas 1941') (*Zeitspiegel*, 14 February 1942); Paul Husserl, 'Gedanken am Meer' ('Thoughts by the Sea') (*Young Austria*, 29 July 1944); Arthur West, 'Zwei Gedichte an der Front' ('Two Poems at the Front') (*Zeitspiegel*, 23 December 1944) and 'Meinem Freund in Österreich' ('To My Friend in Austria') (*Young Austria*, 30 June 1945); and, finally, Heinz Karpeles (later known as Heinz Carwin), 'Das große Glück' ('Great Happiness') (*Zeitspiegel*, 20 January 1945).

Of these contributors, Erich Fried, who arrived in London in 1938 straight from school in Vienna, has subsequently received the most recognition, although recently Heinz Karpeles has also become better known.[44] Fried was an enthusiastic member of Young Austria and 'Das tote Haus' ('The House of the Dead'), the first poem he published in London, appeared in *Young Austria* at the end of January 1941. In May of that year, 'Jugend' ('Youth'), a poem in praise of the organization and its members, was included in a two-page flyer distributed with *Zeitspiegel* in an attempt to recruit young people to Young Austria. Fried's contribution to the periodical's Soviet hagiography the following year was 'Wir stürmen das Land' ('We're Storming the Land'), a call to arms written for a performance of the Young Austria Choir during the Austrian-Soviet Friendship week, and 'Traschenkos Tod' ('Traschenko's Death'), a heroic tale of the eponymous commissar who acted as a human bomb to destroy a German tank. Fried also published in *Zeitspiegel* including, in August 1941, an essay on Nazi poetics.[45]

In January 1942 *Zeitspiegel* conducted a survey of its readers, asking them which parts of the newspaper they liked best. Many indicated their appreciation of the cultural coverage[46] for, although there was no formally designated *Feuilleton*, readers could usually expect pages six and seven to be devoted to cultural issues. Books and plays – particularly the Laterndl productions – were reviewed, works of exiled writers appeared and there were essays devoted to exponents of Austrian culture. Nor must the contribution of the classified section be forgotten. After the introduction of printing, large boxed display advertisements regularly informed readers of books available at the Centre through Free Austrian Books, which could also be purchased by mail order. While the majority of the works advertised were in-house publications, left-wing literature from other publishers was also included, as these examples indicate: *Im Namen der ewigen Menschlichkeit* (*In the Name of Eternal Humanity*), Louis Fürnberg's cantata in praise of the Soviet Union, published by Willi Verkauf in Jerusalem in 1943; and two examples from *Einheit*'s 1944 list, Paul Reimann's *Das Großdeutschtum und die böhmische Kulturtraditionen* (*Pan-

Germanism and the Bohemian Cultural Tradition) and *Stimmen aus Böhmen* (*Voices from Bohemia*), the anthology in memory of Rudolf Fuchs edited by Paul Reimann and Rudolf Popper.[47]

Newly published works were regularly reviewed: in October 1942, Robert Neumann's novel *Scene in Passing*, in August 1943, *Verbannt aus Österreich* (*Banished From Austria*), a volume of poetry by Theodor Kramer; in December 1943, *The World of Yesterday*, the English translation of Stefan Zweig's autobiography; in March 1944, *Into Exile*, Ernst Sommer's history of the counter-revolution in Bohemia; in September 1944, F.C. Weiskopf's *The Firing Squad*; and in October of that year *Revolte der Heiligen* (*The Revolt of the Saints*), Ernst Sommer's study of Jewish resistance to Nazi oppression.[48]

In the trenchantly entitled article 'Österreichische Kulturarbeit – eine Kampfaufgabe' ('The Fight for Austrian Culture') which appeared on 30 May 1942 the editor-in-chief Jenö Kostmann subjected the Austrian literary canon to a sternly dialectical evaluation. Only those authors who can be said to foster the 'spirit of opposition' are admitted to the pantheon, their function being to draw 'fresh nourishment [...] from the treasures of our national culture' (p. 8). From this scrutiny, Nestroy, Raimund, Grillparzer and Schnitzler emerge triumphant, the satire of the last named on the effete mores of the officer caste and excoriation of anti-Semitism ensuring Kostmann's approval. A preview of the Laterndl production of Schnitzler's *Professor Bernhardi* which described the play as attacking the 'deplorable way of thinking of the Austrian intelligentsia, riven by German arrogance and anti-Semitic racism' illustrates the point categorically.[49]

While it is not difficult to find further examples of this insistence that literature should be reinterpreted for an exiled community in wartime, there is also evidence of some appreciation of the subtlety which characterized so much Austrian writing and art, a realization that values could be implied as well as baldly stated. For example, while Remarque's *Flotsam*, published in 1941, received the following robust condemnation in a review probably written by the Communist Ernst Fischer – 'The book is a caricature of emigration and the antifascist struggle [...] It depicts emigrants merely as hunted, broken men and says nothing of the struggle against Hitler'[50] – a review of Max Hermann-Neisse's posthumous *Letzte Gedichte* (*Last Poems*), possibly from the pen of Rudolf Fuchs, exonerates the author from the imputation that his work lacked explicit 'Kampflosungen' ('watchwords for the struggle') and so was not relevant to wartime: 'Those who, like this author, bemoan the enslavement of freedom and the denigration of human dignity so eloquently, do not need to engage in anti-Prussian rhetoric.'[51] Similarly, Albert Fuchs, writing on the first anniversary of Stefan Zweig's death, defends his subject against charges of producing trivial and superficial biographies: 'What do we mean when we accuse an author of writing superficially? Zweig writes as vividly and as graphically as his illustrious predecessors.'[52] And again, whereas the reviewer of *Unentschuldigte Stunde* (*Little Ladyship*) by the Österreichische Bühne could dismiss the choice of material as 'too harmless and trivial for an émigré production',[53] it is very much in the spirit of Karl Kraus, a writer whose light, confident touch masked biting satire, that the reviewer of the Laterndl production of *Goldregengäßchen* (*Laburnum Grove*) claims that the typically banal lower-middle class world of J.B. Priestley, with its allotments, open fires and the wireless 'at the same time illuminates the incomprehensible depths of the superficial'.[54] For the superficial need not obliterate social comment. Once this had been realized, the Austrian classics could be re-examined to reveal what lay below the surface polish characteristic of so much Austrian art, and thus reinterpreted in the light of contemporary struggles.

Zeitspiegel's support for contemporary writers did not extend to serializing novels. The newspaper's practice in this respect was different from that of other exile newspapers and periodicals published in London, such as *Die Zeitung* or *Einheit*. But, as we have seen in the case of Bruno Heilig's *Menschen am Kreuz*, contemporary novels were excerpted, and the following examples give some indication of the range in subsequent years: F.C. Weiskopf, *Vor einem neuen Tag* (*Before a New Day*) (10 July 1943), Ernst Sommer, 'Gerichtstag' ('Day of Judgement'), from *Revolte der Heiligen* (25 December 1943), Ernst Lothar, *The Angel with the Trumpet* (15 July 1944). Instead of serialized novels there appeared short pieces of imaginative prose, interpreting and commenting on recent history, among them contributions from established writers such as Ernst Sommer[55] and Hermynia Zur Mühlen,[56] as well as several pieces by the journalist Eva Priester, a member of the *Zeitspiegel* editorial board who had contributed poetry to *Die Vertriebenen* and *Zwischen gestern und morgen* (*Between Today and Tomorrow*). Typical examples of this kind of writing are: Priester's 'Die Mauer' ('The Wall'), published on 6 February 1943, which illustrates the inadequacy of the German Social Democratic resistance to Hitler in the months prior to his assumption of power; Sommer's 'Der Maler Egger-Lienz' ('Egger-Lienz, the Painter'), published on 24 June 1944, an account of the 19th Century Tyrolean painter who depicted peasants resisting foreign occupation; and Zur Mühlen's 'Pferde-Mobilisierung' ('Mobilizing the Horses'), published on 9 September 1944, a stylized and idealized depiction of the sensibilities of village people who, observing horses entraining for the war zone in 1938, draw an analogy with the fate of their sons. Finally Rudolf Fuchs's short story 'Der Henker Heydrich und die böhmische Königskrone' ('The Hangman Heydrich and the Bohemian Crown') appeared on 17 January 1942, exactly one month before the author's untimely death.

Despite the undoubted interest of *Zeitspiegel*'s editorial board in fictionalized documentary material, an outstanding example of this genre, Sommer's 'Die Gaskammer' ('The Gas Chambers'), the first account of this method of liquidation to appear in German literature, based on information provided by the World Jewish Congress in London, appeared not in *Zeitspiegel* but in *Einheit* in December 1942.[57] However, Sommer's chilling autobiographical vignette of the Nazification of the Sudetenland, 'Die Tragödie des Komikers' ('The Tragedy of the Comedian'), which offered an insight into the background to the author's emigration, had appeared in *Zeitspiegel* some months earlier, on 24 January 1942. Sommer recounts how a satirical remark made by the Austrian comedian Paul Morgan when performing at a theatre in Karlsbad in 1937 had been blown up out of all proportion by the political editor of the local paper, who asserted that it had injured 'the most sacred feelings of the German people'. When consulted, Sommer (who ran a legal practice in the town) totally misjudged the situation, assuming the paper would settle out of court. In the heightened atmosphere preceding the German invasion, this course was refused for, as the paper's young lawyer declared, 'in a case where German honour is impugned there can be no compromises'.[58] Later Sommer received a postcard from his client instructing him to withdraw from the case written, he strongly suspected, from a concentration camp. In this assumption Sommer was probably correct for Morgan had been arrested in March 1938, sent to Dachau and transferred to Buchenwald, where he died in December of that year.

In addition to the examples outlined above, *Zeitspiegel* had an even more distinctive contribution to make to Austrian letters: one-page essays on aspects of Austrian culture which appeared in the later years of the publication. The influence of Hermann Ullrich, Albert Fuchs and even Ernst Fischer (at that time resident in Moscow) must be noted here, as must the continuation of the didactic impulse, for this material was used in the formal training sessions which prepared young Austrians to return home.[59] Concomitantly, the perception of many in the host country that Austria 'consisted entirely of Salzburg and Apfelstrudel, with perhaps a waltz thrown in'[60] was a view that needed some correction, and to this end the veil of the gracious outward form was lifted to reveal the grim reality beneath for, in the words of a Grillparzer epigram quoted to this purpose, 'Germany is smaller than it thinks/Austria is greater than it seems'.[61] Thus Nestroy's comedy is seen as a reaction to Metternich's censorship – 'Nestroy used humour like a hand grenade to attack Metternich's dictatorship' – and this author's experience of the darker side of Austrian life, which led him temporarily to embrace silence as a form of protest, 'shows us that the much vaunted Viennese *Gemütlichkeit* is a misconception'.[62] Similarly, Hermann Ullrich, examining the origins of the waltz, declared that when this sophisticated version of popular music first arrived in the salons of Vienna and Paris it was seen as an 'expression of the democratic *Zeitgeist*'.[63]

Music featured prominently in the exploration of Austrian identity; an article on Schubert, for example, which appeared in *Zeitspiegel* in 1942 represents an early but characteristic example of the short essay, where biographical information is combined with an evaluation of the artist's work and an assertion of his specifically Austrian identity, emphasizing the political, social and economic factors which informed his life and work. The essay opens with an account of the musician's death in dire poverty, which is then contrasted with the nostalgic interpretation of his work in the Biedermeier period. Schubert's music, the author asserts:

> is less the expression of an untrammelled *joie de vivre* than a reaction to the hectic pleasures of this misguided age which serve merely to mask pain, sorrow and the unending yearning for a better world.[64]

This hope for a better world, so evocative of the aspirations of exile, was to remain typical of the cultural politics of *Zeitspiegel*. The three editors, Jenö Kostmann, Eva Priester and Hilde Mareiner, all returned to Austria soon after the end of the war, and before the Austrian Centre closed. They were leading by example, following the course of action advocated by the Free Austrian Movement. All three eventually worked for the Communist Party press in Vienna, and could congratulate themselves that *Zeitspiegel*, the newspaper they had edited in London had, in concert with *Young Austria* and *Austrian News*, popularized the political aims of the Austrian Centre and the Free Austrian Movement.[65] Arguably, too, these journalists enjoyed greater success in wartime Britain than they ever achieved later, in their homeland, where the eradication of the Fascist legacy proved so slow, partial and inadequate.

Notes

1   *Zeitspiegel*, 3 October 1942.

2   Eden to Vansittart, 7 September 1942, National Archives[NA], FO 371/30911; see also interview with Jenö Kostmann, 24 January 1983, in Wolfgang Muchitsch, ed., *Österreicher im Exil: Großbritannien 1938-1945: Eine Dokumentation*, Vienna 1992, pp. 378-79.

3   *First Annual Report of the Austrian Centre*, London 1940, pp. 13-14.

4   The second anniversary of the Austrian Centre had been marked by a special edition of *Zeitspiegel* in May 1941.

5   Originally entitled *Austrian News*, from 1942 *Austrian Centre News*, from 1943 *Austrian Centre*.

6   *Austrian Centre*, February 1945, p. 3.

7   *Austrian Centre*, June 1945, p. 2

8 Originally *Österreichische Jugend*, it was called *Junges Österreich* from July 1939; after July 1940 it became *Young Austria* and from October 1944 *Jung-Österreich*.

9 See 'Neue Redaktion', *Young Austria*, early January 1942 ('Sondernummer zur Landeskonferenz'), pp. 2-3.

10 On this, see for example, Georg Breuer, *Rückblende: Ein Leben für eine Welt mit menschlichem Antlitz*, Vienna 2003, pp. 82 ff.

11 As the target group was clearly different, Muchitsch's description of *Austrian News* as a relaunch of *Österreichische Nachrichten* (*Österreicher im Exil*, p. 359) is misleading.

12 See Richard Dove, '"KZ auf Englisch": Robert Neumann's internment diary', in Charmian Brinson *et al.*, eds., *England? Aber wo liegt es?*, Munich 1996, pp. 157-67 (pp. 164-65).

13 W. Scholz, 'Solidaritat', *Zeitspiegel*, 14 September 1940, pp. 2-4.

14 Hans Probst, 'The Camp Youth', *Young Austria*, early August 1940, pp. 1-2.

15 'Unsere Freunde schreiben', *Young Austria*, early August 1940, pp. 4-5; 'Was sie uns schreiben', *Young Austria*, mid-August 1940, pp. 3-5, and two pages of replies, 'Und wir schreiben ihnen', *ibid.*, p. 5; 'Unsere Freunde in den Lagern', *Young Austria*, mid-September 1940, pp. 3-4; 'Briefe aus den Camps', *Young Austria*, mid-October 1940, pp. 3-4.

16 'Wie leben unsere Freunde in Australien?', *Young Austria*, early March 1941, p. 3.

17 'In Australien', *Young Austria*, end May 1941, pp. 1-2.

18 '400 Australien-Internierte frei', *Zeitspiegel*, 6 December 1941, p. 12.

19 'Unsere Freunde schreiben', *Young Austria*, early August 1940, pp. 4-5.

20 E.R., 'Canada inside out', *Young Austria*, 21 June 1941, pp. 3-4.

21 'Eine Woche der großen Leistungen', *Young Austria*, end November 1941, pp. 1-2; 'Deutsche Emigranten für Rußland', *Zeitspiegel*, 8 November 1941, p. 3; 'Freie Deutsche helfen Rußland', *Zeitspiegel*, 6 December 1941, p. 5; 'Der Tageslohn vom 22. Juni gehört der Sowjetunion', *Young Austria*, early June 1942, p. 1; 'Zwei österreichische Röntgenwagen werden verwundeten Rotarmisten helfen', *Zeitspiegel*, 4 July 1942, p. 1 (cf. Hilde Mareiner, *Eine österreichische Stimme gegen Hitler*, Vienna 1967, p. 20).

22 See Maimann, *Politik im Wartesaal: Österreichische Exilpolitik in Großbritannien 1938-45*, Vienna/Cologne/ Graz 1975, pp. 121-43.

23 See *ibid.*, p. 120.

24 FAM Landeskonferenz, 27-28 November 1943, not reported until 14 December; Cultural Conference on Post-war Reconstruction, 22-24 October 1944, reported 29 October and 4 November.

25 E.g. *Landeskonferenz des Free Austrian Movement*, [December] 1943; cf. also, the following chapter of this volume on the publications of the Free Austrian Movement.

26 See the present author's '*Einheit*', in William Abbey *et. al.*, eds., *Between Two Languages*, Stuttgart 1995, pp. 169-88 (p. 176).

27 These events are covered in greater detail in Mareiner, *op. cit.*, pp. 23-35. See also Wolfgang Muchitsch, *Mit Spaten, Waffen und Worten: Die Einbindung österreichischer Flüchtlinge in die britische Kriegsanstrengungen 1939-1945*, Vienna/Zurich 1992, pp. 23-71.

28 See Friedrich Scheu, *Die Emigrationspresse der Sozialisten 1938-1945*, Vienna/Frankfurt/Zurich 1968, p. 23.

29 Cf. Mareiner, *op. cit.*, p. 26.

30 See *Austrian News*, December 1942, p. 6.

31 For list of volunteers, see NA, FO 371/38830, 16 August 1944.

32 This, and all subsequent *Zeitspiegel* references in this paragraph, are from p. 1 of the newspaper.

33 Editorial, *Austrian News*, 16 November 1943, p. 3; unless otherwise stated, all the articles referred to subsequently are anonymous.

34 Bruno Heilig, *Men Crucified*, London 1941.

35 'Austrian Literature in Exile', *Austrian News*, January/February 1945, p. 4.

36 Anzengruber, First December issue 1939, p. 2; Lenau, mid-August 1939, pp. 5-6; Bertha von Suttner, First November issue 1939, pp. 3-4, this last signed F.W. (= Fritz Walter).

37 'Ein großer Österreicher – Ludwig Anzengruber: Zum 100. Geburtstag und zum 50. Todestag', *Junges Österreich*, First December issue 1939, p. 2.

38 'Joseph Roth', *Österreichische Jugend*, June 1939, p. 7.

39 E.g., *Young Austria*, 20 November 1943, p. 3; *Young Austria*, 25 December 1943, p. 3; *Young Austria*, 29 January 1944, p. 4; *Young Austria*, 26 February 1944, p. 4; cf. also, articles on local history, 'Wien', *Jung-Österreich*, 21 April 1945, p. 3; 'Salzburg', *Jung-Österreich*, 19 May 1945, p. 3.

40 'Stefan Zweig', *Young Austria*, early March 1942, p. 2.

41 Cf., 'Vineta', *Jung-Österreich*, 5 May 1945, p. 4.

42 Another was *Mut*, London 1943; on this, see also following chapter.

43 *Young Austria*, mid-August 1941, p. 8; *Zeitspiegel*, 24 August 1941, p. 10; both volumes were reviewed in *Zeitspiegel*: 'Die Vertriebenen – Dichtung der Emigration', 29 June 1941, p. 7; E.P. (= Eva Priester), '*Mut* – eine Anthologie der Jugend', 27 November 1943, p. 9.

44 See Jörg Thunecke, ' ... und wo die Synagogen brennen, erzittern auch schon die Kathedralen in ihren Grundfesten', in Ian Wallace, ed., *Aliens – Uneingebürgerte: German and Austrian Writers in Exile*, Amsterdam/Atlanta 1994, pp. 195-206; Jörg Thunecke, 'Schuldig ist ja nur, wer tat, was irgendeiner hätte tun können', in Brinson *et al.*, *England? Aber wo liegt es?*, pp. 193-206.

45 The full references are: 'Das tote Haus', *Young Austria*, end January 1941, p. 6; 'Jugend', in flyer distributed with *Zeitspiegel*, May 1941, p. 1; 'Wir stürmen das Land', *Young Austria*, early July 1942, p. 3; 'Traschenkos Tod', *Young Austria*, end August 1942, p. 5; 'Die Todesmystik in der Nazilyrik', *Zeitspiegel*, 28 August 1941, p. 8; for these observations on Fried, I am indebted to Steven W. Lawrie, 'Between Austrian Centre and Free German

League of Culture: Erich Fried's Literary Beginnings in London', *New German Studies*, 17 (1992-1993), pp. 109-31,

46   'Ihre Meinung zum *Zeitspiegel*', *Zeitspiegel*, 17 January 1942, p. 11.

47   The advertisements appeared in *Zeitspiegel* on 2 February 1944, 23 September 1944 and 6 January 1945 respectively.

48   The full *Zeitspiegel* references are respectively: J.M.S., 'Lieber Herr Neumann', 17 October 1942, p. 7; Albert Fuchs, 'Theodor Kramers Gedichte', 14 August 1943, p. 9; Albert Fuchs, 'Stefan Zweigs letztes Buch', 25 December 1943, p. 14; anon., 'Böhmen und Österreich vor 300 Jahren', 25 March 1944, p. 6; Ernst Sommer, 'Psychologie der Barbarei', 2 September 1944, p. 8.

49   '*Professor Bernhardi* im Laterndl', *Zeitspiegel*, 10 June 1944, p. 9.

50   E.F., 'Treibgut der Zeit', *Zeitspiegel*, 12 October 1941, p. 9.

51   R.F., '*Letzte Gedichte* von Max Hermann-Neiße', *Zeitspiegel*, 6 December 1941, p. 9.

52   Albert Fuchs, 'Stefan Zweig', *Zeitspiegel*, 10 April 1943, p. 7.

53   -d, 'Unentschuldigte Stunde', *Zeitspiegel*, 25 April 1942, p. 9.

54   U., 'Priestley-Uraufführung im Laterndl', *Zeitspiegel*, 3 April 1943, p. 7.

55   For bibliography, see Stefan Bauer, *Ein böhmischer Jude im Exil*, Munich 1995, p. 376.

56   For bibliography, see Manfred Altner, *Hermynia Zur Mühlen: Eine Biographie*, Berne 1997, pp. 231-32.

57   See Bauer, *op. cit.*, pp. 208-09.

58   Ernst Sommer, 'Die Tragödie des Komikers', *Zeitspiegel*, 24 January 1942, p. 8.

59   See Fritz Walter's letter to Bruno Frei, 24 October 1944, quoted in Muchitsch, *Österreicher im Exil*, pp. 344-45.

60   Willi Scholz, 'Tourist Travesty', *Young Austria*, August 1941, pp. 7-8 (p. 7).

61   H[ans] E[berhard] Goldschmidt, 'Grillparzers österreichisches Vermächtnis', *Zeitspiegel*, 4 March 1944, p. 4.

62   Bruno Frei, 'Nestroy – der revolutionäre Witzbold', *Zeitspiegel*, 27 November 1943, pp. 6-7.

63   Hermann Ullrich, 'Der Wiener Walzer: Ein Kapitel österreichischer Kulturgeschichte', *Zeitspiegel*, 13 November 1943, p. 7.

64   Alfred Rosenzweig, 'Franz Schubert: Zu seinem Todestag', *Zeitspiegel*, 28 November 1942, p. 7.

65   Cf. Muchitsch, *Österreicher im Exil*, p. 359.

PUBLISHING WITH A PURPOSE
FREE AUSTRIAN BOOKS

CHARMIAN BRINSON AND RICHARD DOVE

In a booklet published in May 1944 marking the Austrian Centre's fifth anniversary,[1] Georg Knepler summarized the aims of the Centre under four headings:

- to organize the Austrians in the fight against Hitler
- to promote friendship between the British and the Austrian people
- to foster the cultural life of the Austrians in this country
- to provide help, support and advice for Austrians.

Among the most important means of achieving these aims, and of advancing the political agenda which underpinned them, were the weekly newspaper *Zeitspiegel*, and the series of publications which appeared under the programmatic imprint Free Austrian Books.

The publications of the Austrian Centre, issued firstly under its own name and subsequently under the imprint Free Austrian Books, were intended to make the political voice of Austrian exiles in Britain more widely heard. At first sight they seem a disparate and even random list, ranging from literary works (verse anthologies, short prose, autobiography), political pamphlets concerned with contemporary issues regarding Austria, to more general publications which reviewed Austrian culture and history. On closer examination they are revealed as a conscious and roughly continuous exposition, providing a political and cultural statement of Austrian identity and aspiration during the Second World War.

The term 'books' is perhaps something of a misnomer, since most of the publications were in fact pamphlets or booklets, their format determined largely by wartime paper shortage – although some of the literary texts were longer, comprising up to a hundred pages. They were published in German or English, the English-language texts aiming broadly to raise British awareness of Austria's specific cultural and political identity, while the German-language publications were (until 1944-45) largely literary or cultural texts, intended to foster Austrian national consciousness, particularly amongst younger Austrians. However, the distinction between English-language and German-language publications was not always clear-cut, at least as regards readership: English-language pamphlets, for example, were at one point apparently widely read by young Austrians serving in the British forces. Texts in either language were intended to serve the overriding political purpose: the post-war re-establishment of an independent Austria.

The very first publication of the Austrian Centre was its *First Annual Report*, issued in March 1940. Comprising some thirty pages, the report was published in English, both to comply with censorship requirements and to make it accessible to British supporters. Though primarily a functional document, it was also intended to raise awareness of the Austrian Centre, and hence Austria, amongst British sympathizers. To this end, it contains messages of support from prominent British patrons, such as D.N. Pritt, Eleanor Rathbone and the Bishop of Chichester, which preface the detailed report on the Centre's first year of activity. The report itself is unsigned, but to the latter-day reader its most striking feature is its political neutrality.[2]

This first publication by the Austrian Centre was also its last for nearly two years, during which it confined itself to the production of the weekly newspaper *Zeitspiegel*. The reasons for such studied reticence were both political and practical. Although the Communists had played an important role in establishing the Austrian Centre and occupied leading positions within it, the Nazi-Soviet Pact of August 1939 had imposed considerable tactical constraints on them. Wartime conditions precluded public support for the official line propagated by the Comintern that this was a war between rival imperialist powers which Communists had a duty to oppose; public opposition to the policy of the British government would have meant rapid internment. These difficulties were further exacerbated by internal political developments in Britain; as indicated earlier, the mass internment of 'enemy aliens' ordered by the British authorities in May 1940 forced the Austrian Centre to concentrate on immediate practical tasks, such as lobbying for an end to internment and dealing with the subsequent problems of accommodation and employment.[3] Conversely, the publication programme which the Austrian Centre launched at the beginning of 1942 was a result of its new-found tactical freedom after the entry into the war of the Soviet Union.

The first book publication with which the Austrian Centre was associated was the verse anthology *Die Vertriebenen: Dichtung der Emigration (The Exiles: Poems of Emigration)*, published late in 1941 in collaboration with the Free German League of Culture and Young Czechoslovakia.

Jenö Kostmann's booklet *Restive Austria* (1942), published at the Austrian Centre

Claiming to be 'the first book published in the German language in this country since the war began', this slim volume contains a selection of poems by refugee authors, aiming 'to give the British public an insight into the intellectual strivings of the refugees'. The ideological thrust of the publication is implicit in the sub-title: '37 German Poems – but not written by our enemies.' As a collaborative venture, it sought to represent all German-speaking exiles, avoiding any assertion of a specific Austrian cultural identity. However, the Austrian Centre seems to have played a leading role in this publication. The two major contributors (numerically), Eva Priester (five poems) and Erich Fried (four poems), were both closely connected with the Centre.[4] The cover design was by Wolfgang Schlosser, and the poems selected by Albert Fuchs, both leading members of the Centre, while the publication address was that of the Centre's premises at 126 Westbourne Terrace.

Political conditions for Austrian exiles were transformed in December 1941 with the founding of the Free Austrian Movement (FAM). Its emergence signalled the introduction of an overt political agenda, pursuing the aim of the post-war re-establishment of an independent Austria and profiling Austrian cultural achievements as an assertion of a separate Austrian identity. Shortly after, in the spring of 1942, the Austrian Centre finally launched a publishing programme which was gradually to gather momentum throughout the rest of the war.[5] By the end of the year the Centre had published five booklets encompassing various aspects of its political platform, an agenda most explicitly enunciated in three pamphlets entitled *Zurück oder nicht zurück? (To go back? Or not?)* (April 1942), *Restive Austria* (May 1942), and *The Austrian Ally* (October 1942).[6]

Zurück oder nicht zurück? reprints the text of an address given at the Austrian Centre by its President, F.C.West.[7] In a speech originally given under the title 'Zurück oder nicht zurück – das ist keine Frage' (To go back - Or not? There's no question'), West made a strong appeal for total commitment by Austrian refugees to the British war effort, arguing that only the defeat of Hitler could create a situation in which the question posed in the pamphlet's title had any real meaning. While this text was clearly intended for West's Austrian compatriots, the next two pamphlets were equally clearly aimed at actual or potential 'British friends'. *Restive Austria* was the first of several pamphlets which sought to challenge the prevailing perception of Austria in Britain. British public opinion had hitherto made little distinction between Austria and Germany, an attitude reinforced by the British government's diplomatic recognition of the *fait accompli* of the Nazi annexation of Austria in 1938. Diplomatic recognition had been endorsed by bureaucratic anomaly. Austrians entering Britain after September 1938 had been admitted with German passports and therefore registered with the Aliens Department as Germans.

Restive Austria is intended to modify this perception. The programmatic preface (again by F.C. West) seeks to establish Austria as

Jury Herman's *Viel Glück* (1943), translated from the Russian by Eva Priester,
first publication in the series Free Austrian Books

the first victim of Nazi aggression: 'Austria too belongs to occupied Europe' (p. 2). The actual text, written by Jenö Kostmann, the editor-in-chief of *Zeitspiegel*, claims 'to give a report of the Austrian powder-barrel', i.e. to document the Austrian struggle for freedom. It paints a picture of a country oppressed and exploited by its Nazi occupiers, and reports growing passive resistance and acts of sabotage: a picture probably coloured by political optimism. The pamphlet's reports of incipient Austrian resistance were to be repeated and embellished in later publications, becoming a common-place of KPÖ war propaganda, intended both to bolster morale amongst Austrian refugees and to influence Allied attitudes towards Austria. That the Communists were also influenced by their own propaganda seems probable – and may help to explain the bitter disillusionment they suffered on their return to Austria after the war.

The Austrian Ally, published later that year, sought to make the case for Allied recognition of Austria as an occupied country and therefore as an ally. More specifically, it aimed 'to achieve a better understanding of the forces operating inside Austria [...] and a proper comprehension of the position of the Austrians in Great Britain, worthy allies as they are'. It consequently deals in turn with 'Austria Within' ('Guerrilla warfare has at last reached Austria', [p. 3]) and 'Austrians in Britain', telling 'the story of the participation of Austrian refugees in the war effort of this country' (p. 9). The pamphlet bears eloquent testimony to the need Austrian émigrés felt to explain themselves to the British: equating themselves with the anti-Nazi opposition within Austria itself. The concluding page of the pamphlet contains notes intended for Austrian readers, confirming that it was not aimed exclusively at a British audience. Kostmann's essay in the booklet ends by invoking the example of Andreas Hofer, leader of the Tyrolean struggle for freedom against Napoleon (p. 8). The reference to Hofer undoubtedly rested on the assumption that his name would be known to British readers from the sonnets of William Wordsworth.[8] However, this overt reference to an icon of Austrian patriotism suggests an ideological ambiguity which can also be detected in other publications.

It is perhaps most striking in the booklet *This is Austria*. Published shortly before Christmas 1942, and 'dedicated to all British friends of Austria by the two largest Austrian organizations in this country', the booklet was produced as an inexpensive Christmas present for Austrians to give British friends. It was intended to promote the concept of an Austria which was historically, culturally and politically independent of Germany. Subtitled 'The Story of a Beautiful Country', the booklet offers a tourist's eye view of Austria as a small country of outstanding natural beauty and cultural achievement. Consisting of text and pictures, it seeks to challenge the Nazi view of a German 'Eastern Province' by tracing the historical antecedents of a separate Austrian identity. In so doing, it appropriates much of the iconography of Austrian nationalism, presenting a conception of Austria similar to that propagated by the *Ständestaat* of Schuschnigg.[9] The front cover shows a mountain village in winter, the back cover a country girl in traditional dress, framed by fruit blossom. This tourist's eye view of Austria is completed by views of mountains and lakes, and above all by pictures of Salzburg, the festival town which had come to symbolize Austrian high culture. There are also attempts to convey a different tradition (that of 'Red Vienna') through illustrations of the ambitious municipal housing projects in Vienna, such as Karl-Marx Hof or the Matteoti Hof, but even these are undercut by the accompanying text, which emphasizes the emergence of the patriotic front of Catholics, Socialists and Communists in Vienna immediately prior to the Anschluss.

The presentation of such images was not of course arbitrary. The primary political reason, as stated above, was that the Austrian Centre itself represented a broad patriotic front. However, this was a booklet intended for British readers, and the images of Austria presented were calculated to confirm current British preconceptions, reinforcing a view of Austria derived from the cinema and musical theatre. Probably the best-known Austrian living in Britain in the 1930s was Richard Tauber, whose films such as *Blossom Time* and *Land without Music* had helped to create a perception of Austria as a country of scenic beauty and song: a natural backdrop for operetta. It is no accident that one of the photos in the booklet is of the original White Horse Inn (p. 15) – the operetta of the same name having achieved enormous popularity in London in 1931/32.[10] There were undoubtedly also practical explanations for the choice of images, not least the limited supply of available photographs. Certainly, tourist photographs could be obtained more easily – and more cheaply – than news agency pictures. The overall effect, however, remains culturally regressive.

Austria, produced a year later (November 1943), is both tourist brochure and political tract. A page of photographs, captioned 'Tourists' Paradise', are juxtaposed with an essay ('Britain's Friends in the Alps') which describes the Austrian Freedom Conference held in autumn 1942. The essay concludes that 'as the first victim of Nazi aggression, it is absolutely vital for Austria that she be recognized by the Allies as an associate' (p. 14), and raises the political demand for the foundation of a Free Austrian Fighting Force. Elsewhere, the contents include essays on Mozart, Beethoven and the Salzburg Festivals, confirming its cultural conservatism.

The crucial place assigned to culture in the political discourse of Austrian exiles, and above all of the Austrian Centre, is illustrated by the Austrian Cultural Conference held in London on 29-30 August 1942.

Convened by the Free Austrian PEN, and chaired by its President Robert Neumann, the conference was attended by representatives of all the main Austrian exile organizations. The keynote address was given by Albert Fuchs, a leading member of the Austrian Centre. Reporting the conference in *Zeitspiegel*, Jenö Kostmann asserted 'that the nurturing of the Austrian cultural heritage is a weapon in the struggle against Nazi domination'.[11] Fuchs's speech, published later that year as *Über österreichische Kultur (Concerning Austrian Culture)*, gave a more subtle, if no less Marxist, analysis of Austrian culture, offering a dialectical reading of cultural development.

Refuting the Nazi claim that Austria was an artificial creation, 'ready to return home to the Reich', Fuchs reviews the 'main stages' of Austria's history, emphasizing precisely the points at which it diverges from Germany's. Within this historical perspective, he seeks to delineate a distinct Austrian culture (and thereby an Austrian cultural identity). 'We want to demonstrate, to ourselves and to others, the *particularity* of the Austrian spirit. Nothing more.' The course of Austrian culture is both the product of social change and the harbinger of political revolution. Thus the cultural achievements of the early nineteenth century record the economic ascent of the 'rising middle classes' – and presage the political revolution of 1848:

> *One* difference is certainly unmistakeable: the courtly way of thinking has gone. Schubert, Strauss senior, as well as Waldmüller, Raimund, Nestroy, and even Grillparzer have their roots in the suburbs, draw from there the impulse for their work. Their works frequently mirror the running battle with the feudal regime (p. 10).

Fuchs does not fail to mention the brilliant flowering of Austrian culture around 1900, nor the social achievements of the First Republic – 'these were new forms of expression of the Austrian spirit, of the spirit of the progressive class in Austria' (p. 13).

1942 ended with the publication of the verse anthology *Zwischen gestern und morgen, (Between Yesterday and Tomorrow)* which represents something of a milestone in Austrian Centre publications. The volume is subtitled 'New Austrian Poetry', though the unsigned foreword (written in fact by Georg Knepler)[12] clearly defines 'Austrian' in cultural, not ethnic terms: 'Not all these writers were born in Austria; all of them spent decisive years there; for most of them Austria supplied their material – and perhaps something more than that. – Austrian authors' (p. 2). Ten poets are represented, ranging from established writers such as Berthold Viertel, Franz Werfel and Theodor Kramer, to younger poets like Erich Fried and Jura Soyfer. While the quality of the poems is uneven, the volume itself is significant as the first anthology of *Austrian* verse to be published in Britain during the war.

In May 1943 the Austrian Centre officially launched its imprint Free Austrian Books with the short novel *Viel Glück* (*Good Luck*)[13] which was translated by Eva Priester from the Russian original by Jury Herman (i.e. Yuri Pavlovich German). The reasons for choosing this particular text to inaugurate the new imprint were explained in a short foreword:

> It gives us special pleasure to be able to publish the first German translation of a Soviet novel from this war, all the more since this book, which portrays the fighting comradeship of Russian and British airmen, reflects the growing friendship between the peoples of the Great Alliance.[14]

The text was published at a time when Anglo-Soviet friendship and cooperation were flourishing. The entry of the Soviet Union into the war had transformed it from a hostile power into a heroic ally. British convoys bringing weapons to the new ally were sailing the hazardous Arctic supply route to Archangel; British factories were producing 'Tanks for Russia'. The shift in the perception of the Soviet Union had also altered official British attitudes to German and Austrian refugees. Enjoying a new-found freedom of action, the Austrian Centre had launched its first 'Aid for Russia' campaign in November 1941. The following June saw the conclusion of a further campaign to raise funds for the purchase of mobile X-ray vans for the Soviet Union.

Viel Glück, subtitled 'From the Diary of a Soviet WAAF', is a literary artefact of this brief political rapprochement, concerning the experience of a Russian fighter squadron and the British pilots who arrive to train them to fly Hurricane aircraft. Written in the conventional style of Soviet realism, the novel portrays the growing comradeship of men and women fighting for a common cause. The atmosphere is one of subdued heroism, in which personal lives are subordinated to the overriding aim of winning the war.

The introduction of the new imprint heralded a sharp increase in publishing activity. By far the greatest number of Austrian Centre publications is concentrated in the years 1943-45, a progression reflecting a growing sense of political urgency. Most of the pamphlets published in this period are concerned with topical political events. *The House of Lords on Austria* (February 1943) reprinted speeches made in the Lords debate (2 February 1943); *Ein Weg ins Leben* (*A Way into Life*) (February 1943) is a discussion of the Jewish question, taking up the appeal made by British bishops to 'make room' for Jewish refugees. It was the duty of the civilized nations 'whether neutral or Allied [...] to do their utmost to find a place of refuge for these victims' (p. 3). The pamphlet's author was

Willi Scholz, the General Secretary of the Austrian Centre, who – as a non-Jew and (more importantly) a Communist – took a strong anti-Zionist line.

According to Georg Knepler, the two most widely-read pamphlets of the Austrian Centre were *Austria: Gateway to Germany* (September 1943) and *Moscow on Austria* (December 1943).[15] The former, written by the poet and journalist Eva Priester, and aimed at 'the British friends of the Austrian cause', sought to emphasize the key strategic and military importance of Austria in the wake of the Allied invasion of Italy. It also reported growing Austrian resistance to German rule, illustrated by the formation of the Austrian Freedom Front. *Moscow on Austria* reproduces the text of the Allies' Moscow Declaration in November 1943, which represented the achievement of a major political aim of exiled Austrians. The Declaration pronounced the Anschluss 'null and void' and for the first time included the re-establishment of an independent Austria as an Allied war aim; Austria was, however, reminded that 'account will inevitably be taken of her own contribution to her liberation'. *Moscow on Austria* is therefore at pains to stress the role of the Austrian Freedom Front, calling on Austrians abroad to support it, and raising the political demand for the formation of an Austrian National Committee in exile. Though both pamphlets were aimed primarily at British readers, they had an important subsidiary readership among young Austrians serving in the British forces.

The outstanding literary publication by Free Austrian Books, published at Christmas 1943, was *Ein Sohn aus gutem Hause* (*A Son of a Good Family*) a short volume of autobiography by Albert Fuchs. The author's memoirs of his middle-class childhood in Vienna's IXth district were the evocation of a long-vanished world, all the more poignant for its contrast with wartime London. Moreover, it was a world which lived on in the minds of many of Fuchs's fellow-exiles, who shared his well-to-do Viennese Jewish background. *Ein Sohn aus gutem Hause* is more than a charming memoir. Fuchs goes on to record his conversion to the cause of Communism in 1934/35, lending his text the structure of a *Bildungsroman*.

When Georg Knepler came to write *Five Years of the Austrian Centre* (May 1944), he could therefore look back, *inter alia*, on two years of successful publication. The subtext of his account was of course that the Austrians had escaped from their stigmatization as enemy aliens, and were now free to state their case and even to exercise political influence. During these two years, he reported, the Centre had published eight booklets in English with an aggregate sale of 50,000 copies; the equivalent figure for German-language booklets and pamphlets was 'just under 19,000'. The evident emphasis on English-language publishing confirms that during 1942-43 the primary purpose of publication was the exposition of a political agenda, which sought to influence British public opinion (and government policy) in its favour.

The period up to 1943 had seen a gradual extension of Communist influence within the Austrian Centre. Given the crucial importance which the Party assigned to political education, it is unsurprising that Communist activists should dominate the Centre's publication programme. All of the eight pamphlets cited by Knepler were written by leading functionaries of the Austrian Centre – all of whom were, like Knepler himself, also leading cadres of the KPÖ. They included F.C. West, the President of the Austrian Centre (*House of Lords on Austria*), the General Secretary Willi Scholz (*Ein Weg ins Leben* and *Moscow on Austria*), and the leading cultural spokesman Albert Fuchs (*Über österreichische Kultur* [*Concerning Austrian Culture*]); the editorial team of *Zeitspiegel* – Jenö Kostmann (*Restive Austria* and *The Austrian Ally*), Hilde Mareiner (*The Austrian Ally*) and Eva Priester (*Austria: Gateway to Germany*); and the veteran KPÖ member Anna Hornik (*This is Austria*).

The increasingly visible profile of the KPÖ is demonstrated above all by the publication of several pamphlets by Ernst Fischer, the party's leading cultural theorist, who spent the war in Moscow. The most notable of these was *The Rebirth of my Country*, consisting of a series of broadcasts on Austria which Fischer had made over Moscow Radio. *Zeitspiegel* recommended the pamphlet as eminently suitable for the information of British friends.[16] In fact, during 1944/45 the Austrian Centre shifted its emphasis significantly from English-language to German-language publications, reflecting the progress of the war and the changing political priorities it imposed. These shifting priorities can be clearly read in the titles of such pamphlets as *The Rebirth of my Country* (September 1944), *Die österreichischen Flüchtlinge und ihre Zukunft* (*The Austrian Refugees and their Future*) (November 1944), *Was bringt der Friede?* (*What will peace bring?*) (April 1945) and *Die Heimat ruft!* (*Home is calling*) (July 1945). The last of these, advertised as 'a profusely illustrated pamphlet', was in fact a calculated mixture of pictorial nostalgia and political education, in which pictures of the Stefansdom and Altaussee were juxtaposed with extracts from Ernst Fischer's newly established newspaper in Vienna *Neues Österreich* (*New Austria*), in a clear attempt to win the hearts and minds of Austrian émigrés.

The last recorded publication by Free Austrian Books engages even more directly with the political discourse of post-war Austria. It is a short pamphlet, containing a speech given by Ernst Fischer at the reopened University of Vienna in autumn 1945, under the title *Für Freiheit und Vernunft* (*For Freedom and Reason*). Fischer was by then a prominent public figure, having already become Secretary of State for Culture and Education in a provisional government. Although the pamphlet was printed in London, the place of publication was given as

Vienna/London, further confirming the reorientation of the Austrian Centre towards a liberated homeland, to which all its leading activists were committed to return.

The prospect of an imminent return to Austria also determined a greater emphasis on political education, the need for which was particularly urgent in the case of young Austrians, who had spent crucially formative years in Britain and whose memories of their native country were growing increasingly distant. The youth arm of the Austrian Centre, Young Austria, which had its headquarters in a third Westbourne Terrace house (number 132), had been founded in March 1939; by 1943 it had a total membership of around 1300 and was running groups throughout Britain.[17] It, too, like the Austrian Centre itself, issued numerous publications during the 1939 to 1946 period, initially under the imprint Young Austria in Great Britain, and from 1943, for the most part, under that of 'Jugend voran' (Youth to the Fore).[18] In all, including the joint publishing projects in which it was involved, Young Austria produced some 60 publications, both German and English-language, amounting to a total print run of about 300,000,[19] an extraordinary achievement for a youth press operating in a foreign country in wartime. In general, Young Austria publications catered for a more narrowly defined readership than those of the Austrian Centre, being written principally with youth and youth leaders in mind. A further distinction was that the majority of these were in German, thus targeted largely at an Austrian readership, although British friends were not entirely neglected. However, Young Austria publications followed – if frequently more crudely – a similar political agenda to that of Free Austrian Books.

In 1945, Herbert Steiner, who played a pivotal role in the running of Jugend voran, defined its chief aims as being to produce publications particularly suitable for young people, to provide a forum for matters relating to youth and education, and to offer young writers the possibility of publishing their work. The guiding principle behind all of this was 'to disseminate greater knowledge about our home country'.[20]

The earliest Young Austria publications were almost certainly two song books, *Österreichische Jugend singt* (*Austrian Youth Sings*), which reportedly appeared in 1939,[21] and *Unser Lied* (*Our Song*), published in May 1940, that were intended for use at group meetings. *Unser Lied*, so its preface stated, was to serve as 'a friend and companion in all the happy and dark days that lie ahead' and to afford 'strength and confidence for the better tomorrow'. In 1940, too, an eight-page report on Young Austria's national conference appeared, *Unsere Konferenz* (*Our Conference*), that outlined the organization's mission and aims. A similar pamphlet was published the following year while a further early publication, *Funktionärschule des Jungen Österreich 1941* (*Young Austria School for Functionaries 1941*), was a direct product of its training programme for youth leaders. Though such pamphlets would have been intended principally for internal consumption, an early English-language publication, *Austria and Britain*, clearly had both an Austrian and a British readership in mind and was indeed 'dedicated to the friendship between the Austrian and British Youth', being published to mark the 'Austrians for Britain' campaign of August and September 1942. It portrayed an Austrian people desperate for liberation from Nazi oppression; and, at 'the decisive moment of our lives', Austrian youth in exile, standing shoulder to shoulder with British youth in the fight against Fascism.

Young Austria's publishing programme, while growing from modest beginnings, greatly increased in scope from 1943 onwards. In September of that year, the periodical *Young Austria* announced that the newly instituted Verlag Jugend voran 'was going ahead at full steam', and revealed ambitious plans for the future:

A calendar for 1944, postcards of Austria, a little brochure by Fritz Walter on the situation of youth in Austria, a song book and a small series of six books (Egon Erwin Kisch, from his new book: Market Place of Sensations, Dr. E. Buschbeck: Austrian Economic History, Ernst Fischer: Grillparzer, a small selection by Karl Kraus, a collection of Austrian poetry from eight centuries) [...] An anthology of Jura Soyfer is also planned.[22]

The poetry anthology *Mut* (*Courage*), like the earlier *Zwischen gestern und morgen*, was a collection of Austrian verse, this time by younger poets 'who were born or spent the greater part of their youth in the Austrian Republic'. Opening with a poem by Jura Soyfer who was one of Young Austria's icons, it brought together the poetry of twelve exiled Austrians, ranging in age from 18 to 29, including Erich Fried, Arthur Rosenthal (i.e. Arthur West), Willy Verkauf and Hans Schmeier (who, in the pressured atmosphere of refugee politics, had recently been driven to take his own life). Though the volume was nominally edited by Young Austria's chairman Fritz Walter, the selection was actually undertaken by Herbert Steiner and by Fried himself.[23] In a foreword, the English poet John Lehmann registered the young Austrian poets' determination 'with our help, to build a new Austria on stronger and more hopeful foundations'; moreover their participation in the fight against Hitler served as a reminder 'that there has always been a spirit in their homeland – which we can revive by just and timely action – the very opposite of the barbaric and intolerant militarism with which Prussia has sought to dominate the world' (p. 3). Yet while the anti-Nazi struggle and future Austrian liberation are of course central concerns in the poems, it is notable that, despite the poets' youth, nostalgia for the Austria of the past remains the overriding theme of this collection.[24]

Soon afterwards, reportedly in a large edition,[25] Young Austria also published an English-language pamphlet by Fried which recounted the efforts of young Austrian patriots attempting to resist the German occupation (Jugend voran publications, like those of Free Austrian Books, tended to be unduly optimistic on this score). In keeping with Steiner's belief that reading matter for young people should be amply illustrated,[26] *They Fight in the Dark: The Story of Austria's Youth*, 1944, contains much pictorial material; however, at least one of the illustrations, 'People weeping in Vienna when the Germans marched in, March 1938', an example of Jugend voran's propaganda at its most implausible, would have struck a false note with a readership well aware of the general welcome that the Germans received.[27]

Even while concerning itself with the current situation in Austria, Jugend voran – again, like Free Austrian Books – increasingly looked ahead to the difficulties to be faced there after the forthcoming defeat: thus Vivian Ogilvie's foreword to Emmi Walter's *Die soziale und wirtschaftliche Lage der österreichischen Jugend unter der deutschen Fremdherrschaft* (*The Social and Economic Situation of Austrian Youth under German Occupation*), 1944, already predicted that, as a result of the National Socialist legacy, 'of all the problems of liberated Europe perhaps the most difficult will be the problem of youth' (p. 1). And soon after the end of the war, Georg Breuer's *Forging the Future: Austrian Youth after Liberation*, though recognizing that as part of the heritage of Fascism 'destruction and demoralization' were 'particularly serious in Austria' (p. 5), could nevertheless emphasize the work being done on behalf of and by Austrian youth and end on a highly optimistic pictorial note: a picture of the Vienna parliament (symbol of newly regained democracy) and a drawing of a train proceeding up a mountain track (an image redolent of 'traditional Austrian values') are accompanied by the slogan 'Welcome to Austria'. While the two earlier pamphlets addressed themselves principally to Austrian youth leaders, thus to a specialist readership, the Breuer publication, written in English, served once again to provide information for British friends. In addition, however, it set out to reach the many young Austrians in Britain who had by then lost much of their German. Thus *Forging the Future* formed part of Young Austria's propaganda campaign to attract its young people back home to take part in Austrian reconstruction, quoting from an appeal from the newly founded Free Austrian Youth in Austria as follows: 'We hope that you will soon return home. We are waiting for your hearts and for your hands. Our country needs all its sons and daughters who are devoted to its well-being' (p. 15).

The danger of young Austrians progressively losing touch with their own history and culture had been recognized for some time and a number of publications were produced in an attempt to rectify the situation. Ernst Fischer's pamphlet, *Grillparzer: Ein großer österreichischer Dichter* (*Grillparzer: a Great Austrian Poet*), for example, of 1943 can be viewed in this light as can Hans Tietze's *Abriß einer österreichischen Kunstgeschichte* (*An Outline of Austrian Art History*), 1945, and Paul Reim's (i.e. Reimann's) *Probleme und Gestalten der österreichischen Literatur* (*Problems and Figures of Austrian Literature*), 1945, all three of which stress the separateness of the Austrian cultural tradition from its German counterpart. Though the writing of a specifically Austrian literary history was still in its infancy, Reim contended, Austrian youth was impatient and wanted at least 'a short introduction explaining the most important aspects of Austrian literature' (p. 1).

As already evident, an increasingly important part of Young Austria's work, and that of Jugend voran, was the preparation of youth leaders for the re-education work that would be necessary in post-war Austria. From the autumn of 1944, Young Austria's 'Jugendführerschule' or School for Youth Leaders, which in all trained around 300 functionaries,[28] put out a special series of pamphlets under the Jugend voran imprint. Among these were Stefan Kaufmann's *Ratschläge für Redner und Referenten* (*Advice for Speakers and Lecturers*) and, based upon Young Austria's years of experience in British exile, Herbert Steiner's *Die Organisation einer Jugendbewegung* (*The Organization of a Youth Movement*), both from 1945. Pamphlets that would be particularly helpful for youth leaders in the new Austria in their task of countering the years of Nazi ideology included Erich Schindel's *Über Sexualerziehung* (*Concerning Sex Education*), 1945, and Walter Hollitscher's *Rassentheorie* (*Racial Theory*) of 1944. The ambitions of Young Austria towards Austrian youth, both on the political and social level, are encapsulated in the very title of Jaro Brezik's late 1945 contribution to the series, *Für eine freie und gesunde Jugend im neuen Österreich* (*For a Free and Healthy Youth in the new Austria*).

After the formation of the Free Austrian Movement on 3 December 1941, this organization, too, proceeded to produce a series of around 40 publications from its address at Craven House, Kingsway, ranging from printed booklets, through duplicated lectures and information sheets, to press releases and planning documents for internal FAM use. These set out primarily to publicize the work of the Free Austrian Movement and to propagate its aims, as defined, for instance, at the end of what was probably the first FAM publication, a four-page pamphlet entitled '*In the Victory of the Allies, Free Austria shall find her honoured place*', issued to commemorate the fourth anniversary of the Anschluss in March 1942. Bearing a title derived from the Churchill speech of 18 February 1942 which had accorded Austria the status of 'the first victim of Nazi aggression', the pamphlet requested support in the fulfilment of the Free Austrian Movement's ambitions, namely the abolition of the 'enemy alien' designation for Austrians in Britain; the full inclusion of Austrians in the Allied war effort, both civilian and military (including the formation of a Free Austrian Fighting Force); and the post-war creation of 'a "Free Democratic Austria" in her 1938 frontiers'.

Like the majority of the FAM's publications, it appeared in English, being targeted chiefly at a British readership. So, too, did the thirty-two page pamphlet, *The Case of Austria*, which focuses on the 'contribution to the liberation of the homeland from servitude and distress' (p. 31) to be made by exiled Austrians, a major theme in FAM publications. A further pamphlet from 1942, *A Secret Conference of the Austrian Freedom Front somewhere in the Austrian Mountains*, shifts the emphasis to the other pole of Free Austrian propaganda, that is to the internal anti-Nazi opposition. In stirring tones, it describes the Freedom Front's founding conference, reportedly attended by 40 representatives from all sectors of the Austrian population. The existence of the AFF was to become one of the FAM's chief tenets of faith, as reflected in numerous FAM publications.[29] Presented as an organized body, however – rather than as the isolated pockets of resistance that undoubtedly did obtain in National Socialist Austria – the AFF was largely a propagandist fiction. It is interesting to note that the 1942 AFF conference report, like various other FAM publications, cites as its source the 'Austrian Freedom Station', the radio station allegedly situated somewhere in the Austrian Alps but in fact broadcasting from Moscow.[30]

In 1943, by which time the FAM's publishing programme was in its stride, two illustrated commemorative booklets were issued that were broader in scope than was customary in this publication series. The first, *Five Years Hitler Over Austria*, marking the fifth anniversary of the Anschluss, appeared as a special edition of *Austrian News* and covers a wide range of political, economic and cultural topics. A message from that prominent British friend of the exiled Austrians, the former British Ambassador to Austria, Sir Walford Selby, exhorts them 'to keep alive the spirit of their country in anticipation of the day of Austria's final liberation' (p. 2). While increasingly under Communist control, the FAM was keen to demonstrate its broad political base, as demonstrated by this pamphlet whose authors include not only the Communist *Zeitspiegel* editor Jenö Kostmann but also the Democratic Unionists Emil Müller-Sturmheim and Otto Harpner, and the liberal Hermann Ullrich. A letter from an American professor even proposes that 'Austria and its equally decent neighbours' – not Germany, therefore – might opt in the final peace settlement for federation (p. 5), a view that was favoured in some exile quarters,[31] though certainly not by the Austrian Communists.

The second booklet, this time marking a twenty-fifth anniversary, was entitled *1918-1943: To Commemorate the Foundation of the Austrian Republic*. Like *Five Years Hitler Over Austria*, *1918-1943* sets out to combine a diversity of viewpoints, this time on the achievements during the twenty years of Austrian independence – Hermann Ullrich again on music, the former Social Democratic member of the Austrian parliament Marie Köstler on social welfare, the Honorary President of the Austrian Centre, Professor Walter Schiff on 'The People's Colleges of Vienna', and other pieces on economics and public health.

At the same time, the year 1943 also saw the appearance of a number of considerably less lavish FAM publications that were perhaps of greater immediate relevance. In June, a duplicated report, *The Position in Austria*, was published anonymously (its author was in fact the exceptionally active and well-informed leading FAM functionary, Eva Kolmer). Here Kolmer offers a sombre account of the current political, economic and social problems of wartime Austria before moving on, unusually dispassionately, to the question of Austrian resistance. Basing her account primarily on the Nazi press, but also on BBC, Moscow Radio and Austrian Freedom Station reports, Kolmer compiled the available information on executions for treason, sabotage and guerrilla forces in Austria and dissension among Austrians in the German army. The Austrian resistance movement had, she contended, made 'great headway' in the preceding few months, yet it was hampered by the lack of any 'central direction' and by a deplorable 'tendency to wait [...] because the time for striking is not yet right'; moreover it could not be said to match up either to 'the degree of resistance in other countries' or to 'the requirements of the present period in the whole of the war against Nazi Germany' (p. 15).

At the end of her paper, and here as a subsidiary consideration, Kolmer directs her attention to matters nearer home, the supporting role of the Austrian emigration. But exile affairs were in fact the *prime* focus of a number of FAM publications from around this time. A duplicated statement, *Facts about the Free Austrian Movement and the so-called 'Austrian Representative Committee'*, for one, records some of the bitter ongoing disagreements between the FAM and the Austrian Social Democrats, showing the latter to maximum disadvantage: thus, in the all-important matter of the Moscow Declaration (which the FAM endorsed wholeheartedly), a peevish reaction is attributed to Karl Czernetz, for the Social Democrats: 'We were not consulted. The Moscow Conference brought a dictate [*sic*]' (p. 12).

Another publication, *Landeskonferenz des Free Austrian Movement* (*National Conference of the Free Austrian Movement*), also from late 1943, offers a more general account of the FAM's recent activities, including the important publishing field:

> Literature sales were extraordinarily successful. In the second half of 1943 some 50,000 pamphlets about Austria were sold. The information from Leicester that, in competition with Leeds, literature

to the value of £35 was sold, was greeted with much applause [...] The FAM distributed 20,000 leaflets (p. 2).

Among the lectures delivered at the 1943 conference and reproduced in the conference proceedings was Dr Paul Loew-Beer's 'The Work of the Free Austrian Movement on Post-war Questions', reporting on planning work already being undertaken in a variety of fields. By the following year, as might be expected, several further future-oriented FAM publications had appeared. In May 1944, for instance, for a price of 2/6d., the FAM's Social Welfare Department published its *Gesammelte Vorträge aus einem Kurs über Probleme der Nachkriegszeit* (*Collected Lectures from a Course on Problems of the Post-war Period*), all delivered during the previous few months. Other planning documents issued in the course of 1944, often in both an English and a German version, included *The Establishment of a Public Health Service in Austria During the Period Immediately after Liberation* and *Proposals for First Measures for the Rehabilitation of Austrian Agriculture and Forestry: Austrian Agriculture*.

Copies of a number of these found their way to British Government departments, having been sent there by Eva Kolmer for information purposes and also, undoubtedly, in the hope of having some influence on Allied policy. The British authorities, in general, reacted dryly to such documents, with the War Office passing on its copy of *Austrian Agriculture* to the Foreign Office with the accompanying message: 'Here is an effusion from the Free Austrians. I am sure you will have a suitable drawer in which to put it.'[32] A more considered approach to the paper is found in a letter, marked 'Secret', to the Foreign Office from Economic and Industrial Planning Staff:[33] they criticized what they saw as the FAM's more radical or impractical suggestions, such as the proposals for the immediate and total dissolution of the former Reich Food Estate. As to the paper's recommendation that 'Trustees of the Austrian Freedom Front must immediately be put in charge of all agricultural and forestal co-operatives' (p. 1), the British response is pointed: 'I notice that, while members of the Movement are to appear in key positions, there appears to be no provision for representation of the peasant and farming population in general.'[34]

With regard to events within the FAM itself, the development of the Free Austrian Movement into the Free Austrian World Movement, announced on 11 March 1944 to mark the sixth anniversary of the Anschluss, was celebrated in a publication entitled *Free Austrian World Movement: A Survey of Austrian Organizations Abroad*. It emphasizes the large number of countries in which affiliated organizations were by then to be found, their membership consisting both of:

those who look forward to returning to Austria when it has been liberated, and those who intend to settle down in the country in which they have found refuge, or else to re-emigrate after the war. Both kinds, however, have their place in the Free Austrian organizations (p. 2).

The same distinction between groups of Austrians in exile in Britain was drawn by Jenö Desser in September 1944, at a FAM conference on 'Die österreichischen Flüchtlinge und ihre Zukunft' ('The Austrian Refugees and their Future'), the proceedings of which were published in a booklet of the same name. Other lectures reproduced in the booklet, namely Leopold Spira's 'Die Österreicher in den Alliierten Armeen und ihre Probleme' ('Austrians in the Allied Forces and their Problems') and Eva Kolmer's 'Hilfe für die Österreicher im befreiten Europa' ('Help for Austrians in Liberated Europe'), mirror further FAM concerns of late 1944. Kolmer's paper announced the mounting of a large-scale campaign for impoverished Austrian refugees who had managed to survive the war, in camps or in concealment or disguise, in countries such as Italy or France. Some of them, Kolmer maintained, had succeeded in playing a more active role in the prosecution of the war, fighting with the Italian partisans or the Maquis; and to these Austrians, in December 1944, the FAM devoted a separate publication, The Free Austrian Movement in the Occupied Countries, which begins with a statement on the subjects that formed the basis of the FAM's publishing programme:

We have on previous occasions given accounts of the activities of Austrian organizations in the free world that arose on the basis of national unity for the restoration of a democratic and independent Austria. We have described the formation and steady growth of the Austrian Freedom Front in the homeland. Now, as the Allied armies of liberation drive the German invaders from one occupied country after another, we receive news of the heroic struggle carried on by our countrymen in those countries against the common enemy. It is a story which we are proud to tell.

While the Free Austrian Movement/Free Austrian World Movement continued publishing throughout 1945, it is possibly accurate to suggest that a German-language publication, Heimat Österreich (Our Austrian Homeland), which appeared right at the beginning of the year, represented a more or less final word from the FAM to its mass membership. With the end of the war in sight, the attractively produced booklet – 'dedicated to the Austrian antifascists' – sought to bear testimony to the Austrian resistance movement inside Austria and the anti-Nazi activities of Austrians abroad and, on this basis, to campaign for the reinstatement of an independent Austria. These were, of course, well-worn themes; but by January 1945 there was a true urgency about them. 'Now everything will depend on our own efforts,' exhorted Ernst Fischer in his contribution 'Österreichs unvollendete Symphonie' ('Austria's Unfinished Symphony') (p. 7). Apart from the by now customary selection of evocative visual images, other items included a Wildgans poem 'Mein Österreich' ('My Austria'), a statement of the 'peace goals of the Austrian Freedom Front', a message from an 'Austrian in the Army of Liberation' (i.e. the British army), a timely reminder of the terms of the Moscow Declaration and an announcement concerning the setting up of an Austrian Battalion in the Slovenian Liberation Army. Meanwhile a passionately written piece on 'The Austrian World Movement' has distinct echoes of an apologia about it:

> We did not leave our homeland voluntarily, the Germans and their Austrian accomplices drove us out of Austria. Like tens of thousands of freedom fighters from all oppressed peoples we left our country to join the struggle for the liberation of our people from German tyranny. In emigration we have ended up in practically every country in the free world. Everywhere, where Austrians settled they began, after a short time, to unite in order to remain Austrians, even while abroad, in order to preserve the very Austria that the Germans wished to destroy, and to work for the day when our country will be once more free and independent (p. 2).

Nothing as compelling as *Heimat Österreich* was to appear again in the Free Austrian Movement series. The FAM continued, post-war, to produce information sheets, such as its *First Currency Measures in Austria* of mid-1945, in the enduring if optimistic hope of having some influence on British policy towards Austria. In addition, three more substantial publications were still to appear in 1945 under the Free Austrian Movement imprint and on three specific areas of Austrian national life, on its medical provision (*The Health Services in Austria: Problems of Medical Reconstruction and Rehabilitation*), its economy (*Austria's Economy Past and Future*) and its science (*Science in Austria*). Each of these works, written in English, was produced with an eye to enlisting support for the new Austria. *The Health Services in Austria*, for instance, sought to draw up proposals on how best 'to restore the medical services to the oppressed, misguided and maltreated Austrian people' which could be 'put [...] before the medical profession, before the British authorities, and before the authorities of other Allied Nations' (p. 4).[35]

Even as the publications of the Free Austrian Movement, like those of Free Austrian Books and *Jugend voran*, increasingly focused on political and indeed practical matters at the close of the war and after, cultural issues were not neglected. Since 1942, the Austrian Centre had been producing a duplicated monthly magazine, *Österreichische Kulturblätter*, which had reflected both its own and Young Austria's cultural activities, had published carefully selected literary texts and had provided its speakers and dramatic groups with material from Austrian literature and history for cultural propaganda work. It was out of this, at the beginning of 1944, that the *Kulturblätter des FAM* developed (later that year renamed *Kulturelle Schriftenreihe des Free Austrian Movement*). These were edited by the lawyer and music critic Dr Hermann Ullrich, a leading activist in the Austrian Centre and in the Free Austrian Movement who, as well as contributing regularly to *Zeitspiegel* on cultural matters, had reportedly also played a part in producing the earlier *Österreichische Kulturblätter*.[36]

The new journal, however, represented a radical departure from the loosely-structured and heterogeneous *Österreichische Kulturblätter*, with Ullrich choosing both to raise significantly the level of cultural debate and to focus in each issue on a single cultural field: music, art, science, history, historiography, humour, the contribution of women, the great cities of Vienna and Salzburg, and literature (with one number devoted exclusively to Hugo von Hofmannsthal and another to Franz Grillparzer). Unlike the other publications described in this chapter, which set out in varying degrees to shape both exiled Austrian and British opinion, the *Kulturblätter des FAM / Kulturelle Schriftenreihe des Free Austrian Movement* were directed at a very largely Austrian readership.[37]

At the end of 1943, in fact, Ullrich had already tested out his new concept for the *Kulturblätter* with a preliminary number dedicated entirely to Stefan Zweig. In what would become a regular pattern, the issue was made up of a variety of articles on the late writer, introduced, compared and drawn together by a foreword from Ullrich himself. In marked contrast to the more rigid editorial policies of other Free Austrian publications, it is notable that the articles, by Felix Braun, Victor Fleischer, Alfred Rosenzweig, Siegmund Warburg and Richard Friedenthal, were selected for personal and cultural reasons rather than on ideological grounds (the writers, all formerly close friends of Zweig's, were of diverse political persuasions). Indeed, ideological pluralism remained a feature of the *Kulturelle Schriftenreihe* throughout its existence, a policy that Ullrich, a liberal himself,[38] sometimes felt it necessary to defend, as in his preface to *Österreicher, die Geschichte machten* (*Austrians Who Made History*) of 1945:

> Perhaps the inclusion of one author or another will prove contentious. That is true above all of Srbik, who was undoubtedly a supporter of National Socialist ideas. However, his book on Metternich is a standard work, which no one who concerns himself with the figure of the Austrian Chancellor can pass over (p. iii).[39]

Shortly after the publication of the Zweig number, the first of the four *Kulturblätter des FAM* – 16 more were to follow in the *Kulturelle Schriftenreihe* – would appear, in January 1944, entitled *Wien im Spiegel der Jahrhunderte (Vienna in the Mirror of the Centuries)*. This consisted of a wide selection of poetry and prose extracts – wide enough, indeed, to include even an extract from *Mein Kampf*. In his introduction, Ullrich is unflinching in his juxtaposition of Vienna's glorious past with its wretched present; yet he also calls to mind the earlier occasions on which Vienna had succeeded in throwing off a foreign yoke, adding for good measure: 'If appearances are not deceptive, the days of Nazi tyranny are also numbered and Austria will once again be In ORBE ULTIMA' (p. i). As Ullrich subsequently commented of his intention here: 'To give the doubters and the cowards – and how many there were at that time! – a declaration of faith.'[40]

'Faith has proved its worth' – thus Ullrich would introduce his later *Wien und die Welt (Vienna and the World)*, a revised and expanded version of *Wien im Spiegel der Jahrhunderte*. Yet while the heroic tone had been entirely appropriate in January 1944 when the earlier issue had appeared, a more sober note was in keeping with the Austrian realities of late 1945:

> A considerable change in objectives, structure and selection of the material had certainly become necessary. Anything polemical, anything determined by the contemporary liberation struggle had to be omitted and Vienna's significance in the world and for the world throughout the ages had to be put into the clear light of objective assessment [...] Even the faults and the weaknesses of the city and its inhabitants were not to be overlooked (p. i).

New voices to add to the old, therefore, included the Frenchman Marc Henry, who had criticized the decadence and indifference of Vienna prior to 1914, and the Englishman Edward Crankshaw who had diagnosed a state of terminal decline in Vienna in the inter-war years. Characteristically, though, even in the rigours of the immediate post-war period, Ullrich still chose to reassure his readership as to Vienna's present and future: 'Even from this crisis, perhaps the most serious in its history, Vienna will emerge stronger and more beautiful, older and more serious but also made more humane and more mature by the depth of its suffering' (p. ix).

From the combined issues of the *Kulturblätter des FAM/Kulturelle Schriftenreihe des FAM*, it is evident that the Austrian culture with which Hermann Ullrich was most conversant and which he felt to be most appropriate to his cultural propaganda purposes was the high culture of past centuries. In later numbers of the *Kulturelle Schriftenreihe*, it is true, he attempted to broaden the range, as in *Die Frau in der Österreichischen Kultur*

(*Women in Austrian Culture*), 1945. He himself, however, in a lengthy preface, admitted to feelings of hesitancy in such an area; and it was left to the ex-Social Democratic deputy Marie Köstler, in a plain and practical foreword, positively to endorse the issue's subject-matter as well as to express her conviction that, as in the past, so women would play a full part in Austria's national life in the future. Ullrich's cultural perspective may also explain why not only the number entitled *Österreichische Wissenschaft* (*Austrian Science*) of 1945 but also the two issues on *Österreichische Schriftsteller im Exil* (*Austrian Writers in Exile*) which appeared near the end of the *Kulturelle Schriftenreihe*'s life in 1946 and which obviously consisted entirely of contemporary literature, contained no contribution from their editor.

Be that as it may, Ullrich's achievement under wartime and immediately post-war conditions in bringing out a wide-ranging and high-level cultural journal – what he himself has termed a 'bibliophile rarity'[41] – that both fostered the Austrian cultural tradition and promoted new work by exiled Austrian writers and scholars, should not be underestimated. As Ullrich would write in the final issue, in his 'Farewell to the Reader':

> It exceeded the powers and capabilities of one individual to show all the facets of this jewel. And I worked as an individual throughout these three years, despite the help (which can never be adequately acknowledged) of so many splendid Austrians in the free world.

Chief among the difficulties he experienced were those in obtaining the material he required, noting in his preface to *Wien im Spiegel der Jahrhunderte*, 'that many works were, in the present circumstances, unobtainable even in that enormous reservoir of human knowledge known as the British Museum' (p. i). Moreover, until the end of 1945, quite apart from the problems associated with the wartime paper restrictions, circulation was limited by the duplicating process by which the journal had to be produced.[42] Yet despite Ullrich's essentially lone position in this venture, he could, as he himself conceded, call on the services of a wide range of experts from among his fellow exiles to assist with selection and to write for the journal. A leaflet advertising the *Kulturelle Schriftenreihe* in mid-1945 included in a list of contributors the writers Felix Braun, Albert Fuchs, Mela Hartwig, Eva Priester and Martina Wied; the artists Georg Ehrlich and Oskar Kokoschka; the musicians Hans Gál, Bruno Walter and Egon Wellesz; as well as others active in science and medicine.[43]

For its last four numbers, from the beginning of 1946, the *Kulturelle Schriftenreihe* was brought out as the 'Literary and Cultural Supplement' to *Zeitspiegel,* published for the FAM by Free Austrian Books at the Austrian

Centre, and thus managed to increase its circulation figures. It was in this, its final printed form, that the *Kulturelle Schriftenreihe* was to become permitted reading for Austrian prisoners in the British Prisoner of War camps. In addition, copies were at last being sent into Austria – although without much success, to judge from Ullrich's lament to Viktor Matejka of 21 February 1946: 'A shame that the numerous copies of the *Kulturelle Schriftenreihe* which we have sent into the country since liberation have obviously been lost.'[44]

For the redoubtable Marie Köstler, the value of the *Kulturelle Schriftenreihe* lay in the fact 'that in every issue it confronted us with a fragment of home and showed us that we have reason to be proud of our country and our nation'.[45] Ullrich himself defined as his motivating force the conviction 'that our homeland and above all the youth of today, uprooted and spiritually undernourished by eight years of exile or tyranny, has a right to our work'; his task had been 'to serve Austria'.[46] The issue in which his valedictory piece appeared, in June 1946, was devoted to Franz Grillparzer, 'Austria's greatest writer', a choice which in Ullrich's view bore the greatest relevance to the current Austrian situation:

> But how contemporary Grillparzer is, how many of his observations are still valid today and how little has basically changed in Austria since his times! He, a man who did not want to be a German but an Austrian, even a Lower Austrian, or above all a Viennese, would soon get used to the Austria of today. And thus the task of this copy of the journal is to encourage consideration of this poet, not to lead readers *back* to Grillparzer but *forward* to him.

It was on this forward-looking note that Hermann Ullrich took leave of his readers. The time had come, so he wrote, for him and many others to return to the *Heimat*; others, who had decided to remain in their country of exile, would now strive to assume the culture of their new land. 'There is no further need for a revue, which arising from the necessity of the time, matured with it and now sees that time fulfilled.' Like Ullrich, many of those who had contributed to Free Austrian publications in Britain would indeed soon return to Austria, where they undoubtedly hoped to set up the post-war cultural guidelines. These hopes were largely unrealized. Austrian cultural identity was eventually redrawn, not according to the precepts of the Free Austrian Movement, but the ideological expediencies of the Cold War.

Notes

1   Georg Knepler, *Five Years of the Austrian Centre*, London: Free Austrian Books, 1944.

2   The report on the first year of activities was almost certainly written by Eva Kolmer, who sent a draft copy to Friedrich Otto Hertz in February 1940 (cf. Friedrich Otto Hertz Papers, Archive for the History of Sociology in Austria, Graz).

3   See Eva Kolmer, *Das Austrian Centre: 7 Jahre österreichische Gemeinschaftsarbeit*, London: Austrian Centre [1946], pp. 4-7. Cf. also *Zeitspiegel*, 25 January 1941.

4   Among the other contributors were: Kuba (i.e. Kurt Barthel) (3 poems), Max Zimmering (2), Max Herrmann-Neisse (2), Rudolf Fuchs (2), and Rolf Anders (4).

5   Eva Kolmer's list of publications in her commemorative booklet (see note 3 above) starts in 1942. The early publications appeared under the imprint Austrian Centre or Austrian Centre/Young Austria; from March 1943 most appeared under the imprint Free Austrian Books.

6   In her booklet (see note 3 above), Eva Kolmer suggests that *Restive Austria* was published in April and *Zurück oder nicht zurück?* in May 1942, but a contemporary diary of Austrian Centre activities confirms that they actually appeared in the opposite order (see Wolfgang Muchitsch, ed., *Österreicher im Exil: Großbritannien 1938-1945: Eine Dokumentation*, Vienna 1992, p. 292).

7   F.C. West's speech, due to be held at Paddington (i.e. 124-126 Westbourne Terrace) on 31 March, was advertised in the weekly *Zeitspiegel*, 28 March 1942, p. 10.

8   William Wordsworth, 'Hofer', from 'Poems dedicated to National Independence and Liberty'. See *The Poetical Works of William Wordsworth*, vol. 3, ed. by E. de Selincourt and H. Darbishire, Oxford 1954, p. 129. Cf. the translation of this poem by Eva Priester, under the title 'Andreas Hofer', in *Zeitspiegel*, 13 March 1943, p. 6.

9   For a comprehensive discussion of the iconography of Austrian exile publications, see Ursula Seeber-Weyrer, '"Ergötze dich am längst nicht mehr Vorhandenen": Österreich-Bilder des Exils', in Ursula Prutsch and Manfred Lechner, eds., *Das ist Österreich: Innensichten und Außensichten*, Vienna 1997, pp. 123-40.

10   *The White Horse Inn*, described as 'a musical spectacular', was given 651 performances at the Coliseum Theatre between 8 April 1931 and 23 April 1932.

11   *Zeitspiegel*, 5 September 1942, p. 7.

12   According to Knepler himself (letter to the authors, 9 April 1998).

13   Although Free Austrian Books was not officially launched until May 1943, the imprint had already been inaugurated with the booklet *Kleines Magazin*, a miscellany of poems, short stories and political essays.

14 Jury Herman, *Viel Glück: Aus dem Tagebuch einer Soviet WAAF*. Aus dem Russischen übertragen von Eva Priester, p. 2.

15 Georg Knepler, *Five Years of the Austrian Centre*, p. 5.

16 *Zeitspiegel*, 30 September 1944, p. 8.

17 See 'Sieben Jahre "Junges Österreich"', *Jung-Österreich*, 28 August 1946, pp. 4-5.

18 *Jugend voran* was also the title of a periodical for Austrian youth in Great Britain as well as that of the journal of the Austrian World Youth Movement.

19 'Sieben Jahre "Junges Österreich"'.

20 Herbert Steiner, *Die Organisation einer Jugendbewegung: Organisationsformen und Erfahrungen des 'Jungen Österreich' in Großbritannien*, London: Jugend voran (Jugendführerschule des Jungen Österreich), [1945], p. 10.

21 According to the preface of *Unser Lied*.

22 'Der Verlag der österreichischen Weltjugendbewegung', *Young Austria*, 25 September 1943, p. 1. All these plans were realized with the exception of the Jura Soyfer volume.

23 See Herbert Steiner, 'Mein Freund Erich Fried', in Volker Kaukoreit and Heinz Lünzer, eds., *Erich Fried und Österreich: Bausteine zu einer Beziehung: Eine Ausstellung der Dokumentationsstelle für neuere österreichische Literatur und der Internationalen Erich-Fried-Gesellschaft für Literatur und Sprache im Literaturhaus*, in *Zirkular*, Sondernummer 33, November 1992, p. 10.

24 For a discussion of *Mut*, see Jörg Thunecke, '"Doch wer den Mut verliert ist besser tot!"': Young Austria and the Problem of Political Poetry', in Edward Timms and Ritchie Robertson, eds., *Austrian Exodus: The Creative Achievements of Refugees from National Socialism (Austrian Studies* VI), Edinburgh 1995, pp. 41-58.

25 According to Steiner, 'Mein Freund Erich Fried', p. 10.

26 Steiner, *Die Organisation einer Jugendbewegung*, p. 10.

27 The picture had previously appeared in *Five Years Hitler over Austria*, the special edition of *Austrian News* marking the fifth anniversary of the Anschluss.

28 'Sieben Jahre "Junges Österreich"'.

29 See, for example, *Documents of the Austrian Freedom Front* and *Three Years of the Austrian Freedom Front*, both from 1944.

30 On this, see Karl Vogelmann, 'Die Propaganda der österreichischen Emigration in der Sowjetunion für einen selbständigen Nationalstaat (1938-1945)', unpublished doctoral dissertation, Vienna 1973.

31 By the pro-Habsburg Legitimists of the Austrian League, for example, who were still affiliated to the FAM at the time that *Five Years Hitler Over Austria* appeared.

32 Ripman to Chaplin, 16 October 1944, National Archives [NA], FO

371/38833.

33   An interdepartmental body set up early in 1944 to study the economic aspects of plans for liberated or occupied territories in Europe.

34   Mountrie to Butler, 7 November 1944, NA, FO 371/38833.

35   Dr Erich Schindel, the booklet's editor, has in recent years spoken candidly of the realities of the situation, however: 'We were not, of course, under any illusions, we already knew that what we were setting out in programme form and as *desiderata* would play no role in the reconstruction of Austria, yet it achieved the desired object because it aroused interest among the Socialist doctors and the organization "British Friends of Austria" […] Our aims were to win friends for this work and for the reconstruction of Austria, and help for the doctors who wanted to return,' Documentation Archive of Austrian Resistance, [DÖW], Vienna, Interview 170.

36   See Helene Maimann, *Politik im Wartesaal: Österreichische Exilpolitik in Großbritannien 1938-1945*, Vienna/Cologne/Graz 1975, p. 73.

37   Nevertheless, see Ullrich's report in *Der Turm: Monatsschrift für Österreichische Kultur*, I, July 1946, p. 408, in which he claimed that the *Kulturelle Schriftenreihe* had also served the purpose 'of showing German-speaking English friends that there is a large consciously Austrian cultural movement'.

38   According to Georg Knepler, Ullrich 'described himself as a Liberal, Austrian patriot, antifascist, as someone who had sympathy for Socialism, without himself being a Socialist' (letter to the authors of 9 April 1998).

39   It is notable that the inclusion of Srbik did not find favour with J.K. [Jenö Kostmann], for instance, in *Zeitspiegel* who termed it 'a serious mistake' (12 October 1945, pp. 6-7).

40   Hermann Ullrich, preface to *Kulturelle Schriftenreihe des Free Austrian Movement: Wien und die Welt. Urteile und Vorurteile in Berichten, Briefen, Dokumenten und Beschreibungen aus acht Jahrhunderten*, 1945, p. i.

41   See Hermann Ullrich to Herbert Steiner, 29 April 1968, in Steiner Papers, Exile Library of the Literature House, Vienna.

42   Ullrich, 'Abschied vom Leser'.

43   Flyer reproduced in Muchitsch, *op. cit.*, p. 398.

44   Hermann Ullrich to Viktor Matejka, 21 February 1946, DÖW 18.861/147.

45   Köstler, 'Vorwort', in *Kulturelle Schriftenreihe des Free Austrian Movement: Die Frau in der österreichischen Kultur: Literatur, Kunst, Frauenbewegung, Staat und Politik*, 1945, p. ii.

46   Ullrich, 'Abschied vom Leser'.

ACTING FOR AUSTRIA
THE LATERNDL AND OTHER
AUSTRIAN THEATRE GROUPS

RICHARD DOVE

When the Austrian exile theatre Das Laterndl (The Lantern) opened on 27 June 1939 with the revue *Unterwegs* (*On the Road*), few would have predicted that, apart from two enforced breaks in 1939/40, it would remain open for the next six years, presenting Austrian cabaret and theatre in the unlikely setting of wartime London.[1] The Laterndl was the brainchild of three actors – Fritz Schrecker, Franz Hartl (i.e. Franz Bönsch) and Franz Schulz – who, meeting at the Austrian Centre in March 1939, agreed to propose to the Centre's management committee the establishment of a small theatre.

The Laterndl was conceived as a distinctively Austrian theatre, intended to recreate the typically Viennese 'Kleinkunstbühne', or small theatre performing political cabaret. Cabaret theatres such as 'Der liebe Augustin', 'Literatur am Naschmarkt', 'Die Stachelbeere', and 'ABC' had flourished in the years of the 'Ständestaat' (corporate state), only to be ruthlessly suppressed by the Nazis. Most of the Laterndl's original collaborators had actually worked at one or other of these theatres, including the actor/director Martin Miller, the stage designer Carl Josefovics, and the writers Hugo Koenigsgarten, Rudolf Spitz and Franz Hartl. The programme for the opening revue indicated the theatre's *raison d'être*, expressing the hope that 'the LANTERN will preserve one of the characteristic forms of Austrian culture':[2] the Laterndl was to be an explicitly *Austrian* theatre, a symbolic assertion of national identity at a time when Austria had vanished from the political map.

The name chosen for the new theatre was equally symbolic, though there has been some disagreement as to where it came from. However, it was a name primarily intended to encapsulate the theatre's function, as spelt out in the verses of the 'Lantern Man', on which the curtain was brought down:

Listen, folks, and hear me say:
In darkest night and fearful day
We shall strike a tiny light,
Which speaks of far-off future bright.
That's the Lantern![3]

The Laterndl was therefore to represent a beacon of hope, keeping the light of Austrian culture burning while darkness reigned in Austria itself.

The theatre was registered as the Austrian Theatre Club, the device of club status enabling it to avoid censorship by the Lord Chamberlain's office to which all public theatres were subject, and perhaps more importantly to avoid the need to secure work permits for actors. The Austrian Centre placed two rooms in its building in Westbourne Terrace at the disposal of the theatre. The auditorium was made by knocking down the wall between these two rooms, creating a theatre space which held a tiny stage (five metres by three metres), and seating for an audience of sixty to seventy.[4]

Even before it opened, the Laterndl had managed to gain some influential friends. The theatre's letter-heading confirms that it opened under the patronage of the London PEN Club, its individual sponsors including the playwright Ashley Dukes, the film actress Luise Rainer, whose Hollywood roles had brought her two Oscars in successive years (1936/1937) and the well-known journalist Wickham Steed. Among the audience for the first night were such literary luminaries as Stefan Zweig and Robert Neumann, H.G. Wells, with his companion Baroness Budberg, and J. B. Priestley.[5]

This opening production, which ran until the end of August, was performed largely in German, but English guests in the audience could orientate themselves via the master of ceremonies whose brief commentary linking the various short sketches was given in English. (In this first production, it was spoken by an American actress, Margaret March, though the role was later performed by Hanne Norbert.)

The revue consciously followed the format of the Viennese cabaret, alternating short dramatic sketches and songs, the serious and the comic. The songs included Jura Soyfer's 'Lied des einfachen Menschen' ('Song of the Simple Man') sung by Martin Miller. Soyfer, the young poet and dramatist who had died earlier that year in Buchenwald, was to be an emblematic figure in the early productions of the Laterndl. Among the original sketches written for the programme was 'Bow Street' by Rudolf Spitz, portraying events in the waiting-room and interview-room of the Aliens Office where all refugees had to register. The sketch 'Wiener Ringelspiel' ('Merry-go-round'), by Hugo Koenigsgarten, mocked the Nazi occupation of Austria, portraying a Vienna which had embraced in turn the Romans, the Turks and the French: 'They all wanted to stay there for ever, and they all had to leave. But Vienna is still there. It seems to me that they won't be the last.'[6] The audience greeted this programme, which enacted their own experience and hopes, with predictable enthusiasm. Less predictable was the enthusiasm with which the production was greeted in wide sections of the British press: *The Times* (28 June 1939), *Daily Telegraph*, *Manchester Guardian* (29 June 1939), *News Chronicle*, *Reynolds News*, *The Star*, *The New Statesman* and *The Spectator*.[7] *The Times*, for example, wrote that the revue 'made an extremely favourable impression', calling it 'an entertainment which reflects the grim present and is yet delightfully informed with traditional Viennese gaiety'.[8] The young critic Goronwy Rees, writing in *The Spectator*, was even more effusive, declaring that: 'We should be grateful to Herr Hitler for the Lantern. Austria's loss has been our gain.' He continued:

> The Lantern, besides being a delightful addition to London's entertainments, can perform a valuable function in this country. I hope that when its players become acclimatized here [...] they will turn their wit upon us; no country ever needed satire so much as this or provided such abundant material for it.[9]

Unterwegs was a resounding success, playing to full houses for almost sixty performances. The Laterndl would continue to play regularly for the next six years, apart from the two enforced breaks, the first of which came with the outbreak of war, when the Laterndl, like all other theatres and cinemas, was forced to close for a period of two and a half months as a measure of public safety. It reopened in November in a new location, the original building having failed to satisfy LCC fire regulations.[10]

The new premises in Finchley Road, which had formerly housed the Hampstead Concert Studio, were larger than those in Westbourne Terrace, seating about 150 people. While catering principally to Austrian refugees, the Laterndl also hoped to promote awareness of Austria with the English public. *PEN News*, for example, in reporting the reopening of the Laterndl ('The Little Theatre from Vienna is now firmly established at 153 Finchley Road'), emphasized that 'it welcomes English members with open arms'.[11] However, it must be said that since all performances were largely in German, English visitors never numbered more than a handful, the vast majority of the audience being the members of the Austrian Centre.

The new theatre was opened with a second revue *Blinklichter (Beacons)*. This included a sketch by Albert Fuchs entitled 'Wo liegt Deutschland?'('Where is Germany?'), in which a group of Martians travelled throughout Germany to decide whether the German people bore collective responsibility for Nazism, a thesis famously espoused by

'The Führer Speaks': Martin Miller in the second Laterndl review *Blinklichter*

Sir Robert Vansittart. The revue also contained Martin Miller's famous Hitler impersonation 'Der Führer spricht' ('The Führer Speaks'), in which 'Hitler' recorded Columbus's discovery of America, 'based on the experiments of German scholars and using German apparatus and instruments'. He went on to make territorial claims to the United States, announcing:

> Since 1492 [...] I have remained silent and left this problem untouched in the interests of peace. But now my patience is exhausted. Let Herr Roosevelt take note that it is my unshakeable will finally to occupy the seat destined for me by Providence in the White House – and thereby transform it into the Brown House.

Miller's 'Hitler speech' resounded far beyond the Laterndl, earning him an invitation to broadcast the speech on the BBC early in 1940. According to one contemporary source, the revue *Blinklichter* was attended by some 6000 people over the three months of its run.[12]

The third programme *Von Adam bis Adolf* (*From Adam to Adolf*) comprised the usual mixture of songs and sketches, once more featuring the talents of its resident writers. It also included Jura Soyfer's short play *Der Lechner Edi schaut ins Paradies* (*Edi Lechner glimpses Paradise*). This too was a highly appropriate choice, since – like most of Soyfer's one-acters – it had originally been written as the 'Mittelstück' or centre-piece of a revue, a short play of roughly 35–40 minutes, usually performed between the two intervals when customers could order or pay.[13] Soyfer's work had already been performed at the Austrian Centre on three successive Monday evenings in January 1940 as part of a programme called *Little Theatre of the World*.

The Laterndl's fourth programme *Der unsterbliche Schwejk* (*The Eternal Schweik*), comprising a montage of scenes from the life of its eponymous hero, attracted wide attention, including a double-page photo spread in *Picture Post*.[14] Schweik, played by Martin Miller, was one of the traditional figures of Viennese cabaret, the archetypal little man, enmeshed in red tape, put upon by police, doctors, clergy and officers, but always emerging triumphantly. *Der unsterbliche Schwejk*, which opened on 23 March 1940, was once more directed by Martin Miller, and scripted by the resident writing team of Koenigsgarten, Spitz, Hartl and Fuchs, with music written and arranged by Georg Knepler. It was this small group which met regularly to decide the artistic content of the Laterndl programme. There were often heated debates which reflected the political differences between Austrian émigrés: Knepler and Fuchs were committed Communists, Spitz an equally committed Social Democrat.

During this early period, the Laterndl had to contend with the day-to-day difficulties of wartime, exacerbated by the particular problems which

Hanne Norbert and Fritz Schrecker in Stefan Zweig's adaptation of Ben Jonson's
Volpone, Laterndl, March 1942

inevitably confronted an exile theatre. While offering actors and other
theatre workers the chance to practise their craft, the Laterndl could
scarcely provide them with a living. Actors worked on a cooperative
basis, receiving a percentage of the box-office takings, after the expenses
of the production had been met.[15] In addition, some actors had
exhausting daytime jobs, particularly after 'enemy aliens' were absorbed
into British war industries.

One early problem was the loss of leading actors, some of whom re-
emigrated, while others received offers of more lucrative roles in the
English theatre. Thus Peter Preses, one of the outstanding performers in
the early revues, eventually re-emigrated to New York. Martin Miller
acted and directed only during the early period until the offer of lucrative
roles on the West End stage forced him to resign. (He played, for
example, for three and a half years in *Arsenic and Old Lace.*) Fritz
Schrecker, the Viennese character actor who had been one of the original
founders of the Laterndl, was working for the German Service of the
BBC, playing the role of the eponymous hero in the series *Die Briefe des*

Gefreiten Adolf Hirnschal (*The Letters of Corporal Adolf Hirnschal*). Hirnschal was to become a legendary figure in the history of the BBC German Service: the simple front-line soldier whose letters to his wife in Zwieselsdorf faithfully repeated the Nazi slogans of the day in such a way as to expose them to ridicule. However, Schrecker was not lost to the Laterndl. At the height of his success as Hirnschal, he returned there, appearing regularly from May 1943 to 1945.[16]

In 1940, the greatest single problem confronting the Laterndl was internment. The performance of *Der unsterbliche Schwejk* was followed by a production of Brecht's *Dreigroschenoper* (*Threepenny Opera*), but by the time the play opened on 26 May 1940, the British government had already begun the widespread internment of 'enemy aliens'. No fewer than three actors rehearsed in turn the role of Mack the Knife, the first two being interned before the part was finally assigned to Jaro Klüger.[17] With the internment of many of its leading actors and the majority of its audience, the Laterndl went dark again, this time for a period of fifteen months.

September 1941 – January 1943

When the Laterndl finally reopened in September 1941, it was at another new location, but one which would remain the theatre's home for the rest of its existence. The Austrian Centre had acquired a house at 69 Eton Avenue, Swiss Cottage, which had previously belonged to the Hon. John Collier, a prolific amateur artist, who had courted notoriety in public disputes with the sculptor Jacob Epstein and the Royal Academy. The critic of the London *Evening Standard*, who attended the opening revue *Laterna Magica* (*Magic Lantern*), recorded his impressions of the new premises:

> A minute from Swiss Cottage is the large house where the Hon. John Collier lived. The Austrians have taken it over: an odd Anschluss. As you enter the front door, your nose meets the savoury whiff of Viennese cooking, your eyes the pictures that the Hon. John painted untiringly.[18]

The pictures lined the stairs, leading up to the former owner's studio on the top floor, which had been turned into a theatre space seating an audience of just over a hundred. There were no footlights; scenery and properties were reduced to a minimum. The walls of the theatre were still lined with Collier's pictures, including the portrait of George Bernard Shaw, which had caused great controversy when it had been rejected by the Royal Academy. (Shaw himself had not liked it, suggesting that it had been painted 'with a brush attached to a fishing rod'.) Theatre performances in the new venue were limited to only four days a week

(Thursday to Sunday) largely because some of the actors, and many of the audience, were also engaged in war work.

The decision to reopen the Laterndl with the revue *Laterna Magica*, produced by Martin Miller, was intended to signal continuity with the theatre's opening season, but in fact the political context had changed enormously, and with it attitudes to the Laterndl. The reactions to *Laterna Magica* revealed sharp differences of opinion within the Austrian Centre as to the function of an Austrian exile theatre, a debate which was to continue over the coming months. Reviewing the production in *Zeitspiegel*, under the heading 'The Lantern Shines Again', the critic Paul Reimann recorded the unbridled enthusiasm of the audience, but pronounced a mixed verdict on the production itself.[19] He indeed praised some of the sketches: 'And in fact the programme contained a series of things which are an enrichment of the exile theatre repertoire.' He had particularly commended Erich Fried's one-acter *Ring-Rund* (*Round the Ring*), 'which is not only good and pointed, but also expresses the spirit of resistance of the Viennese'.[20] However, he had distinct reservations about some of the other sketches: 'We cannot deny that some things could be better.' His criticism was levelled at Hartl's sketch 'Napoleon greift nicht ein' ('Napoleon does not intervene'), and particularly at Koenigsgarten's 'Wiener Jause' ('Viennese Afternoon Tea'), in which the jokes were 'somewhat stale and hackneyed'. Nor were the musical contributions spared: 'Even the Linden Tree and the parody of the Song of the Flea were unappealing.'

The reservations expressed by Reimann, a leading member of the Czech Communist Party since 1929, were undoubtedly shared by several of the leading figures in the Austrian Centre. However, his critique proved controversial: it was felt by many to be too harsh, forcing Eva Priester to publish a 'Self-critique of the Critique' in the following number of *Zeitspiegel* in which she tried to mitigate the force of the criticism while maintaining that 'objectively it was not entirely unjustified'.[21] She defined the central problem of the theatre critic in exile as a (necessary) lack of critical detachment: the critic was in the same boat as the actors and the audience. ('We are not critics seated on a high chair. We and you are comrades who for some years have been working in a common cause [...]') Acknowledging that the Laterndl had made some outstanding achievements, she nonetheless demanded a more prescriptive political agenda: 'It's not enough to say: "Hitler is a scoundrel and a fool", you must also say: "You, the man in the stalls, you, the refugee worker must do this and this, so that we defeat him".' Theatre therefore had to depict the current situation of the exiles and tell them what had to be done. She conceded the difficulty of this but went on to declare, invoking Schiller: 'Cabaret too is a moral institution and by "moral" the classical authors meant help in understanding and indications for action.'

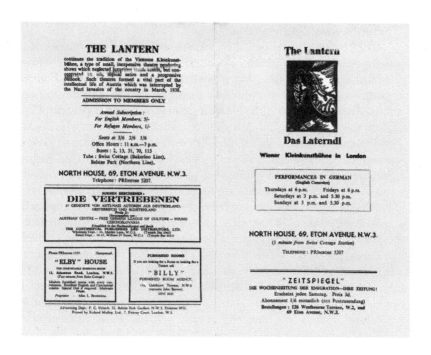

Laterndl programme for *Laterna Magica*, September 1941

The debate surrounding *Laterna Magica* had practical consequences, resulting in a discernible change in the programme of the Laterndl, which continued to perform 'cabaret evenings', but began to alternate them with the performance of full-length plays. One reason for this was certainly that the resident house authors had moved on, Rudolf Spitz to the BBC, Hugo Koenigsgarten to Oxford, where he had found a teaching post at New College School. Some later suggested that their inspiration had flagged, reflecting the difficulty of writing satire in a place remote from its social roots. Others may have felt that satire had lost its edge in a situation where its inherent exaggerations had been outstripped by a reality so brutal that it had placed itself beyond parody.

Moreover, there were also influential figures within the Austrian Centre who considered cabaret to be unnecessarily restricted, and even inappropriate to a wider political agenda. The tension between the conflicting demands of entertainment and political education is implicit in Eva Priester's review of *Der Hauptmann von Köpenick* (*The Captain of Köpenick*):

Here we see once more that the Laterndl can go beyond the somewhat rigid framework of cabaret – it can perform 'proper' plays and it *should* perform them. But 'proper' plays also mean plays for today. Zuckmayer's satire, set in Germany in 1930, was a warning about the old German reactionaries. [...] The warning delivered in 1930 pales in comparison to the horrors of the German militarism of 1941.[22]

Der Hauptmann von Köpenick was produced by Arnold Marlé, a well-known actor and producer who had already worked with the Free German League of Culture in London. It was the first of a succession of German-language comedies at the Laterndl; these were interspersed with 'cabaret evenings', produced by Martin Miller, thus guaranteeing, for a time, a certain continuity.

In January 1942 the Laterndl produced a new revue, *Here is the News*, consisting of a series of dramatic sketches, loosely linked by the compère's commentary. Juxtaposing the comic and the serious, the revue reopened old arguments as to the *raison d'être* of an (Austrian) exile theatre. Should it offer an escape from the present or attempt to impose political coherence on it? Should it merely seek to entertain or to articulate a more overt political message?

Particular controversy centred on Franz Hartl's short play *Brennende Erde (Scorched Earth)* which confronted its audience with the consequences of total war. In one scene 'German soldiers rest for a short while in their trench when once again the order to attack is given. On the verge of mutiny guerrillas attack.'[23] In other scenes a partisan leader is shot for refusing to cooperate; German soldiers appear as the morally and physically mutilated victims of war. Hartl's often brutal realism, heightened by its juxtaposition with comic sketches and songs, polarized opinion between those who felt exile theatre should offer an escape from the grim reality of war, and those who thought it should seek to engage with that reality. The opening shots in the argument came from the veteran theatre critic, Monty Jacobs, in a hostile review in *Die Zeitung*:

> In harsh times, no one wants to wrap the audience in cotton wool [...] But only strong art can portray a strong present, and *Scorched Earth* is a weak and awkward piece of work which is unable to take the step up from propaganda to poetry, from rhetoric to dialogue, from the painful to the moving. [24]

Zeitspiegel attempted to widen the debate by asking its readers to respond to the question 'What do we expect from theatre?'.[25] Among the leading contributors to the subsequent debate conducted in its columns were Oskar Kokoschka and the writers Bruno Heilig and Robert Neumann.

Marianne Walla and Hanne Norbert in Eva Priester's *Das Urteil* from third
Laterndl revue, *No Orchids for Mr Hitler*, October 1942

The latter was unequivocal in his praise: 'The play is by far the best thing
that Hartl has written so far, in fact it is the best thing produced by any

Austrian exile so far.'[26] Exile theatre, Neumann affirmed, was not merely an excuse for nostalgic entertainment, but also a forum for moral and political debate.[27] Kokoschka was equally forthright.

The political background to this debate in 1941/42 was the entry into the war of the Soviet Union and the founding in December 1941 of the Free Austrian Movement (FAM), the umbrella organization intended to coordinate the political activities of Austrian refugees in London. Significantly, both Kokoschka and Neumann were among the prominent signatories of the founding declaration of the FAM – who also included the Laterndl stalwarts Fritz Schrecker and Martin Miller.[28]

Hartl's short play remained the exception rather than the rule. *Here is the News* was followed by a succession of comedies, beginning with Nestroy's *Der Talisman* (*The Talisman*) and Zweig's adaptation of *Volpone*, continuing with four one-acters by Schnitzler under the title *Wiener Miniaturen* (*Viennese Miniatures*), and followed by Ferenc Molnar's *Spiel im Schloss* (*Play in the Castle*) and Bruno Frank's *Sturm im Wasserglas* (*Storm in a Teacup*), two light comedies chosen primarily for their entertainment value, though both had the additional virtue of being written by exiled authors.

Spiel im Schloss was reviewed by Eva Priester under the headline 'Holiday Comedy at the Laterndl':

> All theatres, even the biggest, have a holiday in the summer when they perform light and harmless plays which are not otherwise part of the repertoire. The Laterndl is following this custom and giving its audiences a few weeks' holiday from problems, contemporary plays and, so to speak, 'serious art'. Molnar's *Spiel im Schloss*, which is itself about people who are on holiday, is a real holiday play.[29]

The play was evidently well received, Priester reporting that the audience laughed so heartily that for minutes on end the dialogue was inaudible. *Spiel im Schloss* was followed by Bruno Frank's comedy *Sturm im Wasserglas*, which was advertised as 'the comedy triumph of the German Volkstheater in Vienna'.[30] The play had indeed been a success in Vienna, Berlin and Munich, but also, in an adaptation by James Bridie, had run for over a year on the London stage, being voted 'best comedy of the year' by English critics in 1936. The choice of these two plays – and Priester's comments on the first – highlights the dichotomy between those who saw the Laterndl stage as a vehicle for a broad political agenda, and the majority of the Laterndl audience who wanted to be entertained.

Between the performance of these two plays, the Laterndl presented another revue *No Orchids for Mr Hitler*, a title playing on that of the well-known thriller by James Hadley Chase. The revue was greeted by ecstatic audiences and enthusiastic reviews: 'The Laterndl is performing cabaret again. And – notwithstanding its great success with Schnitzler und Molnar – that's where it feels most at home. As if automatically, the Viennese cafe atmosphere, which stems from the cabaret, establishes itself.'[31] There were obviously still many who thought that in resuming its performance of *Kleinkunst*, the Laterndl was reverting to its true metier, but despite this *No Orchids for Mr Hitler* proved to be the last revue to feature in the main programme of the Laterndl.

February 1943 – March 1944

The production of *Thunder Rock* in February 1943 marked a first step in the evolution of the Laterndl towards the performance of full-length plays, and the adoption of a more direct political agenda. Written by the American author Robert Audrey, *Thunder Rock* had enjoyed great success, having run for two years in the West End, and having subsequently been filmed. The main character was a Spanish Civil War veteran who, despairing of persuading his compatriots of the threat of Fascism, had withdrawn to the sanctuary of a remote lighthouse on Lake Michigan. During his stay there, he is visited by the spirits of those who had been shipwrecked while attempting to escape Europe in the aftermath of the 1848 revolution. This spiritual encounter with refugees from the past convinces him that he must rejoin the fight against present oppression and injustice. The relevance of the play's message to Laterndl audiences was unmistakeable, dealing as it did with the very question of the proper response to Fascism which many felt the Laterndl should long since have addressed. The play was in fact already very familiar to some refugees, having been performed by internees in Hutchinson Camp on the Isle of Man in August 1941, where the cast had included Otto Tausig who, after his release, was to play a leading role in the Young Austria Players.

The production none the less represented a new departure for the Laterndl. The reviewer in *Zeitspiegel* felt it had been a risky experiment to transfer the play to the tiny stage of the Laterndl, but one which had justified itself: 'The experiment succeeded. The Laterndl production can stand comparison with those of the leading English theatres in which the play ran for two years and with the recently released film version.' She went on to emphasize that the production represented a conscious departure from the Laterndl's previous repertoire: 'The Laterndl has shown that it can perform serious drama and the Laterndl audience has shown that it also wants to see serious plays and not just to be amused.'[32]

The last assertion was questionable since the play had failed to attract large audiences, provoking Robert Neumann to write an open letter to *Zeitspiegel*, chiding his compatriots for their indifference. He too praised the production as a risky but successful experiment, comparing it favourably to its West End counterparts: 'It is a long time since I spent such an interesting and exciting evening. But I spent it in a room in which there were roughly thirty people. The rest was empty.' Emphasizing the vital role of theatre in the anti-Fascist struggle, Neumann concluded by asking sardonically when *Zeitspiegel* would bring its readers on a conducted tour of the Laterndl.[33]

The production of *Thunder Rock* inaugurated a repertoire of international theatre which included plays by J. B. Priestley, Niccolò Machiavelli, František Langer, Louis Verneuil and a Soviet drama by Leonid Rachmanov. This repertoire of international modern plays correlates to a more direct political agenda, reflecting the alliance of national liberation movements in London. In fact it was a theatrically varied programme, which included, for example, the comedy *Die Bekehrung des Ferdisch Pistora (The Conversion of Ferdisch Pistora)*, by the Czech author Frantisek Langer, as well as the Soviet play *Professor Poleshajew*, Arnold Marlé acting the title role in both plays. Both productions were performed in an explicitly political perspective. *Professor Poleshajew* opened its run with a gala performance in honour of the 26th anniversary of the Red Army, given in the presence of representatives from the Soviet Embassy and other Soviet organizations such as the news agency TASS.[34] Similarly, *Ferdisch Pistora* received a special performance at a Friendship Evening held by Austrian PEN for Czech writers, at which the play's author was among the audience. Czech-Austrian cooperation was very much a watchword of the Free Austrian Movement and in his introductory speech, Robert Neumann stressed the close links between Czech and Austrian culture: 'This play, which is set in Prague, could be produced in Vienna, as a play set in Vienna – but not in Berlin or in Munich.'[35] The translation of the play had been made by the Czech writer Rudolf Popper, a practical demonstration of cultural cooperation. In fact, the lack of serviceable German texts was a persistent problem throughout this period, frequently forcing the theatre to commission its own translations. Thus *Thunder Rock* was played in a German version by Rudolf Spitz, Priestley's *Laburnum Grove* in a translation by Richard Duschinsky.

Cabaret did not entirely disappear from the Laterndl stage. The productions of full-length plays were still interspersed with weekly 'cabaret evenings', under such titles as *Lachendes Laterndl (Laughing Laterndl)*, *Von Babylon bis Kischinew (From Babylon to Kishinev)*, *Das Laterndl einmal anders (The Laterndl – differently)*. However, the emphasis remained on the production of full-length plays: cabaret had taken a back seat.

April 1944 – August 1945

The tension between entertainment and political education, between nostalgic self-indulgence and ideological prescription, was perhaps best resolved in the last eighteen months of the Laterndl's existence. Between April 1944 and August 1945 the theatre presented a programme consisting almost exclusively of modern Austrian plays, performing works by Schnitzler (twice), Anton Wildgans (a former director of Vienna's Burgtheater), Karl Schönherr (twice), the 'peasant dramatist' Ludwig Anzengruber, Hermann Bahr and Raoul Auernheimer. Virtually all these productions were directed by Paul Hardtmuth.

In April 1944 the theatre's production of three one-acters by Schnitzler, Wildgans and Auernheimer prompted *Zeitspiegel* to comment: 'Encouraged by the great success of *Professor Poleshajew*, the Laterndl has resolutely turned back to its real domain – the cultivation of the Austrian dramatic repertoire [...] It proves once again the strength and liveliness of Austrian drama.'[36] True to its origins, the Laterndl was therefore returning to an Austrian theatre tradition.

The Laterndl's adoption of an exclusively Austrian repertoire was not an independent development, but a corollary of the wider political agenda espoused by the Free Austrian Movement, and more specifically the deliberations of the two Cultural Conferences, held in August 1942 and October 1944, which had established a cultural agenda whose immediate objectives were to reassert an Austrian cultural identity and to reclaim the Austrian cultural heritage suppressed or appropriated by the Nazis. These objectives were based on the political assumption that most émigrés were going to return to Austria after the war, a judgement which ultimately proved false.

If the Laterndl sought to explore a specifically Austrian theatre heritage, it also had to satisfy its audience's hunger for entertainment. Thus in November 1944 it staged a musical revue *Österreichische Rhapsodie* (*Austrian Rhapsody*), written by Paul Knepler, a former librettist for Franz Lehar: a production which fulsomely indulged its audience's need for nostalgia, while seeking to demonstrate the distinctiveness of Austrian culture. *Zeitspiegel* reviewed the production under the caption 'We're just different.'[37] Similarly, Hermann Bahr, one of the dominant literary figures in *fin-de-siècle* Vienna, was represented by his most frequently performed comedy *Das Konzert* (*The Concert*), while he was simultaneously presented, in a *Zeitspiegel* profile, as an Austrian patriot.[38]

To celebrate its fifth anniversary in June 1944 the Laterndl gave a special performance of Schnitzler's *Professor Bernhardi*, with Arnold Marlé once more appearing in the title role. The choice of play was considered particularly appropriate both because of its topical theme of anti-Semitism and because of its past history of controversy:

> The Laterndl [...] has thus rendered Austrians in this country an important service and simultaneously achieved everything that it is the duty of an Austrian émigré theatre to do: to show or remind the audience of the things they are working and fighting for, and to maintain the living link between them and their home.[39]

Significantly, the review devotes more space to the ideological significance of the play than to the actual production. *Professor Bernhardi* was followed by Anzengruber's comedy *Der G'wissenswurm* (*The Worm of Conscience*). Anzengruber's pioneering achievement in dramatizing the problems of peasant life and his anti-clericalism were used to justify the conscription of author and work to a progressive theatre agenda: 'The time has finally come to give Anzengruber the major place in Austrian dramatic poetry which he deserves. Anzengruber is not simply a dramatist of peasant life and certainly not an author of "Blood and Soil".'[40]

More difficult to justify was the inclusion in this theatrical canon of Karl Schönherr, author of naturalistic peasant dramas set largely in his native Tyrol. Schönherr was a figure of some ideological ambiguity. In March 1938 he had greeted the Anschluss with enthusiasm, publishing an effusive poem in the *Neue Freie Presse*. After his death in March 1943, *Zeitspiegel* (10 April 1943) had published a short obituary calling him 'a master of the stage', and attempting to absolve his work from the stigma of 'Blood and Soil' affinities. When Schönherr's one-acter *Die Bildschnitzer* (*The Wood Carvers*) was chosen for production in May 1944, it was billed as a 'Volksstück' (dialect folk play), reclaiming the piece for a progressive theatre repertoire. *Zeitspiegel* commented: 'With the production of the *Bildschnitzer* by Karl Schönherr the Laterndl is continuing the important and valuable work it began some time ago: making Austrian dramatic literature accessible and comprehensible to an Austrian audience.'[41] A year later, the performance of Schönherr's *Weibsteufel* (*Devil Woman*) was to be the Laterndl's final production.

The Laterndl's repertoire during its final year was therefore calculated to re-introduce Austrian exiles to their cultural patrimony, aiming particularly at younger exiles, whose memories of Austria were now faint. It also had an ideologically more ambitious aim: to propose a new canon of Austrian dramatic literature suitable for performance in a post-war democratic Austria.

The Executive of the Free Austrian Movement wrote officially to congratulate the Laterndl on fulfilling its duty as an exile theatre, namely in

> faithfully cultivating Austrian drama and in preserving the best of Austrian tradition. The decisive adoption by this theatre of the fulfillment of a national mission, the conscious emphasis on the task of being custodian and preserver of Austrian dramatic literature in exile has the full approval and acknowledgement of the Executive.[42]

The statement was intended as a valedictory tribute. The programme for the winter season 1945/46, including Grillparzer's *Wehe dem, der lügt* (*Woe*

to him who lies), Schnitzler's *Liebelei* (*Flirtation*) and a further play by
Anzengruber, had already been planned – only to be abandoned. The
theatre's final production, Schönherr's *Der Weibsteufel*, reopened at the
beginning of August, running for a final four weeks.[43] After that the
Laterndl went dark, the final curtain coming down on Sunday, 26 August
1945. Members of the Laterndl ensemble sent a letter of greeting to the
Minister of Education and Culture in the new Provisional Government,
Ernst Fischer, expressing their hope of an early return, and their
readiness for 'joyful collaboration'.[44] Among the signatories were some of
the Laterndl's best-known actors, such as Marianne Walla, Arnold Marlé,
Fritz Schrecker and Jaro Klüger, but none of them would ultimately
return to Austria.

Other Austrian Theatre Groups

While the members of the Laterndl ensemble were theatre professionals,
eager above all to practise their craft, the Austrian Centre also fostered
various amateur dramatic groups, whose aims were more directly aligned
with the Centre's political agenda. The earliest of these was an *ad hoc*
group formed by members of Young Austria at the beginning of 1941,
which gave at least one performance at the Austrian Centre. The young
actors chose a programme attuned to their audience of fellow-refugees,
performing a scene from *Floridsdorf*, Friedrich Wolf's dramatization of the
events of February 1934, which they supplemented with a scene of their
own devising called *Die Frauen kämpfen weiter* (*The Women Fight On*). The
polemical nature of both pieces needs little emphasis.

During 1941, as more and more Austrians were released from
internment, the Austrian Centre established several amateur dramatic
groups in London and elsewhere. In June, it announced in the columns
of *Zeitspiegel* that it was setting up a 'Drama and Singing Group'.[45] If the
raison d'être of the Laterndl was to maintain the traditions of the Austrian
theatre for a largely émigré audience, the new dramatic group aimed
principally to raise awareness of Austria and Austrian issues amongst the
British public. Calling themselves the Austrian Centre Players, the group
devised its opening revue, *Return Ticket Vienna–London*, during the
summer of 1941, first performing it in the auditorium of the Austrian
Centre on 28 September.[46] Though the cast were all amateurs, they had
the benefit of professional advice: the revue was directed by the actress
Koka Motz, and included music specially composed by Georg Knepler,
the Musical Director of the Laterndl.[47] Devised specifically for *English*
audiences, the revue was performed in English, consisting of a sequence
of nine scenes 'with music, dance and song', which portrayed the actors'
own experience of persecution and exile. The dramatic sequence began in
Vienna in 1930, continuing with scenes, helpfully titled, showing 'How
Hitler raped Austria' and 'Hospitality in England', or enacting the

integration of the refugees into the war effort ('From Charity to Productive Work'), before finally returning to its point of departure: 'Inside Austria'. The theatre programme, written in both English and German, stressed that

> these are shows with a difference. Our members have no ambition to be stars of the stage, our only ambition is to tell our British friends in a new and perhaps more impressive way of our experiences as refugees, how our people stood up against the Nazi menace, how we want to carry on the fight beside our British friends and how we want them to understand our problems.[48]

Reviewing the performance, the journal *Young Austria* called it 'a strange sort of show, partly acted, partly danced and partly sung', describing the finale as a 'Dance of the War Effort'.[49]

Despite reports of its publication, the text of *Return Ticket* has disappeared.[50] Only one short scene has survived, published in *Österreichische Kulturblätter* under the title 'Priest Scene', but probably corresponding to Scene 8, listed on the theatre programme as 'Inside Austria'.[51] It enacts a meeting between a priest and a woman whose husband has been killed on the Eastern Front. She is sitting clutching his jacket, the only possession of his to have been returned, but it is precisely this which the priest wants her to give him. He explains that he will give it to a young man who has gone absent from his army unit, one of a group of deserters who are hiding in the forest.

Although the first performance of *Return Ticket* took place in the Austrian Centre, the Drama Group was anxious to reach a wider public, clearly hoping to escape the cultural ghetto of émigré circles to put the Austrian case to the British. By the end of the year they had performed the revue fifteen times, to audiences totalling 1250.[52] Using little in the way of scenery or properties, they were able to perform wherever there was a stage – or even where there was not. One of their recorded performances was given in an air-raid shelter in King's Cross, a location which emphasized the common fate of both players and audience:

> There were children, students, workers, business people among the audience, who followed the performance of our enthusiastic group with close attention and gave it tumultuous applause. The performance made clear to us the great importance of the work of our drama group.[53]

Whatever such performances may have lacked in professional polish, the troupe's appearances drew favourable attention. In February 1942 they were invited to take part in the annual Drama Season at Toynbee Hall in

London's East End, a festival at which numerous British amateur dramatic societies used to appear. Performing in English, the Players were well received, being invited to perform again the following year.

By March, having given *Return Ticket Vienna–London* no fewer than twenty-five times, the Players were already working on a second revue. They took the opportunity to hold a recruitment week in search of new actors, singers, dancers and musicians, attracting no fewer than fifty-two new members.[54] It was reported that the new revue they were devising would deal with 'the unity of Austrians', a theme proposed by the Austrian Centre.[55] Keen to encourage writing and acting with a political message, the Centre held a competition for the best scenes publicizing the recently founded Free Austrian Movement or the current tasks of Civil Defence and War Work.[56] Prizes were subsequently awarded to Erika Wachtl, Erich Rattner and the twenty year old Erich Fried.[57] Although not specifically named, Fried's contribution may have been the sketch 'Wiener Neustadt 1942', published in the Austrian Centre's duplicated monthly journal *Österreichische Kulturblätter* earlier that year.[58] The sketch is a stirring, if somewhat optimistic portrayal of the solidarity of Austrian workers, evoking the example of the munitions workers' strikes in January 1918 as a precedent for resistance to German occupation.

The Players' second revue, *We from Austria*, again directed by Koka Motz, and including scenes by Fried, Wachtl and Rattner, was first performed at the Austrian Centre in Westbourne Terrace on 25 October 1942.[59] The difficulties frequently encountered in documenting the activities of an exile theatre group, such as the lack of artefacts like theatre programmes and reviews, are mitigated in the case of the Austrian Centre Players, whose early activities are documented to an unusual degree. The Austrian Centre's journal *Österreichische Kulturblätter*, which dealt at length with the work of cultural propaganda, made repeated attempts during 1942 to encourage the formation of amateur dramatic groups and to offer appropriate material for performance. The article 'ABC of a Drama Group', written by Koka Motz, was an attempt to give advice on devising and staging plays and sketches, drawing on the early experiences of the Austrian Centre Players to guide the first steps of new drama groups.[60] It therefore incidentally confirms how the first two revues were devised, how they were staged and what results they aimed to achieve. Under the heading 'How do we write our Scenes?', it describes the devising sessions which produced the 'Salvage Scenes' in the revue 'We from Austria':

> We wanted to write about our war effort. The entire drama group (35 young men and women) met under the direction of a writer. We chose the theme 'Saving und Salvage': a scene, which was a serious appeal

designed to show our positive reaction. [...] And now the group's work began. Jokes and ideas flew back and forth and were noted by the 'collector', as well as a series of stories from our friends, who forced through savings measures in the factories where they were working. It was one of the most stimulating and positive evenings our drama group has had. One colleague took the responsibility of sorting out all the stories and devising an effective scene out of these building blocks.

The writer also notes that in the three months since their publication, the scenes had been performed frequently and successfully, adding: 'Half of our revue *Return Ticket* was devised in this way.'

Once again, the elements of music, mime and dance contained in the scenes were stressed. Some of the scenes enacted items reported in the press, a technique obviously influenced by the idea of the 'living newspaper', popular amongst left-wing theatre groups during the 1930s. Material was not only topical, but could be adapted to local circumstances; when performing in factories, the group tried to introduce local events or problems.

The writer also recommended the use of 'speech choruses' or mass declamation, another technique used by agitprop groups, particularly to deliver strong propaganda messages. She cited the use of mass declamation in a scene which appealed for volunteers for Sunday harvesting work, which 'not only achieved artistic success but also – which was more important – produced a large number of volunteers'.

Koka Motz also enumerated the difficulties encountered by such groups, particularly in wartime, such as actors becoming unavailable at short notice, so that scenes had to be rewritten, dialogue reassigned or characters written out. Stage sets, and even properties were minimalist, since the group often performed in locations lacking a stage or, in the case of an air-raid shelter, even a hook in the wall. In such cases, an easel and flip charts were used to indicate changes of date, time or place, but performances such as that at the Empress Hall, an 8000 seat arena normally used for sporting events, presented entirely different problems.

The actual content of *We from Austria* can also be documented, several scenes having already been published in *Österreichische Kulturblätter* a couple of months earlier.[61] These included the various short 'Salvage Scenes', which were punctuated by the choruses of the 'Salvage Song':

Save, save and use your wits,
Save, save the ends and bits,
Which you do not need
But which will help indeed
Make us win this war much quicker.

There was also a 'Second Front Scene', set in a 'large prison cell somewhere in occupied territory', in which prisoners from various occupied countries, all under sentence of death, called for the creation of the Second Front – thus enacting one of the political demands of the FAM. As with the first revue, song and dance were both woven into the dramatic action.

The scenes published also included Erich Rattner's playlet *Post S27*. This short dramatic sketch portrays an incident in occupied Yugoslavia, as a young Austrian soldier decides to desert and join the partisans: a strong, if crude political message. It was this sketch which the Players Group chose to perform when they once more took part in the annual Drama Season at Toynbee Hall. The performance was positively received, not simply because of its powerful propaganda message. The judges were quick to compliment the actors on their achievement in performing in English, remarking on the ease with which they had carried this off.[62]

In the pamphlet *Five Years of the Austrian Centre* Georg Knepler stressed that the Centre made concerted attempts to reach British friends and sympathizers, and that the Players Group played a key part in this endeavour, alongside the Speakers Department which provided speakers at the request of British organizations.[63] However, the available records do not suggest that there was any continuous or coordinated programme.

It is clear that the Players were not the only drama group fostered by the Austrian Centre. Others, performing for a local audience, included the Swiss Cottage Players, under the direction of the actress Lily Hammerschlag, whose opinions are of more than usual interest since she was also a member of the Executive Committee of the Austrian Centre. In an interview with *Zeitspiegel*, she summarized the aims of an 'Exile Theatre' as 'using acting, theatre and song to make Austria's liberation struggle comprehensible to the English public, to keep alive Austria's great culture and to make it accessible not only to the English but also to the Austrians'. To achieve this, she recommended plays from the classic Austrian theatre repertoire: 'I consider the performance of Nestroy, Grillparzer and Schnitzler to be good political propaganda.'[64] They were held to be especially appropriate, since they represented not only Austria's cultural heritage but also the country's struggle for liberation. Lily Hammerschlag's statement must be seen in the perspective of Austrian cultural propaganda at that time: the Laterndl was to revert, a few months later, to a programme of specifically Austrian plays.

One of the first productions of the 'Swiss Cottage Players' was of scenes adapted from Schnitzler's *Der junge Medardus* (*Young Medardus*), the play's setting during the French occupation of Vienna in 1809 providing a historical parallel which was considered particularly apposite. The play was directed by the actress Marianne Walla, well known for her performances at the Laterndl.[65] Nor was Nestroy overlooked. The group's second production was of the one-acter *Frühere Verhältnisse* (*Earlier Conditions*), performed in June 1943, apparently with great success. It was announced that the group's future plans included plays by Ferdinand Raimund and Karl Schönherr, though there is no evidence that these were ever realized.

After 1942, indications of the activities of the Players Group are sparse. One recorded production of theirs was *Hope for Tomorrow*, a play adapted from the short novel *Hostages* by the young Stefan Heym, later to achieve literary success in the GDR. The action, originally set in Czechoslovakia, was transferred to Vienna 'und set between the Gestapo Headquarters and the places where the underground struggle of the Austrian people continues'; the performance was greeted with 'tumultuous applause'.[66]

In October 1944, the two groups joined forces to perform the dramatic revue *The Red Eagle of Austria*, written largely by Erika Wachtl.[67] Subtitled 'Scenes from the Austrian Liberation Struggle', the revue sought to deliver a strong political message. The title refers to an Austrian resistance group in the mountains of the Tyrol calling itself 'Rote Adler', which appealed for 'a fighting unity of all, peasant and worker, Catholic and Communist'. This group's activities had been reported in *Young Austria* over a year earlier.[68]

The play was clearly written to demonstrate the reality of Austrian resistance to German occupation which the Allies had laid down in the Moscow Declaration as a prerequisite for post-war Austrian independence. The political focus of the Players Groups is underlined by the contrast with the Laterndl, which at this time was staging the musical entertainment *Austrian Rhapsody*, which was very much an exercise in cultural nostalgia. *The Red Eagle of Austria* was certainly intended to stimulate political debate. It was performed to a mixed British and Austrian audience, who were invited to participate in a discussion after the performance. While British members of the audience were apparently impressed with what they had seen, the Austrians were more sceptical – perhaps with some reason, since the portrayal of fierce Austrian resistance to Nazism seems to exemplify the exaggerated optimism prevalent amongst politically committed exiles, especially those close to the KPÖ, at this stage of the war.[69]

Spielgruppe des Young Austria/Young Austria Players: 'From the Danube to the Thames'

Parallel to the work of the two groups run by the Austrian Centre was that of the Young Austrian Players, a drama group under the auspices of the youth organization Young Austria. The activities of the group are well documented, largely due to the records preserved by the actor Otto Tausig, who became its leading member. Tausig, who had come to

England on a Kindertransport, had joined the group after his release from internment on the Isle of Man.[70] He had been held in Hutchinson Camp, where he had been a member of the drama group formed by Fritz Weiss, which performed German classics like *Nathan der Weise* (*Nathan the Wise*) and *Die Räuber* (*The Robbers*), as well as modern English plays such as Galsworthy's *The Silver Box* and Robert Ardrey's *Thunder Rock*. These had been performed in German or English, a precedent for the work of the YAP. Tausig had first joined the group in late 1942, after attending a performance of Jura Soyfer's *Columbus oder Broadway-Melodie 1492* (*Columbus or Broadway Melody 1492*) at the Austrian Centre. He quickly set about refining its performance – he described it as 'an amateur group, but an ambitious one'.[71]

The group's dual identity – it was known both as the 'Spielgruppe des Young Austria' and as the 'Young Austria Players' – reflected their dual objectives. They sought both to acquaint British sympathizers with Austria and its political situation and to cultivate the Austrian theatre heritage by performing plays from the Austrian repertoire.[72]

The first aim was pursued through the medium of revue, devised by the group, and performed in English to bring their message to English audiences, particularly youth groups. One such production was the revue *From the Danube to the Thames*, 'a really lively and rousing revue', in which Otto Tausig gave an outstanding performance.[73] A year later they produced the revue *Humour is a Weapon Too*, in which the spirit of Johann Strauss appears to the Director of the Vienna waxworks to complain that his own waxwork figure is to be melted down for soap by the Germans. 'For a whole witching hour, he leads the Director through occupied Austria and shows him how Austrian humour and *Gemütlichkeit* drive the Germans crazy. The result is a decline in German soap production.[74] The final revue performed, with the apt title *Cheerio England*, was written by Eva Priester.

To foster the Austrian theatre heritage, the group had performed Austrian dramatists such as Nestroy, Ferdinand Raimund and above all Jura Soyfer. Their productions included Nestroy's *Einen Jux will er sich machen* (*He Wants to Do it for a Joke*) (1943) and two plays by Raimund: *Der Verschwender* (*The Spendthrift*) (1944),[75] and *Der Diamant des Geisterkönigs* (*The Diamond of the Ghost King*) (1945).[76]

Perhaps their outstanding production was of Jura Soyfer's *Vineta*, a play which had been written and performed in Vienna in 1937. According to Tausig, the group devoted extraordinary time and trouble to the play, rehearsing it for nine months before finally performing it at the Austrian Centre in February 1945,[77] giving a repeat performance a month later. Both performances were in German.

In early May, only days before the end of the war, the group gave a festival performance of *Vineta* which, though also played in German, was aimed at a specially invited audience of 'English and other Allied celebrities'.[78] Among these were the playwright Jack Lindsay (well known for his connections with Unity Theatre), W. P. Coates 'whose writings on the Soviet Union many of us know' and the writer John Lehmann, who had known Jura Soyfer in Vienna and had translated his poems for English publication.

Though *Vineta* was probably the group's most notable production, it was not their last. In November 1945, they performed Raimund's *Der Diamant des Geisterkönigs* in a production by Otto Tausig, who also played the leading role.[79] It proved to be Tausig's farewell appearance with the Young Austria Players. He returned to Vienna early in 1946, fulfilling his ambition to study at the Reinhardt Seminar. Continuing the work he had begun in London, he helped to achieve a renaissance of Jura Soyfer's work in Vienna, publishing an edition of his collected works in 1947 – an edition intended to serve as a collection of practical play texts.[80]

Tausig's departure did not herald the immediate collapse of the Young Austrian Players. They staged one further production, in July 1946, performing another Soyfer play, *Weltuntergang (World's End)*, which was directed by Hans Ungar. The cast was reinforced by members of the Austrian Centre Players, an experiment undoubtedly dictated by dwindling numbers, but nonetheless deemed successful by the reviewer in *Jung-Österreich*.[81] However, this was their last recorded production.

The amateur theatre groups fostered by the Austrian Centre petered out as their political aspiration of an independent Austria was realized. The political agenda had moved back to Vienna, where most of the remaining members of the groups eventually also returned. The Laterndl had long since gone dark. Founded as an assertion of Austrian cultural identity at a time when Austria had been struck from the political map, it disappeared with the post-war re-establishment of Austria. Its existence closely circumscribed by political events, it was inevitably a political theatre. From an initial programme of political cabaret, it shifted, early in 1942, to adopt a repertoire of international plays, symbolic of the alliance of national liberation movements against Fascism, before reverting, in the wake of the Moscow Declaration, to an explicitly Austrian repertoire. However, while its repertoire was committedly anti-Fascist, it was not narrowly prescriptive, still less did it seek to enact a party political line. Its political message was demonstrated by its very existence: theatre was the continuation of Austria by other means. Perhaps its main achievement was to help to maintain morale amongst the exile community and to uphold its cultural links to an increasingly remote homeland. Its abrupt closure in August 1945 caused great dismay among the members of its faithful audience. The Laterndl represents perhaps the outstanding cultural achievement of Austrian exiles in Britain during the war years; it is certainly one of the most fondly remembered.

Notes

1   Although the Laterndl is one of the most successful examples of Austrian culture in exile, little has been written about it. Despite short memoirs by former participants (e.g. Franz Bönsch, 'Das österreichische Exiltheater "Laterndl" in London', in Dokumentationsarchiv des österreichischen Widerstandes and Dokumentationsstelle für neuere österreichische Literatur, eds., *Österreicher im Exil 1934-45: Protokoll des internationalen Syposiums zur Erforschung des österreichischen Exils von 1934 bis 1945, abgehalten vom 3. bis 6. Juni 1975 in Wien*, Vienna 1977, pp. 441-50; Rudolf Spitz, 'Das Laterndl in London', in *Theater im Exil 1933-45*, Exhibition Catalogue, Berlin 1973, pp. 28-30); and references to it in more general surveys of theatre and cabaret in exile (e.g. Reinhard Hippen, *Satire gegen Hitler: Kabarett im Exil*, Zurich 1986; Hugh Rorrison, 'German Theatre and Cabaret in London 1939-45', in Günther Berghaus, ed., *Theatre and Film in Exile: German Artists in Britain 1933-45*, Oxford/New York/Munich 1989), there has been only one (short) publication on the Laterndl in English: Anat Feinberg, 'Das Laterndl in London 1939-1945', *German Life and Letters* 37/3 (1984), pp. 211-17. The only extended academic treatment of the subject remains Erna Wipplinger's interesting doctoral dissertation 'Österreichisches Exiltheater in Großbritannien 1938-1945', Vienna 1984. Though two short articles based on her research did appear (Wipplinger, '"Zünden soll d'Latern": Österreichisches Exiltheater in Großbritannien', *Wespennest*, 56, 1984, pp. 29-38; Wipplinger, 'Von Adam bis Adolf', *Mitteilungen des Instituts für Wissenschaft und Kunst*, ÜL, 1/2 (1985), pp. 30-34), the dissertation itself has regrettably never been published.

2   Copies of theatre programmes for most of the Laterndl productions are among the Martin Miller Papers held at the Institute of Germanic & Romance Studies, London.

3   Franz Bönsch, *op. cit.*, pp. 441-50, here p. 450.

4   *Ibid.*, p. 445.

5   Cf. Laterndl letter-heading; correspondence between Rudolf Spitz and Robert Neumann (Documentation Archive of Austrian Resistance [DÖW], Vienna, 7234/6-7).

6   The text of both 'Bow Street' and 'Wiener Ringelspiel' has been published in Hans Weigl, ed., *Weit von Wo: Kabarett im Exil*, Vienna 1994.

7   Cf. Hilde Spiel, 'Keine Klage über England', *Ver Sacrum: Neue Hefte für Kunst und Literatur*, 72 (1972), p. 21.

8   *The Times*, 28 June 1939, p. 12.

9   *The Spectator*, 7 July 1939, p. 15.

10   Rudolf Spitz to Robert Neumann, 2 November 1939, DÖW 7234/6-7.

11   *PEN News*, March 1940, p. 11.

12   François Lafitte, *The Internment of Aliens*, Harmondsworth 1940 (republished London 1988), p. 56.

13   Cf. Walter Rösler, 'Aspekte des deutschsprachigen Exilkabaretts 1933-1945', in *Exiltheater und Exildramatik 1933-1945*, Maintal 1991, pp. 283-93.

14   *Picture Post*, 27 April 1940, pp. 46-47.

15   Cf. Rudolf Spitz in an interview with *The Star*, 25 November 1939.

16   Schrecker reappeared at the Laterndl after a long absence in Curt Goetz's *Die tote Tante* in May 1943.

17   According to some of his contemporaries, Klüger was an actor of limited range. Georg Knepler, for example, felt that he did not really measure up to the part.

18   *Evening Standard*, 10 November 1941, p. 2.

19   'Das wieder leuchtende Laterndl', *Zeitspiegel*, 5 October 1941, p. 7. The review was signed P.R.= Paul Reimann.

20   The text of *Ring-Rund* was originally published in *Kunst und Wissen: Eine Materialsammlung für Veranstaltungen*, no. 20, London 1941, pp. 20-24 and was reprinted in 'Erich Fried und Österreich: Bausteine zu einer Beziehung', *Zirkular* (Vienna), Sondernummer 33, November 1992, pp. 69-74.

21   Eva Priester, 'Selbstkritik der Kritik', *Zeitspiegel*, 12 October 1941, p. 9.

22   *Zeitspiegel*, 22 November 1941, p. 9.

23   English synopsis of the sketch in the programme for *Here is the News* (Martin Miller Papers, Institute of Germanic & Romance Studies, London).

24   *Die Zeitung*, 6 February 1942, p. 9.

25   *Zeitspiegel*, 21 February 1942, p. 10.

26   *Zeitspiegel*, 7 March 1942, p. 11.

27   Similar views were expressed by the British actor and film director Herbert Marshall: cf. 'Kulturnotizen', *Zeitspiegel*, 21 February 1942, p. 9.

28   See the Founding Declaration of the FAM, reprinted in Wolfgang Muchitsch, ed., *Österreicher im Exil: Großbritannien 1938-1945: Eine Dokumentation*, Vienna 1992, pp. 283-84.

29   *Zeitspiegel*, 15 August 1942, p. 7.

30   *Zeitspiegel*, 5 December 1942, p. 9.

31   *Zeitspiegel*, 17 October 1942, p. 7.

32   *Zeitspiegel*, 6 March 1943, p. 7.

33   *Zeitspiegel*, 6 March 1943, p. 7. The play had been first performed on 11 February 1943 but was not reviewed earlier because *Zeitspiegel* did not appear for two weeks due to paper shortages.

34   '"Professor Poleshajew" von Rachmanow', *Zeitspiegel*, 26 February 1944, pp. 6-7.

35   'Csl. Gäste beim österreichischen PEN', *Zeitspiegel*, 11 September 1943, p. 6.

36   *Zeitspiegel*, 29 April 1944, p. 8.

37   'Wir sind halt anders', *Zeitspiegel*, 2 December 1944, p. 6.

38   'Der Österreicher Hermann Bahr', *Zeitspiegel*, 20 January 1945, p. 6.

39   *Zeitspiegel*, 17 June 1944, p. 3.

40   'Der G'wissenswurm', *Zeitspiegel*, 30 September 1944, p. 8.

41   'Drei Einakter im Laterndl', *Zeitspiegel*, 5 May 1945, p. 6.

42   *Zeitspiegel*, 14 July 1945, p. 6.

43   Cf. the advertisement for the 'final week' in *Zeitspiegel*, 25 August 1945, p. 7.

44   *Zeitspiegel*, 25 August 1945, p. 6: 'A greeting has been sent to the Secretary of State for Education Ernst Fischer by the Laterndl Collective. It expresses their hope of returning home in the near future and their preparedness for enthusiastic collaboration.'

45   *Zeitspiegel*, 29 June 1941, p. 8.

46   Cf. *Zeitspiegel*, 21 September 1941, p. 10: 'This is the first appearance of the newly formed Austrian Centre Players. The revue is intended for our English friends and portrays with music, dance and song in a number of scenes the fate of the Austrian emigration, their wishes and aims.'

47   'Spielgruppe', *Zeitspiegel*, 5 October 1941, p. 7.

48   Programme *Return Ticket Vienna-London*, n.d. [1941], DÖW 7220/1.

49   'Austrians on the Stage', *Young Austria*, 11 October 1941, p. 4.

50   The complete text of *Return Ticket* was reportedly published in *Österreichische Kulturblätter*, cf. 'Kulturnotizen', *Zeitspiegel*, 28 March 1942, p. 9: 'The latest issue of the "Österreichische Kulturblätter" reproduces the complete text of the revue *Return Ticket Vienna-London*. Orders can be placed at the Austrian Centre.' However, the appropriate copy of the *Kulturblätter* could not be traced and seems not to have survived.

51   *Österreichische Kulturblätter*, February 1942, pp. 17-18.

52   'Kulturnotizen', *Zeitspiegel*, 3 January 1942, p. 9.

53   *Austrian News. Monthly Bulletin of the Austrian Centre*, December 1941, p. 2.

54   Cf. 'Kulturnotizen', *Zeitspiegel*, 7 March 1942, p. 9: 'To mark the 25th performance of *Return Ticket*, the Austrian Centre Players will be looking for new members during the week 6-13 March. They hope to recruit new actors, singers, dancers and musicians. Their new programme will be concerned with Austrian unity.' Cf. also, 'Kulturnotizen', *Zeitspiegel* 21 March 1942, p. 9: 'The Austrian Centre Players have attracted 52 new members during their recruitment week. Their newly formed orchestra has already given a performance.'

55   *Zeitspiegel*, 7 March 1942, p. 9.

56   *Young Austria*, early February 1942, p. 4.

57   *Zeitspiegel*, 18 April 1942, p. 9.

58   *Österreichische Kulturblätter*, January 1942, pp. 5-7.

59   Cf. review, signed E.Ft. in *Zeitspiegel*, 24 October 1942, p. 7.

60   'ABC einer Spielgruppe', signed K.M. (= Koka Motz), *Österreichische Kulturblätter*, December 1942, p. 11.

61   *Österreichische Kulturblätter*, August-September 1942, pp. 1-10.

62   'Unsere Spielgruppe im Drama Festival', *Zeitspiegel*, 6 February 1943, p. 7: 'Last year the AUSTRIAN CENTRE Players performed *Return Ticket* and were so successful that they were invited to take part again this year. Our group performed *Post S 27* by Erich Rattner.'

63   'Our "Players' Group" presenting Austrian plays – in English – songs and dances, performed before at least 10,000 British people in 1943 alone' (*Five Years of the Austrian Centre*, London 1944, p. 5).

64   *Zeitspiegel*, 2 October 1943, p. 7.

65   *Zeitspiegel*, 8 May 1943, p. 7.

66   *Zeitspiegel*, 2 October 1943, p. 7.

67   See *Austrian Centre*, October 1944.

68   *Young Austria*, 31 July 1943, p. 1.

69   *Zeitspiegel*, 18 November 1944, p. 7. The revue was performed at least once more, in February 1945, though the performance was not reviewed.

70   Author's interview with Otto Tausig, 7 November 1998. Many of the following details of the work of the Young Austria Players are also taken from this interview.

71   *Ibid.*

72   An early statement of these aims can be found in the manuscript report 'Junges Österreich in Großbritannien: Bericht über die Tätigkeit des Young Austria', DÖW 589A

73   Cf. review in *Young Austria*, 31 July 1943, p. 8; the issue appeared as a supplement to *Zeitspiegel*.

74   *Young Austria*, 15 July 1944, p. 4.

75   The first performance was on 16 January 1944 (see *Austrian Centre*, January 1944).

76   The theatre programme for *Der Diamant des Geisterkönigs* contains a list of previous productions by the Young Austria Players, including Nestroy's *Einen Jux will er sich machen*, *Der Verschwender*, and *Vineta*, as well as the revues mentioned above (see DÖW 20722).

77   Cf. *Jung-Österreich* 10 February 1945, p. 4.

78   *Jung-Österreich*, 5 May 1945, p. 4.

79   See *Austrian Centre*, November 1945.

80   Otto Tausig, ed., *Vom Paradies zum Weltuntergang*, Vienna 1947.

81   Cf. review in *Jung-Österreich*, 20 July 1946, p. 4.

'A TASTE OF TRUE CULTURE, A TASTE OF VIENNA, A TASTE OF LIFE' MUSIC AT THE AUSTRIAN CENTRE

CHARMIAN BRINSON

In an essay of June 1941, 'Musik im Austrian Centre', the Centre's Cultural Secretary and self-styled 'in-house musician',[1] Georg Knepler, makes the following emphatic statement: 'The Austrian Centre is not merely fulfilling an obligation when it attempts to keep a fragment of culture alive in the midst of all the horrors. For us it is a need.' Expressing the wish that more members would seek to take part in the Centre's cultural and musical life, Knepler also seizes the opportunity to publicize some forthcoming events: the 18-year-old Norbert Brainin (later of the celebrated Amadeus Quartet) playing the Kreutzer Sonata, for instance, and a concert by the soprano Erika Storm. Under different circumstances, so Knepler reflects, Storm would be performing at a far more prestigious venue than the Austrian Centre's small-scale theatre. Yet:

> Does that not give a whole new value to her concert? Do not the songs from Krenek's 'Travel Diary from the Austrian Alps' that she will be performing thereby assume a double significance?
> Within our modest premises you are being offered a taste of true culture, a taste of Vienna, a taste of life.[2]

Of all the Austrian cultural achievements, music was without question the one in which exiled Austrian could take most pride, on an international level, and which they could use with effect both to foster the social and cultural life of Austrians in Great Britain and to promote the Austrian cause among their British hosts. Anna Hornik, in her Austrian Centre publication *This is Austria*, which is aimed at an English readership, maintains that 'through her music, Austria has brought the world to her feet, for music is the very element of life for her people'. Indeed Austrian music – and Hornik can claim for Austria such composers as Haydn, Mozart and Schubert, as well as Beethoven, 'a Viennese by choice' – assumes a high degree of symbolic significance in the distinction she draws between Germany and Austria:

> The very last wireless transmission made by a free and honourable Austria, which already felt the destroying hand of Hitler, was of a Schubert Sonata, that had to be interrupted for the news of the entry of the Germans into the country. Thus music was the last message of a free Austria to the world.[3]

Not surprisingly, Knepler, too, in the section of his *Five Years of the Austrian Centre* that celebrates the Centre's cultural achievements, chooses to foreground music:

> Most of our activities in this sphere have been devoted to music. The Austrian Centre was opened with a concert. The number of concerts we have arranged since must be several hundred and numerous famous musicians of many nationalities have performed in our club premises or in concerts arranged by the Austrian Centre in concert halls.[4]

But in fact, collective musical activity on the part of the exiled Austrians can be said even to have predated the Austrian Centre's official opening. In an unpublished memoir, Eva Kolmer recalls the pre-Centre Sunday meetings that she organized for Austrian domestics in premises made available by the Religious Society of Friends: '[I] turned up [...] in my Altaussee Dirndl that I had brought with me from home, with a guitar, and we sang Austrian folksongs together which led to many women crying with homesickness.'[5] And at the 'Meeting of Austrians' that was held at Queen Mary Hall, Great Russell Street, on 11 March 1939 to commemorate the first anniversary of the Anschluss, and to mark the imminent opening of the Austrian Centre, Friedrich Hertz's sombre opening words – 'We are gathered together here today in deepest sorrow'[6] – were accompanied by a programme of music clearly devised as quintessentially Austrian (and, as such, also typical of numerous commemorative concerts to come): Beethoven's String Quartet in E Minor, three Schubert Lieder (including the poignant 'An die Musik'), three more by Hugo Wolf, and the Schubert String Quartet in C Minor.[7] Similarly, when the Austrian Centre was indeed opened soon afterwards, the *Pariser Tageszeitung* reported that 'A Beethoven Trio and some Schubert Lieder concluded the impressive evening'.[8]

Within three months of the Centre's inauguration, at the 'General Meeting of the Club Austrian Centre' on 26 June 1939, an abundance of musical activity could already be reported:

In these three months of the Centre's existence, a large number of cultural events have been put on, for example the Beethoven, Haydn, Mahler, Schubert and Strauss evenings. The Musicians' Group of the Austrian Circle for Arts and Science has devised the cultural programme.[9]

It is interesting to note that the links between the Austrian Centre and the Music Group of the Austrian Circle[10] – in 1939, incidentally, Anna Mahler served as the Austrian Circle's representative on the Centre's 'Club Committee' – seem to have been relatively short-lived, with the Circle soon shifting its adherence to the Austrian Academy,[11] a creation of the centre-right Austria Office (though that still lay some way ahead). In any case, in an attachment to the General Meeting minutes, entitled 'Coming Events', three concerts were announced for the second half of July 1939: the first a Brahms concert (Brahms, like Beethoven, was invariably regarded as a 'Wahlösterreicher', or Austrian by choice, in Free Austrian circles);[12] the second a farewell concert for the singer Charlotte Eisler (former wife of Hanns Eisler) who was moving to Manchester, comprising Lieder by Schubert, Mozart and Mahler; and the third a Verdi programme at which the exiled composer Hans Gál – resident in Edinburgh during most of the Austrian Centre's lifetime, but nevertheless a regular performer there – was to deliver a commemorative prologue.[13]

In addition to the general musical provision for the Austrian exile population, moreover, a special cultural programme continued to be arranged for the Austrian refugee domestics, with the General Meeting minutes referring to some 'Beethoven, Haydn und Mahler evenings' they had enjoyed.[14] The domestic servants also formed a choir and gave performances,[15] though far less has come to light about this than about a slightly later formation, the celebrated Young Austria Choir (see below).

In March 1940, a year after the Austrian Centre's foundation and nine months after that first General Meeting, the Austrian Centre's *First Annual Report* appeared, painting a picture of the remarkably extensive musical programme by then to be found there:

There have been many musical evenings at which pianists, singers, quartettes [*sic*], choirs, etc., performed. The most popular composers whose works had been performed were: Beethoven, Brahms, Schubert, Mozart, Hugo Wolf, Haydn, Johann Strauss, Gustav Mahler, etc. Many musical evenings were arranged for variety. There were 23 such variety evenings, attended by 2770 persons. Music was intermixed with songs, dancing and short sketches.[16]

While all this related to events in London, it was also reported that musical activities for refugees were being organized by the Austrian Centre in Manchester, Glasgow, Edinburgh, Bristol, York, Belfast and Bournemouth. In Edinburgh, where the Centre was promoting activities within the local Jewish Club, the developments were particularly noteworthy:

> The well-known Austrian musician and composer, Gál, has formed a little orchestra and a madrigal quintette [sic] and many gifted Austrians provide most delightful programmes for the socials of the Club.[17]

A year on from that, moreover, the *Zeitspiegel* Special Issue of May 1941 (published to mark the Austrian Centre's second anniversary), suggests that, despite the intervening problems of the Blitz and of alien internment, the Centre's musical provision and its promotion of Austrian music and artists were still proceeding from strength to strength:

> Naturally, due prominence has been given to Austrian music at the Centre. The best representatives of Austrian musical life, Professor Arnold Rosé and Professor Friedrich Buxbaum, have played here. Hans Gál's 'Huyton Suite' was first performed at the Centre. Well known names from the world of music in Austria and on the Continent were to be found on the Centre's concert programmes: Irene Eisinger, Engel Lund, Max Rostal, Ernst Urbach, Dela Lipinskaja, Lea Seidl, Julius Guttmann, Georg Maliniak.
> From the younger generation of artists we have heard the Czech violinist Maria Hlounova, the Viennese pianist Edith Vogel, Gertrud Kaldeck, Heinz Hollitscher, Molly Jonas.
> Josef Plaut performed here; Dr Oskar Adler formed a new Austrian string quartet; countless young artists whose careers had been disrupted by political events were offered the opportunity to perform in front of a discerning audience.[18]

All this was very largely the doing of Georg Knepler, formerly a pupil of Gál's in composition and of Egon Wellesz's[19] in musicology, who was responsible for all cultural events at the Austrian Centre, including the music, and who himself conducted and served as accompanist at numerous Austrian Centre concerts, as well as at Laterndl productions. In a recent interview, Knepler recalled the 'huge demand' for culture among the exiled Austrians; in response, the Centre had been able to offer them 'whatever they had' from among the wealth of exiled musical talent (including some excellent singers, pianists and violinists whom they were fortunate to have at their disposal).[20] Yet, at the same time, there were frequently difficulties associated with mounting an ambitious musical programme in constrained circumstances, that could only be solved by extreme ingenuity, as exemplified by an occasion when Knepler and his first wife, on two pianos, set out to perform the *Dreigroschenoper*:

> Since the space was too small for two grand pianos, we unscrewed the back leg off one of them and placed one on top of the other which meant that my wife had to sit on a raised platform.[21]

A regular feature of musical life at the Austrian Centre were the Sunday morning concerts, again organized and frequently accompanied by Knepler. Artists who took part in the Sunday morning series included the baritone Ernst Urbach – Knepler accompanied him, for instance, in a performance of Schubert's *Schöne Müllerin* in March 1941[22] – the pianist Edith Vogel, who performed a programme of Beethoven, Schumann and Chopin in February 1941, and the singer Margarete Philipsky who later that same month took part, with Urbach and others, in a concert of operatic arias and duets.[23]

Moreover, musical events of this calibre were by no means confined to Sunday mornings. Sunday evenings, too, seem to have been a popular time, with *Österreichische Nachrichten* advertising a Viennese operetta evening for 11 February 1940 and another a fortnight later.[24] In November 1942 Knepler conceived a particularly ambitious Sunday evening event, two concert performances of the *Magic Flute*, 'once again with good singers, it was very good',[25] which, in the words of the programme, consisted of 'Arias und Ensembles with a linking commentary', the latter delivered by Knepler himself.[26] On this occasion, so it is reported, Knepler had to lead from a piano propped up on a soda water crate.[27]

Thursday evenings were also frequently concert nights: in May, June and July 1941, for instance, there was a series of chamber concerts at the Austrian Centre with programmes consisting largely of music of the Baroque and Viennese classical traditions but also including works by Gál (he was invited to London to perform his own compositions on 29 May 1941 in a concert otherwise comprising Bach, Beethoven and Schubert).[28] The previous year there had been other, possibly more adventurous Thursday evening concerts: one on 22 February 1940 at which the English bass Martin Lawrence, who was often associated with Austrian Centre events, had performed a programme of Negro spirituals, and another the following week consisting of music by Schoenberg and Mahler.[29]

In addition, from the beginning of 1943, two Wednesday evenings a month at the Austrian Centre's Swiss Cottage branch[30] were given over to the Austrian Musical Circle, an organization of music enthusiasts whose foundation was reported in *Zeitspiegel* on 30 January:

> Paul Knepler [i.e. father of Georg Knepler and former librettist to Franz Lehar] und Kammersänger [Ernst] Possony have established a musical circle (membership 1/-) which intends to put on regular concerts and musical events at the Austrian Centre, Swiss Cottage. The first evening – a Schubert and Beethoven concert – will take place on 3 February. The [Norbert] Brainin, [Paul] Blumenfeld and [Paul] Hamburger Trio is playing. [31]

Within a matter of weeks, *Zeitspiegel* was reporting on a Musical Circle evening at which a Gál composition, *Variationen über ein Heurigenlied*, had been 'applauded so enthusiastically that it had to be repeated' and, moreover, on the fact that Gál himself would be coming down from Edinburgh to perform a whole evening of his work, together with the well known operatic soprano Claire Born. The Austrian Musical Circle, so *Zeitspiegel* continued, which could already boast many English friends among its members, 'is endeavouring to foster the Austrian musical tradition and is putting on two concerts a month which are attracting general interest'. [32]

Further Musical Circle concerts during 1943 included a concert performance (in Italian) of *The Marriage of Figaro*, 'under the intelligent and measured conductorship of Dr Behrend [i.e. Berend]'; [33] a performance of Bach's *Bauernkantate*, at the end of which 'the audience, filling the hall, showed their keen appreciation of all the performers'; [34] chamber music; and piano and song recitals. In addition, special occasions were commemorated, such as the 100th anniversary of the death of the Austrian conductor and composer Josef Lanner, the programme consisting of a lecture by Paul Knepler and contributions by the singers Alice Hübsch and Margarete Philipsky and the Laterndl actor Fritz Schrecker. [35]

In mid-1944, a reader's letter to *Zeitspiegel* remarked on the fact that the Musical Circle had by then existed for more than a year, and added the following personal appreciation:

> It was a really excellent idea to establish [...] the Musical Circle. Men experienced in the arts have got together and, with the help of outstanding artists, great musical successes have been achieved.
> The Viennese are music enthusiasts but the English, too, are musical connoisseurs as is shown by their increasing interest in our events. We

look forward with keen anticipation to further evenings in the Laterndl auditorium at the Swiss Cottage Austrian Centre.[36]

The Austrian Musical Circle continued along much the same lines throughout the war, as a relatively small-scale 'in-house' organization, catering to the music lovers amongst the Austrian Centre's membership, thus fulfilling a quite different function from the professional Austrian Musicians' Group (see below). On at least one occasion, however, the Circle took it upon itself to assume a more public role: on 28 April 1945 – it will be recalled that Vienna was liberated from National Socialism on 13 April, and the new Austrian Provisional Government formed on 27 April – the Circle mounted a concert in the Queen Mary Hall (the venue, incidentally, where the initial 'Meeting of Austrians' had been held in March 1939). This concert featured the internationally renowned Rosé Quartet, together with the pianist Franz Osborn, who performed a programme of Schubert, Brahms, Dvorak and Chopin.[37] It was undoubtedly no accident, in the new situation in which the Austrians found themselves, that this concert consisted of music by one Austrian, one 'Austrian by choice' and two composers from Eastern Europe.

In her study, *NS-verfolgte Musiker in England*, Jutta Raab Hansen undertakes an interesting analysis of the musical repertoire at Austrian Centre events, according to which the most frequently performed composers were the Austrians Haydn, Mozart and Schubert, and the 'Austrians by choice' Beethoven and Brahms; of these, Mozart enjoyed particular popularity at Free Austrian concerts. The German composers Schumann and Mendelssohn, on the other hand (even given the fact that the latter was banned in Germany), tended to be rather less frequently played. As for the music of Bach, Handel and Telemann, when this was performed at the Austrian Centre it was often by musicians from the Free German League of Culture (FGLC), appearing at the Austrians' invitation. Thus, a typical Austrian Centre concert would have been likely to consist of works of the Viennese classical tradition, up to and including those of Gustav Mahler; Mahler's works, felt to be insufficiently recognized in England, were subject to especial promotion (see below). In addition, it was considered important for the works of exiled Austrian composers such as Wellesz and Gál, Ernst Krenek and Wilhelm Grosz to receive a hearing at Austrian Centre events.[38]

Such concerts, as Raab Hansen also points out, tended to feature a relatively restricted group of singers and musicians, appearing and reappearing in a variety of combinations. Among the professionals – and, of course, it should not be forgotten that amateurs, too, played their part in the Centre's musical life – she totals up a group of 32 Austrians (including the ubiquitous Knepler, Possony and Urbach), though supplemented by British musicians as well as exiled musicians from Germany, Czechoslovakia and elsewhere. [39]

In planning the cultural and musical activities of the Centre, Georg Knepler was, of course, influenced by the ideas of Alfred Klahr on the subject of the Austrian nation,[40] as were the other Austrian Communist Party members in leading positions in the Centre. Hence Knepler felt obliged to maintain a distinction between the music of the Austrian Centre and that of the FGLC, as indicated above, despite the obvious political affinities between the two organizations and his own friendship with Ernst Hermann Meyer (Knepler's opposite number at the FGLC). As Knepler himself has said: 'Since we as Austrians did not wish to recognize that Austria had become a part of Germany, we considered it politically correct to have two organizations that were independent of one another.'[41]

Yet, at the same time, Knepler was well aware that, in the field of music, the more or less indiscriminate appropriation for the Austrian cause of composers from past epochs, while politically expedient, may not always have been historically sound. In August 1941, Knepler himself had written of Mozart's 'Austrianness' in *Young Austria*, as follows:

> There are so many things that endear Mozart to us. He is, to begin with, an Austrian if there ever was one. To melt [*sic*] Italian, French, German and Austrian influences into a style which is entirely new and original could have been only an Austrian's work. [42]

Indeed it is quite possibly this same article that he recalled when reflecting on the problem years later:

> I had, for instance, disagreements with people who claimed that Mozart was an Austrian composer. And I answered that this is too complicated a question, that one simply can't say that. Mozart lived at a time when this question didn't exist. Mozart called himself German and felt himself to be German, so that it is not really possible to term him an Austrian composer. With Schubert, the situation is already a bit different [...] I myself may have even written an article at that time on Mozart as an Austrian composer. But at least I was aware of what the problem was. [43]

Yet the Austrian cause took priority over historical niceties of this sort, and the promotion of Austrian – as distinct from German – music was considered an important weapon in the furthering of this cause. As mentioned above, Mahler was thought by the Austrians, with some justification, to be undervalued in Britain and therefore much time and effort was put into publicizing his music. Indeed, as early as February

1940, Egon Wellesz had published an article on Mahler – who was 'still known too little and rated too low' – in *The Music Review* in which he had offered practical suggestions to British conductors on incorporating Mahler into their repertoires.[44] It was certainly no accident, moreover, that the first of the big public concerts to be organized by the Free Austrians (in this case, more specifically by the Council of Austrians in collaboration with the Free German League of Culture), on 18 May 1941 in the Wigmore Hall, was to mark the thirtieth anniversary of Mahler's death: a programme of Lieder and extracts from Mahler's Second, Third and Fourth Symphonies were performed to general acclaim by the singers Irene Eisinger, Sabine Kalter and Ernst Urbach and the pianists Franz Osborn, Berthold Goldschmidt, Georg Knepler and Paul Lichtenstern.[45]

As part of his publicity campaign for this concert, Knepler had sent two complimentary tickets to Sir Adrian Boult, then the BBC's Director of Music,[46] and with good effect: for Boult had passed them on to the BBC's London representative, Basil Douglas, who had been agreeably impressed, reporting back very favourably on Eisinger and Kalter (if less so on Urbach). The pianists, too, in Douglas's view, 'were all good, and if we include occasional 15-20 minute groups of Mahler songs in our programmes – which I very much hope we shall – I would strongly recommend that one of them be engaged to do the accompanying'. Moreover:

> I am rather sorry that we did not take the opportunity of this anniversary to re-introduce Mahler to programmes [...] May I make a special plea for a discreet, but quite frequent, representation of his music in programmes. [47]

So successful was the promotion of Mahler's music, in fact, that by the end of 1942 *Zeitspiegel* could carry an article, 'London wird Mahler-bewußt' ('London is becoming Mahler-conscious'), listing recent performances of his works (at a National Gallery concert, for instance), and could conclude with some satisfaction: 'Gustav Mahler [...] is finally beginning to get the recognition that is due to him.'[48]

In addition to the task of promoting Austrian music in Britain, however, the Austrian Centre was also committed, as made clear in its 1943 publication *Austrians in Great Britain*, 'to learn to know and understand the cultural life of Britain and her allies'.[49] Where music was concerned, *Zeitspiegel* did its best to scotch the opinion generally prevailing among exiled Austrians of the British as a fundamentally unmusical nation. Typical of articles of the kind was one that appeared on 13 February 1943, 'Musik diese Woche' ('Music This Week'), which recommended various forthcoming musical events in London while stressing the difficulty of selecting 'from among the wealth of good music that London's musical life has to offer' (p. 4). Another article a few months later, 'Musikalische Ereignisse' ('Musical Events'), on the current series of promenade concerts, positively hammered its point home:

> The length of the queue [...] was not at all consistent with the old prejudice, thoughtlessly reiterated by us continentals, that there is no audience for good music in England. And the heartfelt applause demonstrated that this audience was no less capable of an enthusiastic response than our own famous audiences. This audience is above all youthful: students, many blue-collar and white-collar workers at the end of a hard working day, many soldiers, sailors, airmen [...] It would be more appropriate if we spoke less about fostering the traditional musical culture of Vienna and instead played a greater role in English musical life.[50]

As part of the Centre's two-way cultural propaganda – the promotion of Austrian music to the British and of British music to the Austrians – it was considered expedient to stress pre-existing musical links between the two nations. Hermann Ullrich, the musicologist and FAM 'Kulturreferent' or cultural expert, wrote regularly on such topics: in his 'Mozarterstaufführungen in London' ('Mozart First Performances in London'), for instance, in *Zeitspiegel* on 22 January 1944,[51] or his 'Beethoven und seine englischen Freunde und Verleger' ('Beethoven and his English Friends and Publishers') in the *Kulturelle Schriftenreihe des Free Austrian Movement* in January 1946.[52] While these were directed primarily at an Austrian readership, Ullrich's 'Anglo-Austrian Musical Relations through the Centuries', which appeared in *The Music Review* in 1946,[53] aimed to direct the British, too, into the same mode of thinking.

Similarly, as a further aspect of Anglo-Austrian musical relations, practical musical collaboration between Austrian and British musicians was welcomed and remarked upon. One of a number of cooperative concerts, on 30 November 1941 at the Comedy Theatre, Haymarket, was entitled 'Hit Back': arranged in aid of John Lewis's Spitfire Fund, it was announced as 'organized by John Lewis Partnership's Odney Club and Austrian Centre Club' and as being performed 'by British artists and Refugees from Nazi Oppression'.[54]

There were further musical collaborations, too, that were organized together with representatives of other Allied or occupied nations. In Glasgow, for example, the FAM and the local exiled Norwegians gave a concert, featuring both professional (the well known Icelandic singer Engel Lund) and amateur performers, for the benefit of the Norwegian school fund (there were around 60 Norwegian children in Scotland).[55] In London, shortly before, the Austrian Centre had participated in a twelve-nation event, no less, 'Musik der Alliierten' or 'Music of the Allies', in aid of the FGLC's 'Anti-Nazi Fighting Fund' and the British Red Cross fund for the victims of Singapore.[56] In February 1943, a collaborative 'Grand Celebrity Concert' was organized at Porchester Hall by the Paddington Anglo-Soviet Aid Committee, the Austrian Centre, the Czech-British Friendship Club, Free German Youth and Hogar Espanol in aid of Mrs Churchill's Red Cross 'Aid to Russia' Fund: an international group of artists (including the three Austrians Knepler, Brainin and Urbach) put on an equally international programme featuring works by Smetana, Dvorak, Beethoven and the 18th Century English composer Henry Eccles, as well as some French and Spanish folksongs.[57]

Music, then, as an universally understood mode of communication transcending the language barrier, was regarded as a potent propaganda tool both in the promotion of the Austrian cause in exile and as an Austrian contribution to the Allied campaign against Fascism, and was much used as such. It was also employed to expose the deficiencies in Nazi cultural policies, never more powerfully, of course, than when 'banned' music was involved. Thus, on 12 December 1942, Georg Knepler wrote to Kenneth Wright, the Overseas Music Director at the BBC, suggesting a programme of music by the banned Jewish composers Mendelssohn, Mahler, Gál and Offenbach to 'bring home to many that even innocent things like Mendelssohn or Offenbach music are "verboten" in Germany'.[58] The BBC omitted to take up Knepler's suggestion on this occasion (even if it did later – though not until the war had almost ended – broadcast an adventurous concert of music in its European transmission by Austrian exiled composers Hans Gál, Franz Mittler and the FAM's own Hermann Ullrich).[59] Other attempts at publicizing banned music proved more successful, however. On 3 April 1943, for instance, *Zeitspiegel* reported that Gál had organized a concert in Edinburgh within the framework of the FGLC's exhibition 'We Accuse – Ten Years of Hitler Fascism': entitled 'Recital of Music Banned in Germany', the programme had consisted of works by Mahler, Mendelssohn, Hindemith and Gál himself, as well as settings of Heine by Schubert and Schumann.[60] Soon after, in June 1943, the Austrian Musicians' Group, a body still affiliated to the FAM at that point (see below), also put on a concert of 'Banned Composers' – all Austrians this time – at the Wigmore Hall, with a programme comprising Berg, Mahler, Krenek, Grosz, Schoenberg, Wellesz and Gál, performed by Austrian musicians Dea Gombrich, Peter Stadlen and Erika Storm.[61]

In his *Five Years of the Austrian Centre* in 1944, Knepler cited the Austrian Centre's promotion of contemporary Austrian composers as among its cultural achievements.[62] It should be noted, however, that such a policy was not pursued energetically enough in everyone's opinion. On the occasion of the first of the two Cultural Conferences, the accompanying chamber concert of Haydn, Mozart and Schubert was criticized in *Zeitspiegel* by the music critic Alfred Rosenzweig on the grounds that it was 'unrepresentative of the culture of Austrian chamber music in emigration' since it had failed to include any contemporary compositions.[63] Both this event, put on by the FAM-affiliated Austrian PEN Club in Exile, and the second Cultural Conference, organized by the FAM itself, obviously included music among their chief concerns. At the 1942 conference, music was represented by Georg Knepler, the musicologist Hans Ferdinand Redlich and the former critic of the Viennese *Arbeiter-Zeitung*, David Josef Bach.[64] In addition, a lecture by Otto Erich Deutsch

> offered a short survey of the great achievements of Austrian music which, culminating in the classical Viennese School, owed its greatness to the blending of the most disparate influences into a harmonic whole.[65]

On the face of it, the discussion on Austrian music at the two Cultural Conferences, two years apart, appears to have differed markedly: for while in 1942 the focus was still very much on the past, by 1944, with the war as good as over, it had shifted decisively to the future (with the emphasis on the conservation of the Austrian cultural heritage giving way to cultural restoration in Austria after the war). If there is, nevertheless, a central musicological idea linking the two together, then this is perhaps to be found in the line suggested by Deutsch in 1942 and expanded by Egon Wellesz in 1944 of the essentially international nature of Austrian music (a characteristic that was being increasingly promoted in Free Austrian circles as a distinguishing mark between Austrian and German music). It is certainly a theme that Wellesz, in his 1944 keynote speech 'Zum Wiederaufbau des Musiklebens in Österreich' ('On the Reconstruction of Musical Life in Austria'), pursues energetically, and with political as well as musicological effect:

> Austrian music – this was its strength – never positioned itself in national terms. We know that many of Haydn's themes are based on Croatian folk songs. Mozart was strongly influenced by Italian and French music. Haydn and Beethoven harmonized Scottish melodies. Beethoven used Russian themes and Schubert's music frequently reveals Slavonic resonances as does that of Mahler. It was this unique ability to absorb, incorporate, rework and reproduce that made Austrian music great.[66]

The 1944 Cultural Conference was the brainchild of Hermann Ullrich who, together with Albert Fuchs and Egon Wellesz, is singled out by Muchitsch as one of the three outstanding figures in the Austrian Centre and the FAM to dedicate themselves to the defence and propagation of Austrian culture in exile.[67] Both in his own *Kulturelle Schriftenreihe des Free Austrian Movement* and in *Zeitspiegel*, Ullrich wrote regularly to remind exiled Austrians of their musical heritage and to encourage them to believe in its continuing existence in emigration as well as in the possibility of a post-war cultural regeneration. Drawing inspiration, for instance, from the life and work of the celebrated exiled violinist Arnold Rosé, Ullrich writes on the occasion of Rosé's birthday:

> Even now this unbending man, whom age, cares, and the blows of fate are unable to deter, is leading his quartet and helping our country regain those sympathies forfeited by unworthy compatriots. We are delighted to have this 'Grand Old Man' of music in our midst, this great, active and productive musician and good Austrian. May he live to experience the day of Austrian freedom![68]

In his *Österreichiches Pantheon*, in April 1944, he would use the *Magic Flute* to similar symbolic and inspirational effect:

> *The Magic Flute*, at its core, is an Austrian symbol, a symbol of Austria, suffering, struggling and triumphant. And thus this immortal masterpiece by two Austrians, quite apart from its function as a work of art, quite apart from its symbolism, holds a deeper meaning for us that belongs to us alone.[69]

As mentioned above, Hermann Ullrich served the FAM as 'Kulturreferent', with particular responsibility for music. As in other cultural areas, so in music, too, the Austrian Centre and the FAM worked closely in tandem, with the FAM, like the Centre, regularly taking it upon itself to mount concerts marking specific campaigns and occasions. Thus, as part of its ambitious Austrians for Britain Campaign (August to October 1942), the FAM organized a concert in Manchester on 26 September, featuring the Rosé Quartet, that was attended by an audience of 600, including the Mayor, who announced that he was 'very proud to be [...] a friend of the Free Austrians'.[70] A further concert was organized on 16 October at the Lyric Theatre Glasgow to conclude the Campaign; here Scottish and Austrian artists performed to an audience of 500.[71] As part of its general cultural provision, the FAM also organized an 'Anschluss concert' on 9 March 1944 in the Wigmore Hall: an all-Mozart programme, this was performed by the Rostal Chamber Orchestra, with Max Rostal on violin and Dennis Brain on horn.[72] Similarly, though on a more local level, the FAM put on a concert of Austrian music (Mozart, Schubert and Strauss) in Newbury in September 1944, featuring Hilde Zweig, Norbert Brainin and Martin Lawrence with the accompanist Fritz

Berend; attended by the Mayor of Newbury, the concert set out to raise money both for the FAM itself and for Newbury Hospital.[73]

In the *FAM Rundbrief* for October 1943, Hermann Ullrich offers FAM functionaries some useful tips under the heading 'Wie veranstaltet man ein Konzert' ('How is a Concert Organized'). He runs through the basics – choice of venue, acoustic considerations, selection of performers and programme – as well as giving advice on matters of press and publicity. If necessary, so he reminds his readership, the would-be concert organizer can always turn to the FAM, 'whose Cultural Secretariat, in close collaboration with the Austrian Musicians' Group (AMG), is generally able to arrange for the engagement of a suitable artist' (pp. 4–5).

Here and elsewhere Ullrich glosses over the fact that relations between the FAM, as umbrella organization, and the affiliated AMG were not always entirely harmonious (though admittedly the evidence on this is fragmentary). In a memorandum drawn up years later, Ferdinand Rauter sets out the context within which the AMG had come into being: he recalls the difficulties experienced by refugee musicians in pursuing their careers in Britain, the additional problems caused by internment, and then – with the help of some leading figures in the British musical establishment – the formation of a Refugee Musicians Committee that succeeded in freeing individual musicians from internment, certainly, but could do little to improve their employment prospects.[74]

It was Ullrich, according to the Rauter Memorandum, who first suggested that the position of exiled Austrian musicians would be strengthened if they became an organized body, leading to much preliminary activity on the part of Ullrich and Rauter and, on 31 March 1942, to the setting up of a committee, the provisional committee of the new AMG.[75] The initial aims, as set out later in a Rauter *Zeitspiegel* article, were 'to give Austrian musicians the possibility of performing publicly and to raise money to enable gifted musicians to study'.[76] Although Rauter himself had no political affiliation, the AMG was founded within the FAM (in any case, the cultural or political base of the other leading AMG members, Hermann Ullrich and Georg Knepler) which offered the group both financial and professional advantages.[77]

While Rauter is keen to give the impression that the AMG's FAM affiliation was principally a matter of convenience, other sources suggest that, far from this, the setting up of the AMG was actually initiated by the newly founded FAM itself; and that this formed part of a wider FAM campaign to strengthen its own base. Thus, on 16 February 1942, for instance, Ullrich and Knepler were appealing to Egon Wellesz in the following manner:

The urgency of supporting the Free Austrian Movement, about which you will learn more from the enclosed, need scarcely be stressed.

An Initiative Committee under the chairmanship of Robert Neumann has undertaken to organize Austrians living in England, writers and academics, in order to lend the Free Austrian Movement greater weight.

We wish to ask you if you would play as active a role as possible in the preliminary work of the Musicians' Group that is to be established and, in any case, to accept an honorary membership of the group.[78]

The AMG made its first public appearance on the occasion of the 100th anniversary of the foundation of the Vienna Philharmonic, with a concert mounted by the AMG itself, in collaboration with the FAM and Austrian PEN, at the Wigmore Hall on 28 May 1942. This, like the Mahler concert of the preceding year, came to be seen as a landmark event in the life of the Austrian exile community in Britain: 'The centenary celebration,' in *Zeitspiegel*'s words, 'turned into a large-scale demonstration for freedom.'[79] The concert, featuring music by Mozart, Wolf and Dvorak, was performed by the Rosé String Quartet (including Rosé himself, for many years the leader of the Vienna Philharmonic), together with Ferdinand Rauter. The programme included a statement of the concert's symbolic intent:

In celebrating the orchestra's centenary we do not think of the remnant still carrying on under the famous old name but transformed into an instrument to grace Nazi functions. Many of the orchestra's best members have been dismissed, conductors banned; composers disappeared from its repertoire. The orchestra, created as an interpreter of the Austrian spirit, is for the time being dead, struck down by the Nazi invaders. But it lives on in the heart of the Austrians, to whom the restoration of Austria will bring the rebirth of the Vienna Philharmonic as a cultural institution of the nation.[80]

Moreover, the event undoubtedly derived additional weight from the fact that Rauter succeeded in persuading an eminent Englishman – no easy task in wartime conditions[81] – to address the audience in similar spirit. The task fell to John Christie, the founder of Glyndebourne, who 'celebrated the Vienna Philharmonic as part of the great Austrian cultural heritage'.[82]

This successful concert was already behind them when, in July 1942, a second meeting of the AMG was held, confirming the membership of its committee, with Rauter as chairman, Georg Knepler and Alfred Rosenzweig as deputy chairmen, Hermann Ullrich as secretary and Claire Born as treasurer. Among the items to be reported on this occasion was the work already undertaken by Rauter towards the setting up of an English support group, a Society of Friends of Austrian Music.[83]

Rauter, writing of course long after the event, explains the formation of the AMG's support group not only as a financial move – which it undoubtedly was – but also as a means of weakening the FAM's political influence on the AMG about which he himself was uneasy.[84] Muchitsch, in fact, contends that, on the strength of the proposed foundation of its Society of Friends, the AMG withdrew altogether from the FAM at the end of 1942.[85] This version of events is belied, however, by a document from 1944, a report on activities at the Austrian Centre for that year, which carries as a sub-section a 'Tätigkeitsbericht der Austrian Musicians' Group des FAM' ('Report on the Activities of the Austrian Musicians' Group of the FAM'), indicating exactly the same AMG committee composition as in 1942, including Rauter as chairman, and a flourishing membership of 75. Interestingly, the tone of this report suggests that it may well have been considered advisable within Free Austrian circles to define (and thereby confirm?) the relationship between the FAM, the AMG and its Society of Friends (from March 1943 renamed Anglo-Austrian Music Society or AAMS):

> The AMG functions as artistic advisor to the AAMS and fulfils the same function with regard to the smaller-scale Sunday afternoon events which, for technical and financial reasons, have temporarily replaced the larger AAMS concerts during the second half of 1944. Moreover, in the organization of FAM concerts (March celebration, Cultural Conference, 12 November celebration), either the AMG itself or individual committee members have played a direct or an advisory role in engaging the artists. The AMG actively supports the FAM Cultural Department by providing it with artists for concerts outside London and has repeatedly appealed to its members to perform free of charge or to accept a smaller fee such as can be afforded by the FAM's provincial branches.

Moreover, so the report continues on the AMG's 'FAM Work', the AMG was represented 'on the [FAM] Executive Committee [...] and participates in its work', being involved, *inter alia*, in FAM planning for Austrian musical life and education after the war. It should be noted, however, that despite the FAM's evident concern in this document to assert its continuing claim on the AMG, the AMG makes use of the opportunity, for its part, to define its 'Arbeitsprogramm' or programme of work in the following decidedly non-political terms: 'As representative of the professional interests of Austrian Musicians living in Great Britain [...] and, in accordance with its statutes, a non-political body, the AMG has first and foremost to fulfil those tasks that befit a professional organization.'[86]

To conclude this debate as best one can, given the incompleteness of the available evidence: while by the end of the war the non-political Anglo-Austrian Music Society appears to have quietly supplanted the FAM-affiliated Austrian Musicians' Group, as Rauter evidently wished,[87] it would probably be incorrect to suggest that any definite break with the FAM had taken place. On the contrary, the continuing presence of Georg Knepler and Hermann Ullrich within the AAMS suggests that an amicable *modus vivendi* was reached, as does, indeed, as late as September 1945, an invitation extended to the British Marxist composer Alan Bush, at Knepler's instigation, to become one of the AAMS's Councillors.[88]

Politics apart, the AMG and the AAMS between them were extremely successful in the promotion of Austrian music at the highest professional level, a development that was fostered, undoubtedly, by the interest and support of the eminent British musicians – such as Dame Myra Hess, Sir Adrian Boult and Ralph Vaughan Williams – who became the AAMS's patrons. On 15 December 1942, a third landmark concert, this one billed specifically as an 'Anglo-Austrian Concert' – at which, so it was explained in a flyer, 'to demonstrate mutual understanding and appreciation between the two countries the music of each country will be performed by musicians of the other'[89] – was put on by the AMG in the Wigmore Hall. Members of the audience were invited to join the proposed Society of Friends of the Austrian Musicians' Group and, according to Rauter, 'many of those present signed up as members'.[90] Over the following years, numerous concerts were put on by the AMG and AAMS, in which exiled Austrian musicians of the highest calibre – Peter Stadlen, Peter Schidlof and Sigmund Nissel amongst them – performed;[91] prominent British musicians also taking part on occasion included Dame Myra Hess,[92] and Benjamin Britten and Peter Pears.[93]

It was not only the professional musicians, however, who served Austria in this way in British exile, but also the young amateurs who performed for English audiences as members of the Young Austria Players, the folk-dance group and above all the renowned Young Austria Choir under its conductor Erwin Weiss and who became, in Muchitsch's words, 'the most successful instruments of exile propaganda'.[94] Closely tied to the Austrian Centre and later to the FAM, Young Austria had early on set out its aims in this area as being 'to foster Austrian culture and national characteristics among our own members and to propagate these within the host country'.[95] Weiss's Choir was not in fact established until after his release from internment; but there had been musical, including choral, activity within Young Austria from its inception, with singing an important feature of its social programme. Indeed, as already mentioned earlier in this study, in 1939, 1940, and again in 1944 songbooks were issued containing carefully selected songs to be sung 'wherever Austrian youth comes together'.[96] On a more organized level, a

'Singing and Dancing Group of Austrian Youth' was formed which gave its first public performance at an international dance event in Hyde Park on 3 June 1939.[97] Two months into the war, *Junges Österreich* was reporting on the continuing activity of its Singing and Dancing Group and was appealing for additional members in the light of the group's high propaganda value:

> Singing and dancing are not merely fun for us, they also have great significance. We young Austrians abroad must maintain and popularize the culture of our country. The English like our dances and songs and it's easy for us to gain their sympathy in this way. Therefore it's necessary that all friends who enjoy dancing and singing attend our rehearsals regularly (every Friday from 7.30 to 9.30 at the Austrian Centre). This is a really important task for us that we have to fulfil as well as we can.[98]

A Youth choir – though not yet Weiss's choir – as a separate entity from the Singing and Dancing group, appears to have been in existence by March 1940; both, it is reported, 'performed to English audiences on numerous occasions and with the greatest success'.[99] Moreover, there were other choirs, too, operating in and around the Austrian Centre: the above-mentioned choir for domestics as well as a choir formed by the 'Gemeinschaft berufstätiger Frauen' or Working Women's Group[100] and an international choir in which Young Austria participated.[101] In Birmingham, too, a Young Austria Choir was founded of which it was reported in August 1942 that it had appeared '24 times in the last three months to audiences totalling around 2000'.[102] Probably none of these could compare, though, in musical terms, with the London-based Young Austria Choir which, under Erwin Weiss, a brilliant musician and inspirational choir leader, gave many outstanding performances encompassing a range of music that frequently stretched the capabilities of its young members to their limit.[103]

In fact, the links between Young Austria and Weiss went back to pre-war days, as is clear from an exceptionally positive review of Weiss's first London concert in June 1939 that appeared in *Österreichische Jugend*:

> At the beginning of this month, our friend Erwin Weiss, who has frequently been kind enough to take part in the events of our youth group, gave a piano recital. It was extremely successful [...] We are proud that Erwin Weiss is an Austrian and we are delighted at his success. [104]

Weiss was a committed Social Democrat, a member of the Austrian Labour Club in exile, though this – for the time being at least – did not appear to present any impediment to him also working with Young Austria.[105] The first public performance of the Young Austria Choir under Weiss's leadership took place in the Wigmore Hall, on 15 May 1942, with a mixed programme that included Brahms, Schubert, and some folk music, not to mention three songs composed by Weiss himself in internment. In its review, *Young Austria* commented on the remarkable progress the choir had made over the past year, from a youth group whose repertoire had comprised 'more or less the obligatory revolutionary songs and songs for youth', to

a real choir [...] , a unified body of sound, that comes in correctly at the conductor's beat, that has mastered all dynamic gradations and can also perform pieces *a capella* [...], a real choir that is not fearful of tackling pieces by Haydn, Schubert or Brahms.[106]

So enthusiastic had the audience become that the *Zeitspiegel* review of the same concert reported 'that in the end concert goers had to be gently urged to go home by two "Bobbies" in front of the concert hall'.[107] And if *Young Austria* and *Zeitspiegel* might perhaps be accused of bias, the same can hardly be claimed of *The Times Educational Supplement* which also awarded the concert something close to a rave review:

'Young Austria' gave a concert which demonstrated in no uncertain way the determination of these young people to keep alive the spirit of their country during their temporary exile [...] Altogether these young musicians showed themselves very worthy of the great musical tradition of their country and deserve nothing but praise for their initiative and keenness.[108]

Another memorable performance by the Young Austria Choir not long after was at an 'Austrian-Soviet Rally' – part concert, part demonstration – at the Stoll Theatre on 28 June 1942, organized by the (FAM- and Austrian Centre-promoted) Austrian 22nd June Committee, as part of its Austrian-Soviet Friendship Week. A new song, 'Wir stürmen das Land' ('We're Storming the Land') – words by Erich Fried, music by Erwin Weiss – which would become closely associated with the choir, was given its first hearing on this occasion and received a rapturous reception from the 2500-strong audience.[109] As Weiss himself recalled:

That was really a sensational success, the way the song was sung in that particular situation – after all, this was before the opening of the second front. It was a mood that would not easily be evoked again in a different situation.[110]

From this point on, the Young Austria Choir was to find itself in great demand, both for small-scale events at church clubs, youth groups and the like, and for appearances such as the ones described above at more prestigious venues. At a concert at the Conway Hall, for example, on 9 June 1943, the choir combined folksongs with the demanding Brahms' *Song of Fate*, the latter constituting 'an extraordinary achievement for these young people', in Weiss's opinion.[111] This concert was lent additional weight by the presence of the British composer Alan Bush who introduced the choir 'with some kind words' as well as conducting two Russian songs himself.[112] *Young Austria* was well pleased with the concert's success, emphasizing at the same time that

> Anyone who has witnessed the application and persistence with which our singers and their conductor Erwin Weiss have been working over the past few weeks will know that this success was well deserved.

One of the last events over which Weiss presided before parting company with his choir was a visit to Wales, as guests of the Abertillery Six Bells Glee Men, in May 1944. This was evidently a great propaganda success if the enthusiastic report by Paul Sheridan, editor of the *South Wales Argus,* is anything to go by, concerning 'the instantaneous liking and understanding that seemed to grow like a mushroom in the night between you Austrians and we people here' and his recognition of the 'common link between the sufferings and anxieties and desires of Young Austria and the sufferings, anxieties and desires of the men and women of the Welsh valleys'.[113]

Weiss spoke of the events that led him to give up the choir leadership in more than one interview: he had become increasingly uneasy at the growing Communist domination of the Austrian Centre and was particularly affronted by the FAM attacks on Social Democratic leaders Oscar Pollak and Karl Czernetz.[114] Finally, on 30 May 1944, Weiss drew up his letter of resignation, explaining his position in the following terms:

> Since taking over the choir, I have endeavoured not to emphasize the differences existing between our two organizations. My hope that these two would become reconciled over the course of time has unfortunately not been fulfilled. Regrettably their differences have increased still further. The truly low level of your propaganda against my friends of the A[ustrian] L[abour] C[lub] makes it impossible for me to continue to appear on stage with the choir and thereby give the impression, however slight, of being in agreement with it.[115]

Despite the political difficulties, however, Weiss much regretted having to give up his choir leadership – an emotion clearly evident from the letter's conclusion in which he expressed the hope that 'you will find someone who can take over the choir so that all the work that has been done so far will not have been in vain'.[116]

Weiss's departure came as a shock to the members of the Young Austria Choir who had evidently received no prior intimation of the fact that trouble was brewing. For a while Fritz Berend attempted to fill the gap but his seriousness of demeanour, as compared with Weiss's lightness of touch, failed to meet with choir approval. There followed a period in which choir members ran the choir themselves, with Rudi Lenk as accompanist and Schlomo Kesten as conductor; and finally, fairly late on, the Viennese Dr H. Riesenfeld assumed the choir leadership, a post in which he remained until the choir's dissolution.[117]

In the meantime the concerts continued, assuming an increasingly politicized form as the war drew towards its close. There was a rally-cum-concert of Russian and Austrian music, for instance, at the Porchester Hall on 28 June 1944, a month after Weiss's resignation, in aid of the General Vatutin Fund of the Joint Committee for Soviet Aid, at which the Young Austria Choir performed one of its specialities, Khachaturian's 'Song of Stalin', as well as some new Soviet songs and Russian and Austrian folksongs.[118] Another Porchester Hall event, at which the choir, under the baton of Fritz Berend, provided the musical programme, was a FAM mass demonstration on 13 November 1944, to mark the anniversary of the foundation of the First Austrian Republic and to anticipate the forthcoming liberation of Vienna.[119]

The Young Austria Choir finally celebrated the Austrian liberation on 2 June 1945 at the St Martin's School of Art where they were joined by their friends from Wales, the Abertillery Six Bells Glee Men. The jointly conceived programme, conducted by Rudi Lenk, for the Austrians, and by a Welsh conductor, consisted of Austrian, Welsh and international songs (including 'revolutionary songs of various nations'), and was dubbed 'a triumph of Anglo-Austrian friendship' by Hans Ungar, reviewing for *Young Austria*. For the rest, Ungar's piece was, in fact, a coded attack on Weiss (for, by implication, having harboured inappropriate choral pretensions):

> Young Austria can be proud of its choir for being able, singlehandedly and without professional help, to perform such a programme [...] The selection of works performed was, for the first time in the history of our choir, a perfect one. Firstly it was vocally well suited to our choir members and secondly it constituted a good balance of what one expects from an *Austrian youth choir*.[120]

The choir was evidently still flourishing in 1946, being referred to as 'this very active Organization' in connection with a concert it was giving in

March at the Austrian Centre, Hampstead. By then Dr Riesenfeld had
taken over and, in *Zeitspiegel*'s opinion, the new choir leader 'has in a short
time significantly improved precision, intonation and nuancing of
expression'.[121] As former choir member Schlomo Kesten recalls,
however, musically speaking the choir was never the same without Weiss.
Yet if – to quote Kesten again – the choir conceived its principal task as
being to carry out propaganda for Austria,[122] then this it achieved
successfully throughout its existence.

It has already been indicated that detailed plans for a post-war Austria,
in cultural as in other areas, had been drawn up by the Free Austrian
Movement some time before the end of hostilities. As far as music was
concerned, planning was carried out within the FAM's 'Sonderkomitee
für den Wiederaufbau des österreichischen Musiklebens nach dem Krieg'
('Special Committee for the Reconstruction of Austrian Musical Life after
the War'), set up at the Second Cultural Conference under the
distinguished chairmanship of Egon Wellesz.[123] It is recorded that, in
addition to Wellesz, six prominent AMG members also sat on the
committee,[124] one of whom was almost certainly Hermann Ullrich;
however, its further composition is unknown. The Special Committee
had derived its impetus from Wellesz's blueprint speech at the Cultural
Conference in which he had set out his ideas for an Austrian musical life
of the future.

In this, Wellesz had considered the future role of the established
musical institutions, concluding, for instance, that while the Vienna
Opera, with its international repertoire, should be left to continue much
as before the war, both the Volksoper and Ravag (the Austrian
Broadcasting Corporation) were in need of complete restructuring. As for
the Salzburg Festival – an interesting, if incorrect, prediction this, in the
light of future developments – Wellesz found it hard to imagine that this
would resume 'for the foreseeable future after the war'. Moreover since,
in his opinion, one of the great problems of the past had resided in 'the
ageing of Austrian musical life', it would now be essential to breathe fresh
life into Austrian music. One of the ways in which to accomplish this
might be through the resumption and promotion of the 'Arbeiterkonzert'
or Workers' Concert, an institution that had achieved a high standard in
Vienna before the war and that could now perhaps form 'the basis of
musical education in Austria [...] , through which a new generation of
Austrian composers can find an audience'. As for music training, while
future teachers at the universities and music academies should aim to
preserve the great Austrian musical tradition, they should also be
outward-looking and open to new ideas. Furthermore they should include
in their ranks 'staff members from all countries and of European
standing', in keeping with the essentially multicultural nature of Austrian
music, for – the internationalist note was, of course, central to FAM

cultural policy by this point – 'it is in the resumption of its mission to unite nations, interrupted only for a short period, that I see the future of Austrian music'.[125]

By March 1945, the Wellesz Committee had issued a seven-page 'Memorandum über den Wiederaufbau des Musiklebens und der Musikerziehung in Österreich nach dem Kriege' ('Memorandum concerning the Reconstruction of Musical Life and Musical Education in Austria after the War') which was published in English by the FAM and sent out 'to leading Allied authorities as well as to prominent personalities in the musical life of Great Britain and the free world'.[126] Although no copy of the actual Memorandum has come to light, its chief recommendations, which appear to have gone quite some way beyond Wellesz's original suggestions, were reported on in *Zeitspiegel* later that month. First and foremost, all Nazis and Germans, 'without regard to rank and name', together with any institutions that the Germans might have established, were to be eliminated from Austrian musical life. This would be accompanied by the setting up of a 'Musikzentralstelle' or Music Centre, to be composed of delegates representing the various branches of the music profession and answerable to the Ministry of Education. Both in the field of music training and in the devising of concert programmes, it was essential

that greater stress be placed on the Austrian musical tradition and on contemporary Austrian music than was done in the past, and that, in particular, the Austrian character of our music should be emphasized in place of the previous pernicious practice of representing Austrian music as a part of 'German music'. Appropriate attention should be paid to the music of our friendly neighbouring nations, in particular the Slav nations, as to that of the great democratic nations such as the Soviet Union, England and France.[127]

Other recommendations included a short-term and longer-term restructuring of the Vienna Opera, and a series of democratizing measures aimed at improving the Opera House's accessibility – ideas that did not figure in Wellesz's original speech but that would appear rather to derive from a Hermann Ullrich piece, 'Die Wiener Oper' ('The Vienna Opera'), that was published in *Zeitspiegel* at very much the same time, i.e. October 1944.[128] So close, in fact, would the overall similarity of concept – with the exception of the 'Musikzentralstelle' scheme – seem to be, that it is tempting to conclude that Ullrich rather than Wellesz was the Memorandum's chief architect.

It was at around this same time, too, that Hermann Ullrich was involved in another cultural planning exercise within the framework of the FAM's 'Arbeitsgemeinschaft für Zusammenarbeit mit der

Tschechoslowakei' ('Working Group on Cooperation with Czechoslovakia'), and indeed he is known to have prepared drafts on Czech-Austrian collaboration in the fields of both music and theatre.[129] These drafts, like the Wellesz Committee Memorandum, are apparently no longer extant; however, Ullrich's interest in promoting future Czech-Austrian musical collaboration is evident from several of his writings at this time, including the programmatic 'The Vienna Opera', in which he introduces his plan for the internationalization of post-war Austrian opera with a plea for 'the establishment of close collaboration with our friendly neighbours, in particular Czechoslovakia, many of whose problems are similar to ours'.[130]

Georg Knepler, too, continued to address himself to the future of Austrian music in the immediate post-war period. In January 1946, he published an essay in *Zeitspiegel*, in prescriptive though still reasonably optimistic vein, in which he endorses and expands on the Memorandum of the Wellesz Committee, particularly commending, as its central core, the plan for the 'Musikzentralstelle', to be made up, it will be recalled, of representatives from all areas of Austrian musical life. For, while the state had a large role to play in the fields of denazification and democratization, 'a new musical life in Austria can only be established by the Austrian musicians'. Thus he chides those exiled musicians who had delayed making plans to return to Austria, while acknowledging, certainly, that, in the conditions then prevailing, Austrian musicians would be called upon to demonstrate 'a certain pioneer spirit, a small degree of enthusiasm, even perhaps a certain willingness to make sacrifices'.[131] Three months later, however, in a further *Zeitspiegel* piece, this time actually written from Vienna, Knepler would concede that not everything was proceeding in Austrian cultural life quite as had been hoped, or at least not in the crucial area of denazification, citing the following case in point:

> In one of the Viennese Adult Education Colleges there is currently a man teaching who during the Third Reich published a piece on the history of music which was in complete agreement with the spirit of National Socialism [...] Mendelssohn, Gustav Mahler, Schoenberg do not exist for this man, and for him Austrian music is indistinguishable from German music. I wonder what this man is teaching his students today about Austrian music history?[132]

Clearly, after the end of the war, with the question of returning home high on the agenda, *Zeitspiegel* appears to have been keen to present a generally positive picture of cultural developments in Austria, as in 'Kunst, Kultur und Erziehung' ('Art, Culture and Education') on 26 May 1945, for example, which informed readers of the at least partial resumption of theatrical and musical life in Vienna. Among those institutions that had recommenced activity was the Vienna Philharmonic, no less, though a shadow was cast over this otherwise encouraging news by the fact that Erich Kleiber had not been recalled from exile as their conductor, as *Zeitspiegel* would have wished. Instead, the orchestra was to be conducted by the politically compromised Clemens Krauss – though 'one has to assume only temporarily'.[133] Similarly, individual musical exiles in Britain appear to have hoped, at least initially, that their planning for the new Austria had not been in vain, with Ullrich, for instance, on 29 October 1945, returning a radio script to Wellesz that, in his opinion, constituted 'a proof of the fact [...] that Austria has not forgotten you'.[134]

Disillusionment, however, both in the columns of *Zeitspiegel* and in the ranks of the émigrés, was not long in making itself felt. On 4 August 1945, *Zeitspiegel* was reporting with deep disapproval not only that the Salzburg Festival was to resume almost immediately – 'would it not, in the given circumstances, have been more dignified to wait a year?' – but also that 35% of the participating artists were to be Germans, 'precisely what we don't need in Salzburg'.[135] As for the exiled musicians, a letter from Alfred Rosenzweig in Britain to Ernst Krenek in the USA, dated 1 April 1948, speaks for itself:

And Klemperer who was here for a few days [...], told me that, despite all the efforts of his agent in Vienna, he had been unable to obtain a single engagement, and it had been just the same in Salzburg. For the Nazis like Herr Böhm and Oberstandartenführer Karajan, among others, are in control of everything and are already exerting influence on the various organizations. For example, the notorious Gründgens – of course with the agreement of the American military authorities – has been appointed permanent director of opera productions in the Salzburg Festival. Here we can see the results of the insane policies of the Anglo-American military authorities for whom Nazism has by no means had its day but rather is a philosophy of life that they actively promote [...] The situation in Austria has become so confused that for instance Friedrich Wildgans [music consultant to Viktor Matejka, Communist Councillor for Culture and Education in Vienna] said in a discussion with Klemperer: 'Our only hope for an improvement of the situation lies in the division of Austria which will presumably come about along with the division of Germany.' Then Salzburg would become the highly nazified musical centre of the Anglo-American western zone and Vienna the musical centre of the Russian eastern zone and we would finally have the opportunity to bring conductors like Klemperer and Scherchen, whose appointment is still being effectively blocked by the Nazis, back to Vienna.[136]

As Georg Knepler later admitted of himself and his fellow Free Austrians: 'We misjudged the situation completely.'[137]

In Britain, in the meantime, émigré musical life continued for a while along familiar lines. A 'Felix Braun Celebration on the Occasion of the Poet's 60th Birthday', for instance, was put on by the FAM at the Austrian Centre's new Hampstead address, 69 Greencroft Gardens, on 18 November 1945, featuring music by Purcell and Mozart as well as recitations from Braun's writings;[138] and a concert of Schubert, Kreisler, Sarasate and some Austrian folksongs, performed by Emmy Heim, Inge Markowitz and Peter Schidlof, was organized on 15 February 1946 at the Livingstone Hall, Westminster, by the FAM-affiliated Association of Austrian Doctors to raise money for medical supplies for Austria.[139] In the summer of 1946, Ernst Possony was responsible for a concert performance of *Carmen* at the Austrian Centre Paddington, 'a great success' that was attended by Richard Tauber;[140] a repeat performance, by popular request, is advertised in the very last issue of *Zeitspiegel*.[141]

Likewise, Hermann Ullrich continued to publish his *Kulturelle Schriftenreihe des Free Austrian Movement* until permitted to return home in 1946. A letter from Ullrich to Wellesz on FAM notepaper, dated July 1945, on the subject of his planned Beethoven number, allows the reader an insight into Ullrich himself and his cultural calling:

> Even though this publication is only read by Austrians and above and beyond them by perhaps a dozen German-speaking English people, nevertheless my task strikes me as an important one and not one to be neglected. Our compatriots, the exiled Austrians here and abroad, look to us for cultural publications [...] Neither in the provinces nor abroad do the exiled Austrians enjoy the same possibilities as we have, therefore they demand guidance and stimulation from us. I consider it our duty on this occasion to bring Beethoven's significance to the attention of the exiled Austrians and to look at his personality from various points of view. I am sure that you will agree with me on this and that you will regard this task, even though it differs essentially from our original plan that was geared to the English public, as significant and important.[142]

Ullrich, who had already persuaded scholars of the order of Hans F. Redlich, Hans Holländer and Hans Gál to contribute to the volume, was hopeful of enlisting Wellesz as a further contributor.[143]

Later in 1945, Wellesz celebrated his 60th birthday, an occasion that was marked by an appropriate tribute in *Zeitspiegel*, proudly positioning the composer in the ranks of Austria's 'finest sons'.[144] It was obviously of the greatest importance to the Free Austrians in terms of cultural propaganda to be able to count on a man of Wellesz's stature, a fact that is reflected in the FAM's official letter of congratulation to him:

> We Austrians in exile, an exile that we hope will soon be reaching its end, are proud to be able to count as one of us a personality of your importance, a leading representative of modern Austrian music and at the same time an internationally recognized authority in the field of musicology. It is with pleasure and with gratitude that we recall your constant readiness to help in our cultural work, your participation in the Second Cultural Conference and many other occasions on which you gave active and effective support to the Austrian cause.[145]

In their *Orpheus im Exil*, Pass, Scheit and Svoboda observe that, of the cultural programme organized at and by the Austrian Centre, 'the musical side of its activities is perhaps not generally very well known'.[146] Yet the musical provision was extensive: as Georg Knepler recalled, 'at the Austrian Centre we put on hundreds of concerts'.[147] These went some way towards answering the deep cultural needs of the Austrian émigré population, while also fulfilling an important consolatory function: Ernst Possony recorded in the closing number of the *Austrian Centre Bulletin* that artists who performed at the Centre had felt it their duty 'to soothe the deep sorrow of their compatriots, to restore for a few hours what was so sorely missed'.[148]

However, there was very much more to it than that. Whilst all the Austrian Centre's and Free Austrian Movement's cultural endeavours were directed towards the same end, namely the promotion of the Austrian cause, it must be reiterated that music, Austrian music, constituted a particularly powerful propaganda tool, both where the exiled Austrians and where the British were concerned, because of its indisputable international reputation and appeal. Through the medium of music, the Free Austrian cultural aims, defined by Jenö Kostmann as 'to maintain, defend and propagate the Austrian cultural heritage',[149] were convincingly pursued and fulfilled.

Notes

1   Georg Knepler, as cited in Walter Pass, Gerhard Scheit and Wilhelm Svoboda, *Orpheus im Exil: Die Vertreibung der österreichischen Musik von 1938 bis 1945*, Vienna 1995, p. 127.

2   Georg Knepler, 'Musik im Austrian Centre', *Zeitspiegel*, 15 June 1941, p. 7.

3   Anna Hornik, *This is Austria: The Story of a Beautiful Country*, London 1942, p. 20.

4   Georg Knepler, *Five Years of the Austrian Centre*, London [1944], p. 6.

5   Eva Schmidt-Kolmer, 'Exil in England 1938 bis 1946', unpublished ms., c. 1990, in private possession of Ruth Kolmer, Vienna, p. 10.

6   See 'Typoskript der Eröffnungsrede von Friedrich Otto Hertz zur Versammlung der Österreicher zum 11. März 1939 (gemeinsame Veranstaltung der Austrian Self-Aid, der Council of Austrians in Great Britain und des Austrian Circle for Arts and Science)', Friedrich Otto Hertz Papers, Archive for the History of Sociology in Austria [AGSÖ], Graz 18/5.15.

7   For programme, see Friedrich Otto Hertz Papers, AGSÖ, 28/5.15.

8   As reported in 'Österreichisches Emigrantenheim in London', *Pariser Tageszeitung*, 24 March 1939, p. 3.

9   'Generalversammlung des Klubs Austrian Centre, London, 26 Juni 1939', Friedrich Otto Hertz Papers, AGSÖ, 18/5.15, p. 7.

10   The Music Group was founded in April 1939 by and on behalf of Austrian musicians in England, with an opening concert at the Royal College of Music.

11   On this, see for example Wolfgang Muchitsch, 'The Cultural Policy of Austrian Refugee Organisations in Great Britain' in Edward Timms and Ritchie Robertson (eds.), *Austrian Exodus: The Creative Achievements of Refugees from National Socialism (Austrian Studies VI)*, Edinburgh 1995, pp. 26 f.

12   See, for example, Hans Gál, 'Brahms, der Wahl-Österreicher', in *Österreichisches Pantheon: Kulturblätter des FAM*, April 1944, pp. 6-8 (in which he claims that the attraction of Vienna for both Beethoven and Brahms was the 'musical atmosphere of this city which is incomparable and inexplicable').

13   Friedrich Otto Hertz Papers, AGSÖ, 28/5.15.

14   'Generalversammlung des Klubs Austrian Centre', p. 8.

15   See *First Annual Report of the Austrian Centre*, London 1940, p. 24.

16   *First Annual Report*, p. 13.

17   *Ibid.*, p. 30.

18   *Zeitspiegel*, 'Sonderausgabe' (Special Issue) [May 1941], [p. 3].

19   Wellesz was in exile in Oxford.

20   Georg Knepler, interview with Richard Dove, Berlin, 2 November 1996.

21   'Georg Knepler über sein Exil in England: Aus einem Gespräch mit der Hamburger Arbeitsgruppe Exilmusik am 3. Dezember 1992 in Hamburg', p. 8.

22   See 'Veranstaltungen', *Zeitspiegel*, 23 March 1941, p. 6.

23   See flyer entitled '3 Sunday Morning Concerts' (26 January 1941, 2 February 1941, 9 February 1941) in private possession of Georg Knepler, Berlin.

24   See *Österreichische Nachrichten*, February 1940, p. 7.

25   Georg Knepler, as cited in Jutta Raab Hansen, *NS-verfolgte Musiker in England: Spuren deutscher und österreichischer Flüchtlinge in der britischen Musikkultur*, Hamburg 1996, p. 125.

26   Programme for the two performances (on 22 and 29 November 1942) in private possession of Georg Knepler. For review, see 'Die Zauberflöte im Austrian Centre', *Zeitspiegel*, 28 November 1942, p. 7.

27   See Raab Hansen, *op. cit.*, p. 318.

28   For a more detailed analysis of the Thursday evening series, see *ibid*, pp. 311f. Flyer from July 1941 advertising 'A Series of Concerts on Thursdays at 7.30' in private possession of Georg Knepler.

29   See *Österreichische Nachrichten*, February 1940, p. 7.

30   Austrian Musical Circle activities were sometimes also extended to the Austrian Centre's Paddington branch and, from 1944, even to Manchester, where Lotte Eisler served as Secretary (see 'Austrian Musical Circle, Manchester', *Zeitspiegel*, 10 June 1944, p. 4).

31   'Konzerte in Februar', *Zeitspiegel*, 30 January 1943, p. 7.

32   'Musik: Variationen über ein Heurigenlied', *Zeitspiegel*, 29 May 1943, pp. 7-8.

33   'Musikalische Ereignisse', *Zeitspiegel*, 28 August 1943, p. 9. Fritz Berend, in fact a German, played a leading role in Austrian Musical Circle events and in musical activities at the Austrian Centre generally.

34   'Bachs "Bauernkantate"', *Zeitspiegel*, 27 November 1943, p. 9.

35   'Kulturnotizen', *Zeitspiegel*, 31 July 1943, p. 10.

36   'Musical Circle' (letter from S.K., London N.W.3), *Zeitspiegel*, 10 June 1944, p. 9.

37   See advertisement in *Zeitspiegel*, 28 April 1945, p. 9.

38   Raab Hansen, *op. cit.*, pp. 317-18.

39   *Ibid.*, p. 313.

40   Knepler is known to have read Klahr's writings in *Weg und Ziel* while in British exile (see Pass, Scheit and Svoboda, *op. cit.*, p. 133).

41   'Georg Knepler über sein Exil in England', p. 8. Despite this distinction, Knepler and other Austrians still appeared regularly at the FGLC.

42   Georg Knepler, 'What is Mozart to us?', *Young Austria*, August 1941, p. 5.

43   Georg Knepler, as cited in Pass, Scheit and Svoboda, *op. cit.*, p. 133.

44   Egon Wellesz, 'The Symphonies of Gustav Mahler', *The Music Review*, I, no. 1 (February 1940), pp. 2-22.

45   Programme held at Documentation Archive of Austrian Resistance, Vienna, [DÖW], 7207. For reviews, see 'Gustav Mahler: A Memorial Concert', *The Times*, 20 May 1941, p. 6; 'Gustav Mahler Gedächtniskonzert', *Zeitspiegel*, 25 May 1941, p. 4.

46   Georg Knepler to BBC Director of Music (on Council of Austrians notepaper), 5 May 1941, BBC Written Archives Caversham [WAC], R Cont 1, Georg Knepler, Artists, File 1: 1936-62.

47   'Gustav Mahler', Memorandum from B. Douglas to BBC Director of Music, 19 May 1941, BBC WAC, R Cont 1, Irene Eisinger, Artists, 1934-1962.

48   *Zeitspiegel*, 5 December 1942, p. 7.

49   See *Austrians in Great Britain*, London [1943], p. 5.

50   28 August 1943, p. 9. Cf. Knepler on music in England at that time: 'To my surprise there were some excellent musicians performing classical music. During the war, for instance, in bomb-torn London, at the time of the

blackout and the nightly air raids, I heard Mozart's string quintets – performed, I believe, over two or three evenings. It was one of the most impressive musical experiences that I can remember' (cited in Pass, Scheit and Svoboda, *op. cit.*, pp. 130-31).

51 On p. 6.

52 In the issue entitled *Beethoven: zum Gedächtnis seines 175. Geburtstages*, pp. 8-10.

53 *The Music Review*, VII, no. 1 (February 1946), pp. 41-50.

54 Programme in private possession of Georg Knepler (for review, see 'We hit back', *Zeitspiegel*, 6 December 1941, p. 9).

55 See 'Norwegisch-österreichisches Konzert', *Zeitspiegel*, 23 May 1942, p. 8.

56 See A[lfred] R[osenzweig], 'Musik der Alliierten', *Zeitspiegel*, 28 February 1942, p. 9.

57 Programme in private possession of Georg Knepler.

58 BBC WAC, R Cont 1, Georg Knepler, Artists, File 1: 1936-62.

59 See 'Österreichische Lieder im BBC', *Zeitspiegel*, 21 April 1945, p. 5 (the broadcast took place on 11 April 1945).

60 W. Gross, 'Recital of Music Banned in Germany', on p. 7.

61 Programme in the Archives of the Anglo-Austrian Music Society [AAMS], Institute of Germanic & Romance Studies, London.

62 On p. 6.

63 'Kammermusikabend: Wigmore Hall', *Zeitspiegel*, 3 September 1942, p. 7.

64 See 'Österr. Kulturkonferenz', *Zeitspiegel*, 22 August 1942, p. 7.

65 As reported by J[osef] K[almer], 'Österreichische Kulturkonferenz', *Zeitspiegel*, 5 September 1942, p. 7. No transcript of Deutsch's speech has come to light.

66 Speech reproduced in *Zeitspiegel*, 4 November 1944, pp. 6-7.

67 In Muchitsch, 'The Cultural Policy of Austrian Refugee Organisations in Great Britain', pp. 36 f.

68 'Arnold Rosé', *Zeitspiegel*, 16 October 1943, p. 7.

69 '*Die Zauberflöte*. Geschichte, Symbolik und Deutung', in *Kulturblätter des FAM* (precursor of *Kulturelle Schriftenreihe des Free Austrian Movement*), April 1944, p. 18.

70 See '"Austrians for Britain" Campaign', *Austrian News*, November 1942, p. 3. On 15 October 1942, as part of the same campaign, Rosé also performed at the Dorchester Hotel in a big concert organized by the Austria Office (at that time still a constituent part of the FAM).

71 *Austrian News*, November 1942, p. 3 (programme held at DÖW 21218).

72 Programme reproduced in Raab Hansen, *op. cit.*, p. 323.

73 'Konzert in Newbury', *Zeitspiegel*, 14 October 1944, p. 7.

74 Ferdinand Rauter, 'Die Gründung der Anglo-Austrian Musikgesellschaft (Anglo-Austrian Music Society): Zusammengestellt aus Erinnerungen, Tagebuchnotizen und Dokumenten', unpublished ms., n.d. [1973], DÖW 8462. For Refugee Musicians Committee, see also, National Archives, London, HO 213/871.

75   Rauter Memorandum, p. 6.

76   Ferdinand Rauter, 'Die Anglo-Austrian Music Society', *Zeitspiegel*, 28 July 1945, p. 5.

77   See Rauter Memorandum, pp. 5 f.

78   Held at the Austrian National Library [ÖNB], Vienna, Music Collection, F13 Wellesz, 1653.

79   See J[oseph] K[almer], 'Die Wiener Philharmonikerfeier', *Zeitspiegel*, 6 June 1942, p. 7.

80   Programme held at DÖW 19119.

81   See Rauter Memorandum, p. 6.

82   'Die Wiener Philharmonikerfeier', *Zeitspiegel*, 6 June 1942, p. 7. To mark the same centenary, the Austrian Centre and Young Austria put on a second Wigmore Hall concert on 11 June 1942, also featuring Rauter and the Rosé Quartet, with a programme of Schubert, Brahms and Beethoven.

83   See Austrian Musicians' Group, *Mitteilungsblatt für Juli 1942*, 9 August 1942, in AAMS Archives, London.

84   Rauter Memorandum, p. 6.

85   Muchitsch, 'The Cultural Policy of Austrian Refugee Organisations in Great Britain', p. 34.

86   See 'Tätigkeitsbericht Austrian Centre 1944', London 1944, DÖW 0316/23, pp. 14-15.

87   No references to the AMG beyond 1944 have come to light.

88   See Miss F.M. Fairbrother, AAMS Honorary Secretary, to Alan Bush, 3 September 1945, in Alan Bush Papers, in private possession of Dr Rachel O'Higgins, Cambridge.

89   Held at DÖW 8462.

90   Rauter Memorandum, p. 7.

91   See 'Österreichische Konzerte 1941-1945', in AAMS Archives, London.

92   For instance, on 27 October 1943 at the Wigmore Hall, to mark Arnold Rosé's 80th birthday.

93   Britten and Pears performed at an AAMS concert on 21 June 1945 at Cecil Sharp House, with an Anglo-Austrian programme of Purcell, Schubert, Britten and Berg (part of which was transmitted to Austria by the BBC).

94   Muchitsch, 'The Cultural Policy of Austrian Refugee Organizations in Great Britain', p. 30.

95   One of the aims set out in the Young Austria membership card, as reproduced in Völker Kaukoreit and Jörg Thunecke (eds.), *126 Westbourne Terrace: Erich Fried im Londoner Exil (1938-1945)*, Vienna 2001, p. 16.

96   See Preface to *Unser Lied*, London 1940, [p. i].

97   As reported in 'The Singing Refugee', *Junges Österreich*, First December issue 1939, p. 3.

98   'Aus den Gruppen: London – Tanz- und Singgruppe', *Junges Österreich*, First November issue 1939, p. 7.

99   As reported in 'Junges Österreich', *Österreichische Nachrichten*, March 1940, p. 5.

100 See, for example, 'Singen macht froh!', *Frau in Arbeit: Periodical of the Working Refugee Women*, December 1940, p. 6. This choir was open to German and Czech women as well as to Austrians.

101 See 'Internationales Jugendtreffen in Camden Town', *Young Austria*, end March 1941, p. 8.

102 'Kulturnotizen', *Zeitspiegel*, 29 August 1942, p. 7.

103 As reported by former choir member Schlomo Kesten (interview with present author, 2 January 2001, London), and elsewhere.

104 'Ein Konzert von Erwin Weiss', *Österreichische Jugend*, June 1939, pp. 3-4. See also the generally favourable review 'An Austrian Pianist', *Daily Telegraph*, 9 June 1939, p. 12.

105 On this, see Interview with Professor Erwin Weiss, 28 November 1990, DÖW, Interview 732, p. 17, in which the interviewer (Muchitsch) points to the censure meted out by the Social Democrats towards Theodor Kramer for appearing at the Austrian Centre. Weiss surmises that in his own case the Social Democrats valued the links with Erich Fried that his work with Young Austria offered.

106 'Zukunftsmusik in der Wigmore Hall', *Young Austria*, [end May 1942], pp. 1-2.

107 J[oseph] K[almer], '"Young Austria" Konzert in der Wigmore Hall', *Zeitspiegel*, 23 May 1942, p. 7.

108 'Austrian Concert', *The Times Educational Supplement*, 23 May 1942, p. 244.

109 For the song and its reception, see *Jugend voran*, November 1942, pp. 14-15. For the programme for the 'Austrian-Soviet Rally', see DÖW 7207.

110 Weiss Interview (DÖW 1990), p. 17.

111 *Ibid.*, p. 18. For programme, see DÖW 16975.

112 See 'Osterreichisches Chorkonzert', *Die Zeitung*, 11 June 1943, p. 8.

113 'Young Austria visits South Wales', as reproduced in *Young Austria*, 20 May 1944, p. 1.

114 Weiss Interview (DÖW 1990); Interview reported in Pass, Scheit and Svoboda, *op. cit.*, from 28 September 1993, pp. 143-45; Interview with the present author, 25 April 2001, Vienna.

115 As cited in Pass, Scheit and Svoboda, *op. cit.*, p. 143.

116 *Ibid.*, p. 144. Pass, Scheit and Svoboda also cite Young Austria Chairman Fritz Walter's obliquely menacing reply: 'We note not only your resignation as leader of our choir but also your report on your political motives for this. It represents an expression of your hostility towards the Austrian Freedom Front and our organization. As such this letter remains a document of your "political views".'

117 Kesten Interview.

118 As advertised in *Zeitspiegel*, 24 June 1944, p. 10.

119 As advertised in *Zeitspiegel*, 4 November 1944, p. 8. For review of event, see 'Der 12. November: Eine Botschaft Minister Ripkas – Freiheit, Unabhängigkeit und Kooperation mit den slawischen Nachbarn', *Zeitspiegel*, 18 November 1944, p. 3.

120 'Österreichisches Befreiungskonzert', *Jung-Österreich*, 2 June 1945, p. 4.

121 '"Young Austria" – Chor', *Zeitspiegel*, 9 March 1946, p. 8.

122 Kesten Interview.

123 As reported in 'Kulturkonferenz des FAM', *Zeitspiegel*, 28 October 1944, p. 8.

124 See 'Tätigkeitsbericht Austrian Centre 1944', p. 15.

125 Egon Wellesz, 'Zum Wiederaufbau des Musiklebens in Österreich: Rede auf der Kulturkonferenz des FAM Oktober 1944', *Zeitspiegel*, 4 November 1944, pp. 6 f. It was also published in English translation as 'The Reconstruction of Musical Life in Austria' in *Austrian News*, mid-March 1945, pp. 4-6.

126 See 'Mitteilungen des Sekretariats des FAM', *Österreichspiegel*, 7 March 1945, p. 19.

127 'Wiederaufbau des Musiklebens', *Zeitspiegel*, 24 March 1945, p. 7.

128 'Die Wiener Oper: Gedanken und Ausblicke anläßlich des 75-jährigen Bestandes des Hauses', *Zeitspiegel*, 28 October 1944, pp. 8 f.

129 See 'Tätigkeitsbericht Austrian Centre 1944', p. 15.

130 *Zeitspiegel*, 28 October 1944, p. 9.

131 Georg Knepler, 'Ein neues Musikleben in Österreich?', *Zeitspiegel*, 12 January 1946, p. 7.

132 Georg Knepler, 'Gibt es eine Kulturkrise in Österreich? Ein Appell an die geistigen Arbeiter im Radio Wien am 5. April 1946', *Zeitspiegel*, 20 April 1946, p. 14.

133 On pp. 8 f. In the event, Kleiber was not able to reestablish himself in Vienna.

134 ÖNB, Music Collection, F13 Wellesz 1249. In fact, Wellesz remained in emigration for the rest of his life.

135 'Die Salzburger Festspiele', *Zeitspiegel*, 4 August 1945, p. 3.

136 As given in Gerhard Scheit, 'Zwei Arten, das Verhältnis von Musik und Politik zu beschreiben', *Aufrisse*, vol. 5, no. 2 (1984), p. 45.

137 Georg Knepler, as cited in Scheit, Pass and Svoboda, *op. cit.*, pp. 133 f.

138 For review, see 'Felix Braun-Feier', *Zeitspiegel*, 1 December 1945, p. 6.

139 As announced in 'Volkslieder-Abend', *Zeitspiegel*, 9 February 1946, p. 8.

140 See '"Carmen" im Austrian Centre', *Zeitspiegel*, 13 July 1946, p. 11. The performance took place on 7 July.

141 *Zeitspiegel*, 24 August 1946, p. 16. The opera was to be repeated the following day.

142 Ullrich to Wellesz, 23 July 1945, ÖNB, Music Collection, F13 Wellesz 1249.

143 In the event, contributions by Holländer, Redlich, Wellesz and Ullrich himself, though not Gál, appeared in the January 1946 issue of the *Kulturelle*

Schriftenreihe des Free Austrian Movement, entitled *Beethoven: Zum Gedächtnis seines 175. Geburtstages.*

144   Hans F. Redlich, 'Zu Egon Wellesz' sechzigstem Geburtstag', *Zeitspiegel,* 27 October 1945, p. 7.

145   FAM (Eva Kolmer and Hermann Ullrich) to Wellesz, 19 October 1945, ÖNB, Music Collection, F13 Wellesz 1249. It is perhaps surprising that Wellesz's substantial contribution to Free Austrian activities has been overlooked by his biographers (cf., Pass, Scheit and Svoboda, *op. cit.,* p. 199, where a similar observation is recorded concerning Wilhelm Waldstein's otherwise informative biography of Hans Gál).

146   Pass, Scheit and Svoboda, *op. cit.,* p. 127.

147   'Georg Knepler über sein Exil in England', p. 8.

148   'Es nehmen Abschied: Der Kammersänger', *Austrian Centre Bulletin,* 'Abschieds-Nummer' (closing issue), [January 1947], [p. 4].

149   Jenö Kostmann, 'Österreichische Kulturarbeit – eine Kampfaufgabe', *Zeitspiegel,* 30 May 1942, p. 8.

PART THREE

THE 'ROBINSON CRUSOES OF PADDINGTON' AND THE BRITISH: RELATIONS BETWEEN THE FREE AUSTRIANS AND THEIR BRITISH HOSTS

CHARMIAN BRINSON

When the leading Austrian exiles arrived in Britain in 1938, they already possessed a number of ready-made British connections that could be drawn on for assistance and support during the years of emigration. Eva Kolmer, in particular, who would become the first Secretary both of the Council of Austrians and of the Austrian Centre, and who later played a pivotal role in the Free Austrian Movement, was especially skilled in building up contacts within the British host community: even prior to her emigration, largely through her work for the *Wiener Wirtschafts-Woche*, she had cultivated the acquaintance of such prominent Britons as the Liberal feminist Margery Corbett Ashby, the Liberal MP Geoffrey Mander, the editor of the *Spectator* Henry Wilson Harris, and the eccentric but influential Duchess of Atholl.[1] Thus, when Austrian Self-Aid was founded in April 1938, it enjoyed the patronage of Mrs Corbett Ashby and the Duchess of Atholl as well as that of the Cardinal Archbishop of Westminster and the Chief Rabbi, among others. The Council (originally Committee) of Austrians, established a few months later in September 1938, benefited from the support of further prominent British champions of the refugees, including the Archbishop of York, Lord Hailey (the Chairman of the Coordinating Committee for Refugees) and the radical lawyer and Labour MP D.N. Pritt.

On 3 February 1939, Eva Kolmer's letter appeared in *The Spectator* enlisting the British public's help in her 'very ambitious plan', the setting up of the Austrian Centre as a much needed facility for the refugees. In return for assistance from their hosts, the Austrians intended 'to give concerts, arrange all sorts of shows, & c., to give English people some pleasure because they want to do anything to pay back somehow their debt of gratitude towards their country of refuge'.[2] Although this letter evidently met with a positive response, it was soon deemed necessary to issue a further appeal, this time by private circulation, and signed not by Kolmer but by the Centre's British supporters Sir William Bragg (president of the Royal Society), the Hon. Mrs Franklin (a leading light in Anglo-Jewish refugee aid), Sir Felix Clay, Mrs Corbett Ashby, Mrs L. de Bunsen and Lady Jowitt.[3]

In fact, when the Austrian Centre was formally opened by Lord Hailey on 16 March 1939, this took place in the presence of some 150 English well-wishers. However, the successful establishment of the Centre in no way lessened the importance, as the Austrians saw it, of continuing to build up their contacts with the British. As the *First Annual Report of the Austrian Centre* records of the activity in this area during the following months:

> In June and July [1939] the Council tried to extend their circle of friends among Members of Parliament and other well-known members of the British public. The Lord Bishop of Chichester and Captain V. Cazalet, M.P., took a personal interest in the activities of the Council, became patrons, and examined with interest and sympathy the various propositions made by the Council in regard to refugee problems. Close contact was established with Miss E. Rathbone, M.P. (Secretary of Parliamentary Committee for Refugee Problems), with the various Committees at Bloomsbury House, particularly the Coordinating Committee, and the Christian Council for Refugees who made the Council of Austrians a grant of £200 for the development of the Austrian Centre and their other activities.[4]

The *First Annual Report*, with its numerous messages of support from British friends, not only testifies to the Austrians' proficiency in establishing cordial relations with the British but also indicates, as Kolmer's *Spectator* letter had done, that these relations were perceived as mutually beneficial. Thus Stanley Ellis, a former president of the University of London Union – employing a memorable turn of phrase for the Austrian refugees – maintained that 'we in this country have much to learn from you Robinson Crusoes of Paddington who have turned every penny and every talent to good account';[5] while Dorothy Buxton, that redoubtable campaigner for the refugees, went one further: 'The Centre is in fact rendering an irreplaceable service not only to our Austrian friends but to all those English people who wish them well but are impotent to do for them more than a tithe of all they would like to do.'[6]

As the *First Annual Report* makes clear, Members of Parliament were targeted as being of particular potential benefit to the exiled Austrians. In her unpublished memoirs, Kolmer recalls the methods she employed:

> Early on I visited Members of Parliament in the House of Commons [...] to ask for their intervention in this matter or that. To get hold of them, one had to report to a member of the staff in the lobby, in the large entrance hall, request an interview with the appropriate MP and then wait until he was able to absent himself for a short while from the parliamentary sittings that took place almost daily. Sometimes I was then taken into the restaurant or I walked up and down along the Thames Embankment with the MP.[7]

This was work of a kind that would stand her in particularly good stead after the outbreak of war and in the difficult months of alien internment and deportation in 1940.

Within a few days of war being declared, Kolmer was already protesting to the Labour MP Philip Noel-Baker at the application of the 'enemy alien' designation to Austrians and Noel-Baker was putting forward the case to R.A. Butler in the Foreign Office (though without success).[8] The same protest was registered in a memorandum of 18 October 1939, 'Tribunals and Refugees', that was compiled by the Council of Austrians.[9] This document, which commented critically on the workings of the Aliens' Tribunal system in its first two weeks of existence, was brought to the attention both of the Home Office and, through reports in such papers as the *Evening Standard*[10] and *Daily Herald*,[11] of the general British public. The Council of Austrians and Austrian Centre sprang into action still more vigorously with regard to the British policy of mass alien internment in May and June 1940 and the subsequent deportations. The sorts of counter-measures adopted were summarized in an article in *Zeitspiegel* on 14 September: the Centre had appealed to the British public by means of a series of publications, declarations and reports; suggestions for improvements in the camps had been submitted to the British press; bulletins had been despatched on a daily basis 'to all leading figures in the country', and more besides.[12]

In an interview for oral history purposes, Kolmer would later describe how she and her comrades had systematically assembled details of abuses in the internment camps, passing the information on to MPs sympathetic to their cause.[13] A letter was sent to the journalist and politician Vernon Bartlett, for instance, on 13 June, reporting in general terms on problems with the internees' food and postal provision and, more specifically, on the very poor conditions prevailing in the notorious Warth Mills Camp:

The building is full of rats, bugs and other vermin, most of the window panes are smashed. The barbed wire surrounding the building is only two meters away from it so that the men have no possibility of going out into the fresh air.[14]

Of course the fate of the deportees aboard the *Arandora Star* and *Dunera* provided additional ammunition, as Kolmer recalled: 'First we approached the MPs and then the affair was discussed in parliament.'[15] Jenö Kostmann, for one, has spoken of the ensuing parliamentary debates on internment and deportation as 'a success of the Austrian Centre';[16] and it is noteworthy that speakers sympathetic to the refugee cause in the celebrated House of Commons debate on 10 July included MPs with whom the Austrian Centre maintained particularly close ties like Geoffrey Mander, Victor Cazalet, Philip Noel-Baker and Reginald Sorensen.

Although internees began to be released from the summer of 1940 on, the process was slow. In December 1940, armed with letters of recommendation from Lord Lytton (Chairman of the Advisory Council on Aliens) and Bishop Bell of Chichester, Eva Kolmer travelled to the Isle of Man to visit Austrian Centre members still interned there. The degree of security that surrounded her visit, however, testified to the extreme nervousness of the British authorities where the Centre was concerned. A meeting between Kolmer and a representative of the Methodist Church in Port Erin resulted in a police interrogation for the latter. In addition, an unpleasant interview ensued between Dame Joanna Cruickshank, the Commandant of the Women's Internment Camp, and the Methodist minister of Port Erin, Rev. J. Benson Harrison, on which the latter reported back in confidence to Bishop Bell:

> I was with the Commandant for over an hour and quite frankly I regard her attitude as quite impossible. She suspects everyone [...] Mrs Kolmer, by the way, is a 'very dangerous Fascist' and her organization is Fascist in disguise [...] What did interest me was the statement that Mrs Kolmer and her organization are definitely under Home and War Office suspicion. The way Mrs Kolmer was shadowed over here all the time points to the fact that there may be wheels within wheels in Home Office circles of which even you [...] may not be aware.[17]

It is interesting to compare this with an exceptionally positive Home Office endorsement Kolmer had received only the year before, in October 1939, after she had called on Home Office official E.N. Cooper to report on developments in the Council of Austrians and Austrian Centre. Then, Cooper had written most approvingly of her to Sir Robert Vansittart:

I have always considered Miss Kolmer, whom I have known for some time, to be a trustworthy person of moderate views, anxious only that the Austrians in England should show their appreciation of the asylum which has been granted to them by refraining from any political activity which would bring them into conflict with the Authorities here, and that the work of the Committee should be confined to promoting the economic, cultural and social welfare of its members.[18]

It is likely that the first exchange between the Council of Austrians and the Home Office took place a year before that, in October 1938, when an Austrian deputation called on Cooper to ask for British travel papers for Austrian refugees whose passports had expired, rather than that they be forced to apply for German passports – a request that was granted.[19] In June 1939 it was reported at an Austrian Centre meeting that the Council of Austrians had met with Home Office approval and was to be regarded, moreover, as a body 'which could speak on behalf of the Austrians and with which the authorities could make contact in matters affecting the Austrians'.[20]

The British authorities became significantly warier as time went on, however, in particular after the outbreak of war. Indeed, when on 9 September 1939 Kolmer wrote to inform the Foreign Office that the Committee (or Council) of Austrians was the only body authorized 'to represent those Austrians in England who do not recognize the annexation, and to deal with all matters regarding the position of those Austrians, their cooperation in British National and War Service, etc.',[21] the British took a dim view. The Foreign Office official Frank Roberts, for one, noted: 'I do not see any reason why we should recognize this particular group of Austrians as the only representatives of anti-Nazi Austrians in England.'[22]

The growing dissensions between the various Austrian political groups in Britain and the shifting alliances from 1939 on also played their part in the early – and lasting – British decision not, in fact, to recognize any one émigré group as representative of the Austrian emigration in Britain or indeed of political opinion within Austria itself. While claiming a policy of even-handedness towards the rival Austrian groups, the British authorities were nevertheless still charged at various times with showing preferential treatment towards the Habsburgs, the Pollak group of Socialists or the Austria Office. Where the Austrian Centre was concerned, the British authorities had become well aware by late 1939 that the Communists had effectively taken control[23] which, particularly during the time of the German-Soviet Non-Aggression Pact, scarcely served as a recommendation to them.

In fact, during most of the period of the Pact, the Austrian Centre was careful to maintain a low political profile with regard to the British authorities, while remaining extremely active in the canvassing of British support on an individual basis, as already noted. The entry of the Soviet Union into the war in June 1941, however, signalled the start of intensive political activity at an official level on the part of the Austrians: Kolmer, for the Council of Austrians, was soon taking up the question of an Austrian representative body with the Foreign Office once again,[24] as part of the initiative that would lead to the foundation of the Free Austrian Movement in December 1941.

From intelligence reports, the British authorities were well informed both as to the fact that 'the Austrian Centre tail wags the Free Austrian Movement dog'[25] and to the Austrian Centre's and FAM's continuing Communist affiliations, and their response was at least in part informed by anti-Communism and, it might be said, also by a barely disguised anti-Semitism. Philip Nichols, British Minister to the exiled Czechoslovak Government in London, reported to Roger Makins, at the Foreign Office, on a conversation on the subject of the FAM, as follows: 'For my part I pointed out that His Majesty's Government did not believe that the Free Austrian Movement, which was largely composed of Jews and Communists, represented anything of importance whatever in Austria itself.'[26] Similarly, a confidential Foreign Office Memorandum, 'Attitude of His Majesty's Government towards the Various Organizations established in this Country by Emigrés from Germany and Austria', dated 16 November 1942, opined that 'it is scarcely to be expected that the Austrian people would accept the leadership of [...] the unrepresentative and ill-assorted collection of Monarchists, Communists and Jews, who make up the Free Austrian Movement'.[27]

One of the most important tasks of the newly formed FAM, notwithstanding, was to make frequent direct representations to British government departments, in particular the Foreign Office. Chief among its initial concerns were, of course, the aims set out in its founding statement, the 'Deklaration österreichischer Vereinigungen in Großbritannien' ('Declaration of Austrian Organizations in Great Britain') of 3 December 1941,[28] namely that the British should revoke their recognition of the Anschluss; that after the war Austria should be granted the right to self-determination in accordance with the Atlantic Charter; that Austrians in Britain should be permitted to serve in the British fighting forces, civil defence and war work; and that the 'enemy alien' status of Austrians in Britain should be revoked.

Eva Kolmer called on the Foreign Office ten days later, on 13 December 1941, to inform it about the FAM – they would, she advised Geoffrey Harrison, 'like to be regarded as representing Austrians in the United Kingdom and also as being able to speak for Austrians in Austria'

– and to elicit the Foreign Office's response. Harrison, the official with special responsibility for Austrian affairs, had reacted unusually positively, such that Kolmer had 'seemed quite pleased with this'.[29] Within a matter of days, however, official caution had prevailed once again with Harrison noting that 'it remains to be seen how long the new organization will hold together' and Makins that 'we should go slow'.[30] There had also been some contact on the subject between the Foreign Office and the Political Warfare Executive, with Valentine Williams of the PWE's Austrian section making the following view known to Harrison:

> He [Williams] is strongly opposed to the formal recognition of the committee [i.e. of the FAM]. He points out that the representation on the committee in no way corresponds to their influence [...] in Austria. Thus the Pollak Social Democrats and also the Christian Social Democrats are not represented at all on the committee, whereas they probably represent a considerable group of opinion in Austria. Conversely the Monarchists and Communists are strongly represented on the Committee, whereas they have almost certainly very little backing in Austria. Mr Williams also pointed out that there was a fairly strong Jewish representation on the committee (e.g. Winterberg, Eva Kolmer, Scholz and possibly others) and that these would probably not do the committee any good in Austria. His impression was that it would be a great mistake to give the committee undue encouragement or publicity.[31]

It is evident, though, that the British authorities viewed the FAM's formation with all due seriousness since a meeting on the subject was convened on 12 January 1942 and attended by representatives from the Foreign Office, the Home Office, the Security Services and the Foreign Office's Political Intelligence Department (PID). A Security Service representative advised the meeting that 'the Austrian Centre played a preponderant role in the newly organized Free Austrian Movement' in which, by comparison, 'the other groups amounted to very little', and pointed out that, although the great majority of the Austrian Centre's members were non-Communist, almost all of its officers were Communist Party members. It was agreed for this and other reasons that official British recognition, formal or informal, should be withheld from the FAM as it was at present constituted.[32]

There were, however, still some significant differences in Home Office and Foreign Office views that continued to be debated. While the Foreign Office was prepared to continue to receive the FAM on an informal basis, the Home Office was inclined to adopt a less favourable attitude to the new organization, warning darkly: 'We have had experience in the Home Office of the skill with which Miss Kolmar [*sic*] exploits informal contacts.'[33] But Foreign Office staff considered that they had already advanced too far with their offer of informal contacts to withdraw it and moreover, as Roger Makins put it: 'We must remain the judge of who we see & who we do not see.'[34] That this did not in any way signify Foreign Office approval of the FAM, though, is clear from a statement of Anthony Eden's of 13 March 1942:

> I am still rather unhappy about the 'Free Austrian Movement', which is extremely active and is using every device to secure publicity for itself.
> Investigation makes it clear that the Movement cannot claim to be representative of Austrian opinion, either here or in Austria [...] Indeed I am inclined to treat it with some caution.[35]

At around this same time, the Foreign Office also declared itself keen to implement a policy of 'canalization' where the FAM was concerned (whereby approaches to other government departments should be channelled through them) since this would be a method of 'keeping a check on them',[36] moreover a means whereby 'we shall also try to limit their excess of zeal'.[37] There were, as the Foreign Office would still maintain some two years later, definite benefits to be derived from their meetings with the FAM, in particular in terms of the FAM's containment:

> They have a certain nuisance value which we can greatly mitigate by the expenditure of a really fairly small amount of time and paper monthly. So long as they can bring their troubles to the FO, they behave with comparative moderation in public.[38]

However, the FAM – and in particular Kolmer, who combined charm with intelligence, persistence and total dedication – were not always that easy to contain. Early in 1942, for example, after Kolmer had repeatedly telephoned the Foreign Office for an appointment to discuss a possible commemoration of the German invasion of Austria, Makins had noted dryly: 'Mr Harrison had better see Miss K. & defend himself as best he can.'[39] There was at least one occasion, moreover, when she was considered seriously to have overstepped the mark: in February 1942 she had approached the Ministry of Labour and National Service for information and, having failed to obtain the required answer, she had attempted to elicit it from an Austrian working as a temporary clerk in the Ministry (who had reported the matter). Paul Brind at the Ministry of Labour was furious, giving her 'a pretty straight rebuke'.[40] Geoffrey Harrison, however, while of course agreeing that 'Miss Kolmer behaved most improperly', tended towards a more resigned view of the affair, writing to Brind that Eva Kolmer was 'an extremely active woman and I am afraid that you, and we, will have a lot more trouble with her yet'.[41]

The relationship between the FAM and the British authorities, in particular the Foreign Office, can perhaps best be characterized as an almost ritualized battle of wits in which the Foreign Office, generally, if not quite always (see below), managed to retain the upper hand, often by means of evasiveness or inaction. 'I don't think we need hurry to give the FAM answers,'[42] represents a not untypical Foreign Office response, on this occasion in reply to a FAM proposal of December 1943 to form an Austrian Committee 'to represent abroad the Austrian resistance movement and Austrian interests generally'.[43]

In general, then, the British authorities were not particularly well disposed towards what they privately entitled the 'self-styled Free Austrian Movement'[44] even if, as Eden himself made quite clear to the Bishop of Leicester in April 1943: 'We have every reason to believe that the organization is whole-heartedly anti-Nazi.'[45] Characteristic of the official British attitude is a Harrison minute from July of that year commenting on the breaking away from the FAM of the Austria Office, Austrian Democratic Union and Allina group of Social Democrats: 'The "FAM" is, I am glad to say, disintegrating [...]'[46] On the other hand, just occasionally there are surprises to be found amongst the Foreign Office papers, such as a letter from Harrison to Eva Kolmer of 30 December 1944 that ends with real personal warmth: 'May I take this opportunity to wish you a Happy New Year. May 1945 bring Austria her liberation!'[47]

Of course, Foreign Office staff were astute enough to recognize from quite early on that the Austrian Centre 'is not [...]a negligible body since it possesses some influence here'.[48] Interestingly, at the meeting on 12 January 1942 at which the official line to be adopted towards the new FAM was discussed, it was noted that care would be necessary in the manner of the response made to the FAM since 'the movement seemed to enjoy the sympathy of influential persons who might raise questions in Parliament'.[49] Geoffrey Mander, for one, intervened regularly on behalf of the Free Austrian Movement: on 4 March 1942, shortly after the movement's foundation, he requested a statement from Eden welcoming 'the amount of unity already obtained among Austrians';[50] on 15 October 1942, 13 May 1943 and 23 November 1943 he raised questions relating to the registration of Austrians as Austrians rather than as Germans;[51] on 25 April 1944 he wished to know whether, in the light of the Moscow Conference, it was proposed to segregate Austrian Prisoners of War from their German counterparts;[52] and he made a number of other interventions besides. Other sympathetic MPs included Vernon Bartlett who, in June 1944, suggested that Austrian platoons should be established on the same basis of those of the Danes; Lt.-Col. Sir Thomas

Moore who, during 1944 and 1945, raised the matter of an 'Austria' shoulder flash for Austrians serving in the British forces; and Sir Patrick Hannon who on 22 October 1945 pursued the vexed question of when Austrian refugees would be allowed to return home.[53] In the House of Lords, too, the FAM had its champions as was demonstrated in the debate on the position of Austria on 2 February 1943 when Lord Sempill called for the establishment of a clear distinction between Austrian and German refugees in Britain and Lord Strabolgi for the formation of an Austrian Legion.[54] The Foreign Office was clearly disturbed by some of these interventions, as evidenced by the fact that pressure was often exerted on the parliamentarian concerned to withdraw his question – on Lord Sempill, for instance, who, notwithstanding, would not comply with Foreign Office wishes.[55] Tellingly, an internal Foreign Office memorandum of 13 November 1942, conceding that the re-registration of Austrians, were this to be agreed, would actually pose no serious administrative or security difficulties, bears a handwritten marginal note from Geoffrey Harrison: 'Not for Mr Mander's ears!'[56]

However, the FAM was not content merely to leave its affairs in the hands of individual MPs, however supportive these might be, but also chose to conduct its own large-scale propaganda towards the British, sometimes with impressive results. In the summer of 1942, for instance, a propaganda drive was mounted in which Emil Müller-Sturmheim, a leading figure in the Austrian Democratic Union and at that point still acting as General Secretary to the FAM, canvassed a number of influential Britons by circular letter, urging the case for a government statement promising to restore the independence of Austria after the war (in effect a non-recognition of the Anschluss).[57] This the Foreign Office was still not prepared to countenance at that stage. As far as the response from individuals was concerned, however, when on 30 July 1942 a FAM Delegation (consisting of Heinrich Allina, Leopold Hornik and Emil Müller-Sturmheim) came to discuss the matter at the Foreign Office, they could report that their circular had evoked:

> not only friendship and sympathy for Austria, but also an understanding of the significance of the Austrian problem. Many of them share with us a sense of inconsistency between what is said about Austria as a country which did not want to come into the war, and the treatment of Austria as an annexed country and of Austrian refugees as enemy aliens.[58]

More specifically, replies had already been received from 38 MPs and four Bishops, including the Archbishop of Canterbury.[59] Indeed, on 16 September, Müller-Sturmheim could inform the ever helpful Bishop Bell of Chichester that the Archbishop had agreed to see a FAM delegation which Müller-Sturmheim himself would lead 'in my capacity as the political adviser of the Free Austrian Movement'. Would Bell kindly write to the Archbishop, so Müller-Sturmheim continued, to advise him as to his credentials?[60]

The FAM's circular letter also had the effect that on 30 July 1942 Lady Violet Bonham-Carter and Harold Nicolson MP, two more of its prominent recipients, called at the Foreign Office to discuss questions it had raised, in particular 'the manner in which the Prime Minister's statement of 18th February last when he opened the canteen in the yard, a gift of the Austrians had been utterly suppressed by the Foreign Office'.[61] This visit, and the fact that notice had been given of two related Parliamentary Questions (from Geoffrey Mander and John Dugdale),[62] appear to have been among the factors motivating Eden to make a fresh Parliamentary statement on Austria on 9 September, namely that 'His Majesty's Government [...] do not regard themselves as being bound by any change effected in Austria in and since 1938'.[63] It was a statement designed to pacify the FAM's sympathizers and, in the view of the present writer, represented a not inconsiderable FAM success.

A FAM propaganda campaign that was directed at the British public as a whole was the 'Austrians for Britain' campaign from 20 August to 10 October 1942, comprising an ambitious series of Anglo-Austrian meetings, performances and lectures up and down the country. 'Come to these meetings,' a FAM leaflet urged Austrians, 'and bring your British friends, whom you want to give a vivid picture of Austria's culture, Austria's fight, and the aims of the Free Austrian Movement.'[64] While one of the stated campaign aims was to foster the friendship between the Austrians and the British people, the other was to maximize the Austrian participation in the war effort and, to this end, a War Effort Conference was held in London in September 1942.[65] At the end of the campaign, *Austrian News* reported on its scope and successes: 61 meetings had been held, not only in London but also in Aberdeen, Edinburgh, Glasgow, Birmingham, Coventry, Leicester, Manchester, Leeds and elsewhere, and important contacts had been made with civic leaders and other prominent people. At the first public meeting of the FAM in Coventry, for instance, a reception was held under the patronage of the Mayor at which Eva Kolmer addressed City Councillors while Captain W.F. Strickland, the local MP, expressed the wish of the British people to see Austria 'restarted to freedom and happiness'. In Manchester, as already noted, a concert given by the Rosé Quartet as part of the campaign was attended by an audience of about 600.[66]

In fact, the fostering of good relations with the general British public – quite apart from the prominent individuals to whom the Austrian Centre and the FAM so assiduously paid court – was seen as a priority in propaganda terms. In 1941, for example, the Austrian Centre had sent round a circular to British 'clubs, associations and societies interested into [*sic*] international relationships and friendship, interested into social and cultural contact with people other than English', both inviting them to the Austrian Centre and suggesting reciprocal visits by Austrian Centre members, many of whom 'feel very lost and lonely in this tremendous town', to the British clubs. Moreover:

> There is another aspect of our work. Among the Austrians there are a great number of excellent artists, lecturers, musicians, actors, a folk dancers' group etc. They will be grateful for an opportunity to bring their art, knowledge and skill before an English audience. These people who have lost their home, are eager to be useful to the community and to adapt themselves to their new surroundings.[67]

Propaganda to British clubs and organizations was also organized in a more formal way through the Austrian Centre's 'Speakers' Department' on whose work the January 1943 number of *Österreichische Kulturblätter* had the following to report:

> It aims to replace the exchanges of views with a few English friends that have been taking place until now, with educational and propaganda activities for the Free Austrian cause that will reach a larger number of the citizens of our English host nation: the members of English organizations such as the Coops, the trades unions, the Workers Educational Association, etc. They should learn about Austria, the country and its inhabitants, about the national characteristics of our native land, the fight for freedom which runs through both our past and present history and about the aims of the Free Austrian Movement.[68]

Young Austria, too, was particularly active in this area of work, sending out around 20 speakers a week to address British youth clubs during 1944;[69] indeed the final issue of *Jung-Österreich* could claim that, in all, Young Austria's speakers had addressed a total British audience of 180,000, based in 500 organizations in London alone.[70] In August 1944, in an article entitled 'Propaganda und englische Arbeit' ('Propaganda and English Work'), Young Austria functionary Rudi Lappe laid down some fundamental guidelines:

> Great Britain can exert a great influence on the further development of the fight for freedom in Austria, BBC Propaganda to Austria can heighten perception of the tasks of the Austrian people; support of the Austrian Freedom Front by diplomatic and military means would

help our people enormously; the recognition of the FAM would strengthen unity here and at home; the creation of an Austrian formation would make a strong impression on Austrians serving in the German army. We can receive this help when the English public understand Austria's fundamental problem. It is the task of our English work to be effective along these lines. [71]

As well as through lectures, Young Austrian propaganda could also be promoted by means of 'performances, press work, personal contacts, joint socials, club evenings, excursions, etc – and above and beyond that, of course, the publication of pamphlets'.[72]

When the FAM delegation had visited the Foreign Office in July 1942 to urge the British non-recognition of the Anschluss, they had also taken the opportunity to sound out the authorities on a new scheme, the formation of a British support group, outlined in a memorandum thus:

> The Free Austrian Movement intends to approach prominent British people, with whom they are in close contact, to request them to organize the numerous friends of Austria in this country in a special association, 'The Friends of Free Austria'. There is already such an association in Oxford. The delegation asks the Foreign Office to give this scheme its favourable consideration.[73]

In response, a Foreign Office minute recorded the view that, while it would not be possible to prevent the FAM from organizing their supporters in this way, the Foreign Office should certainly not give the scheme its blessing 'which seems to be what the Austrians are after'.[74]

Nonetheless, FAM activity in this area already seems to have been well under way by the end of 1942, with the December issue of *Austrian News* publishing messages of support from individual 'British Friends of Austria' on the occasion of Austria's National Day on 12 November. The British supporters included a number of MPs – John Dugdale, William Gallacher, D.N. Pritt, Eleanor Rathbone, Reginald Sorensen and Geoffrey Mander among them – as well as other prominent people like Vansittart and Wickham Steed.[75] Local groups of Friends of Austria began to be formed soon after; by February 1943 *Austrian News* was reporting on their foundation in the North of England and in the Midlands.[76] By the end of 1943 – it is probable that the Moscow Declaration provided an added impetus here – the organization was fully operational, with *Zeitspiegel* describing the opening of the Hampstead Branch in October: the Chair had been taken by Lt-Col Rowbotham, also the chairman of the Hampstead Anglo-Soviet Committee, while the main speaker had been the British writer Ernest Raymond. Characteristically, the evening had included a speech by Eva Kolmer, on behalf of the Austrians, and a cultural programme provided by Laterndl actor Fritz Schrecker and opera singer Claire Born. Raymond, it was reported, had succeeded:

> in imparting a picture of the Austrian character to the numerous Englishmen and women present. 'The aim of the Friends of Austria', he said at the end of his speech, 'should be to strengthen feelings of friendship between both nations and to work towards recognizing and encouraging the Austrian stuggle against foreign rule.'[77]

Shortly after, in one of its monthly *Rundbriefe* or circulars, the FAM issued advice on the subject 'Wie bildet man ein lokales "Friends of Austria" Committee?' ('How does one set up a local "Friends of Austria" Committee?'), based on its author Ernö Fürst's recent experience in forming the Paddington and West London Committee. The article, written for insiders, offers an unusual degree of insight into the thinking behind the FoA organization as well as the infiltrative *modus operandi* — along typical Popular Front lines — of the FoA groups. Members of a working committee in a particular area had to be recruited from amongst the regular attenders at Free Austrian events, moreover it was necessary that they should be British to facilitate the establishment of 'the necessary connections to local authorities, organizations and figures'. It would create a better general impression if these members were not political figures themselves but rather 'clergymen of local churches, female committee members of local organizations, or of the Women's Voluntary Service and Anglo-Soviet Aid Committee'. For the Paddington and West London Committee, five Englishmen and women of this sort had been found with connections to suitably influential figures in the local community (such as the Secretary of the local Liberal Party, the Chairman of the local branch of the League of Nations Union or a Labour Councillor). The five, 'a strong Executive Committee', had been briefed at length on the Free Austrian Movement, the position of Austria and the Freedom Front before drawing up and putting their names to an appeal. The next step would be to organize a public meeting: one committee member with time to spare had undertaken to approach individuals and organizations while the others were to feed him further addresses and personal recommendations. In addition the Committee had set itself the task of finding a President (ideally the local mayor or Member of Parliament), other people of rank to serve as Vice-Presidents and further influential patrons. The local press would of course be invited to report on the public meeting. Membership subscriptions had been set at the rate of 10/6d. per year or 1/- per month which would be sufficient to cover the costs of postage and printing – 'and the Committee is functioning properly'.[78]

Interestingly, the booklet *Austria*, published by Free Austrian Books that same month, November 1943, is dedicated by the Austrian Centre and Young Austria in Great Britain 'to all British Friends of Austria'. The booklet also carries an advertisement for the Friends of Austria, inviting potential members to apply to the Free Austrian Movement, and setting out the FoA aims as follows:

1. To promote friendship between the British and Austrian peoples.
2. To supply the British public with information about the Austrian people's struggle for freedom.
3. To organize cultural events.
4. To support the Free Austrian Movement in Great Britain.[79]

Within a relatively short space of time, the Friends of Austria appear to have undergone a remarkable increase in size: while the FoA National Conference in July 1944 was attended by delegates from fourteen local branches representing 3000 members, the comparable figures for the following year, August 1945, were given as 23 and 25,000 respectively.[80] Moreover, as the number of local branches grew, so the idea was conceived to unite them under a National Committee. On 20 February 1944, under the Chairmanship of H.J. Blackham of the League of Nations Union, a meeting was held at which it was decided to elect an Executive Committee at national level.[81] This was then carried out at the National Conference in July, with the Committee including Blackham himself and Mrs Corbett Ashby, while the following further items featured on the agenda:

The care of Austrian soldiers in the British Army, the publishing of information aimed at a broad spectrum of the population of this country concerning the resistance movement in Austria and the work of the Free Austrian World Movement, the collaboration of British experts as Friends of Austria with the FAM's Post-war Committees and many other tasks of the greatest urgency.[82]

In the meantime, on 4 June 1944, employing the strategies familiar from Fürst's *Rundbrief* article, the Convener of the Provisional National Committee, H.J. Blackham, had written to T.L. Dugdale, MP, the then Chairman of the Conservative Party, to invite him to become one of the new organization's Vice-Presidents and thereby to 'give us your moral support and sympathy'. The vice-chancellors of Oxford and Cambridge, Lord Lytton, Harold Nicolson and John Christie had also offered their support in this way, Blackham assured him.[83] By October 1944, indeed, *Austrian News* could boast that, in addition to the above, its list of distinguished vice-presidents also included Sir William Beveridge, Sir

David Ross, Professor Seton-Watson, the Dean of Canterbury, Professor Julian Huxley and Dr Ernest Jones;[84] by the following year, Anthony Asquith, Professor G.P. Gooch, Ernest Raymond, the educationalist G.C.T. Giles and the theologian Rev. Dr J.S. Whale had also been recruited.[85] The FAM's outstanding success in enlisting powerful supporters, both British and others, to its cause, is nowhere illustrated more forcefully than in the list of guests attending the first public reception of the Friends of Austria at the Rembrandt Hotel London on 1 November 1944 (in commemoration of the first anniversary of the Moscow Declaration), as reported by *Austrian News*:

> Mrs. Corbett Ashby, the Duchess of Atholl, Miss E.A. Allan (National Council for Civil Liberties), Mr. Ken Baker, President of the Fire Brigades Union, Mr H.J. Blackham, convenor of the Friends of Austria, Mr F.J. Bellenger, M.P., Mr. and Mrs. John Christie, Dr O. Crespo y de la Serna, Secretary of the Mexican Embassy, Lord Farringdon, the Hon. Mrs. V. Grant-Duff, Mr. L. Gundel (Danish Council), Mr. G. Hicks, M.P., and Mrs Hicks, Sir Patrick Hannon, M.P., and Mrs. Hannon, Mr. and Mrs. Somerville-Hastings, Dr. Fr. Herman of the Czechoslovak Foreign Office, M. and Mme. R. Luc of the French Embassy, Mr. K. Lisin of the Tass Agency, the Mayors of Islington and Paddington, Mr. R.C. Morrison, M.P., Mr. Mateescu, the Hon. Harold Nicolson, M.P., Dr. K. Pickthorn, M.P., Lt.-Col. Sir Assheton Pownall, M.P., Mr. Ernest Raymond, Sir Gervais Rentoul, Sir David Ross (Vice-Chancellor of Oxford University), Sir Walford Selby (former British Minister to Austria), Lord Strabolgi, Mrs. Leslie Walker (L.C.C.), and many others.[86]

The Friends of Austria, of course, had to concern itself with its local groups as well as with its illustrious patrons: thus the Austrian Centre put on a regular programme in the form of fortnightly 'At Homes' for the Friends of Austria at all its London branches, with speakers, films or musical entertainment. In January 1944, for instance, the FoA Paddington branch was advertising its opening event as follows:

> The 'At Home' will start with a musical performance, to be followed by a short report by a representative of the Free Austrian Movement and a 'gemütliche' tea. The Club evenings are just the right thing for our British friends who are taking an interest in Austria.[87]

News of local group activities on a countrywide basis, too, was given in the Austrian Centre's 'Tätigkeitsbericht' or Report on Activities for 1944. In the Manchester district, for example, after certain initial difficulties, weekly meetings had been arranged for 'gemütliche Zusammenkünfte' ('pleasant meetings') between Austrians and Britons, with the latter taking advantage of the opportunity to practise their German. In Leicester, a strong, active FoA group had developed in which group members, with some Austrian support, were beginning to offer themselves as speakers on Austrian topics. In Birmingham, where activities had for the most part consisted of 'socials, dances, slide shows, lectures, etc.', an attempt had been made to interest the group's 80 members in political topics such as 'On Czechoslovak-Austrian Co-operation'. This had not proved easy, however: 'One of the greatest weaknesses is that, despite huge efforts, the group has not yet changed from being a tourist organization into a political one.'[88]

So to what extent can the time and energy that went into building up the Friends of Austria be said to have paid off, as far as the FAM was concerned? At the FoA Conference of 23 July 1945, chaired by H.J. Blackham and Mrs Corbett Ashby, a number of successes could certainly be reported, as well as important future plans:

> The Annual Report particularly stressed the partial successes enjoyed by the Executive of the Friends of Austria regarding the treatment of Austrian Prisoners of War. The FoA's intervention played its part in the segregation of Austrian from German POWs and in educating them by means of Austrian pamphlets, newspapers etc. One particular success was the conference on the cooperative system in Austria [...] in which more than 120 delegates from London cooperative branches took part.
> The Friends of Austria organization will shortly be concerning itself with problems of reconstruction in Austria, with the development of cultural, social and economic relations between England and our homeland, but above all with the provision of immediate aid for Austria.[89]

However, despite their best efforts, the FoA were beginning to decline in influence in comparison with a competing organization, the Anglo-Austrian Democratic Society (later known as the Anglo-Austrian Society). This had been formed in July 1944 on the initiative of the Austrian Representative Committee as a counterblast to the Friends of Austria and, like its rival, proved extremely successful in recruiting powerful British sponsors, particularly since it enjoyed support in Labour Party circles.[90] Inevitably, the longstanding antipathy between the FAM and the Socialist London Bureau spilled over into relations between their respective British supporters as well. An exchange of letters in the *New Statesman and Nation*, for instance, in the spring of 1945 between eminent members of the FoA, on the one hand, and of the AADS on the other crossed swords on how representative of Austrian émigré opinion their respective organizations might be deemed to be.[91] Indeed, in FoA statements, regular attempts were made to discredit the opposition, as in *Austrian News* in October 1944, for instance:

> In order to prevent misunderstanding, we should like to state that a recently founded Anglo-Austrian Democratic Society is exclusively sponsored by the pan-German Austrian Representative Committee, and has nothing to do with the 'Friends of Austria'. It was obviously the object of the sponsors to mislead British friends of the Austrian cause and to place obstacles in the path to success of the Friends of Austria.[92]

Even leading British FoA supporters seem to have found the distinction between the two groups hard to fathom: for the AADS's first Chairman was originally to have been Professor Sir Ernest Barker who, so the Social Democratic journalist Friederich (later Frederick) Scheu recalled, 'later turned the position down on the advice of some friends of his representing the Free Austrian Movement'.[93]

The Friends of Austria continued their activities throughout 1946, mounting a reception at Caxton Hall in March of that year in honour of the new Austrian Representative in London, Dr Heinrich Schmid, that was attended by the usual array of high-profile British sympathizers.[94] However, the existence of the two rival bands of British supporters of Austria proved confusing for the British public at large so that a certain degree of cooperation was deemed essential. Thus, from the beginning of 1946, the FAM's Austrian Relief Fund and the AADS's Aid to Austria Fund were merged to form the Aid for Austria Appeal Committee, under the chairmanship of the former British Minister to Austria, Sir Walford Selby, and with one vice-president from the AADS (Jennie Lee) and another from the FoA (Margery Corbett Ashby). Not that this signalled the end to the discord between them: on the contrary, even after the merger of the two funds, there was still much dispute as to who should benefit from the aid, while the AADS also accused the FAM of continuing to make separate collections, contrary to their agreement. At the end of 1946, the Reception Committee for Austrian Children was set up as another joint venture in order to bring needy Austrian children to Britain; but by the time the first group of children arrived, in August 1947, the Friends of Austria no longer maintained a working organization in Britain, though FoA nominees H.J. Blackham and Ella Stacey still served as committee members.[95] According to Scheu, the idea of a full-scale merger between the Friends of Austria and the Anglo-Austrian Democratic Society/Anglo-Austrian Society was always rejected by the latter organization since it 'would have given the Communists a permanent foothold which might have become dangerous in view of the continued occupation of eastern Austria by the Soviet Union'.[96]

The feuding within the Austrian émigré community, with the involvement of British supporters, had been going on, of course, throughout the years of emigration. An earlier well documented example had been the intervention by the TUC in May 1941, with backing from the Austrian Socialists, in which a list of refugee organizations was drawn up that although 'ostensibly undertaking welfare [...] work among internees and refugees' were known to be 'Communist-inspired or Communist- controlled': these included the Austrian Centre, the Council of Austrians in Great Britain and Young Austria, as well as the Free German League of Culture and other German and Czech organizations.[97] The accusations were reported widely in the British press, appearing in the Labour *Daily Herald*, for instance, on 3 May 1941.[98]

Prior to the entry of the Soviet Union into the war, this constituted a serious charge against these refugee organizations, even threatening their continuing existence; and the Council of Austrians, for one, wrote immediately to the TUC and the *Daily Herald* to demand a thorough investigation of the allegations.[99] Friedrich Hertz, though no longer holding a leading position in the Council, wrote off in some anxiety to Margery Corbett Ashby: as far as his time with the Council was concerned, at least, he felt able to 'state with absolute assurance that neither the Council nor the Centre has ever pursued any Communist tendencies'. As for the source of the TUC allegations, Hertz presumed that they had originated with the leaders of the Austrian Socialist emigration, one of whom had already declared to him that 'the publications of the Centre, viz. the [*Austrian*] *News* and a Bulletin containing extracts from the press [i.e. *Zeitspiegel* in its early incarnation] were sufficient proofs'.[100]

Mrs Corbett Ashby was quick to reply that it was essential to 'prevent the development of an anti-alien campaign' and to report that she had lobbied several people on the subject and had protested to the press.[101] In fact, an (undated) draft of a letter she was preparing on the subject is held today in the Bishop Bell papers; in it, she pointed out that:

As regards the attack on the organizations specially mentioned it is noticeable that they are all organizations in which the refugees are helping themselves and are self-governing and therefore are putting into practice in spite of poverty and homelessness the principles of democracy. [102]

At the end of May, the *New Statesman and Nation* carried a letter from Dorothy Buxton in defence of the refugees;[103] the same issue also noted that a similar protest had been received from E.M. Forster, G.P. Gooch, Storm Jameson, Vivian Ogilvie and Ralph Vaughan Williams.[104] An editorial statement commented that, while it was true that some of the officials in the organizations listed were Communists, this did not alter the fact that 'admirable cultural and humanitarian work' was being carried out there.[105]

The *Manchester Guardian* had already published a defence of the refugee organizations and along the same sort of lines, lending further weight to the argument by a reference to their eminent British supporters:

> A responsible English worker among the refugees told me today that these bodies might be 'politically lively' but that they did splendid welfare work. Most of them have distinguished English patrons who are certainly not Communists.[106]

Bishop Bell, as one of these distinguished patrons (both of the Austrian Centre and of the Free German League of Culture), took it upon himself to challenge Walter Citrine on the source of the TUC's allegations, though evidently without obtaining an answer that he found satisfactory.[107] Moreover, further assistance was obtained from the refugees' supporters in Parliament in the form of the Parliamentary Questions submitted by Geoffrey Mander and Reginald Sorensen on 19 June 1941. The former urged the Home Secretary for an assurance that the refugee organizations in question 'are engaged in relief and welfare work and carry out no political activities contrary to the public interest' while the latter called attention to an apparent anomaly: if the Home Secretary did not see fit to condemn trades unions with Communist members, 'why should he make any kind of implied condemnation of these organizations in which there may be a few Communists but whose main work is of a cultural nature?'[108]

Even after the entry of the Soviet Union into the war, the Austrian Socialists continued to do their best to influence Labour Party circles against the Austrian Centre and Free Austrian Movement. Thus, on 28 November 1941, in rather breathless English, Johann Svitanics addressed the Labour Party's International Secretary, William Gillies, as follows:

> I think these Austrian Centre swindle should be stoped as the Labour Party had refused to co-operate with the English Communist Party there should not be allowed local Branches to co-operate with the Austrian Communist Centre [*sic*].[109]

One of the local branches referred to was very probably the East Islington Divisional Labour Party whose Chairman, Councillor A. Baker, a staunch FAM supporter, would inform Gillies on 3 October 1942 that he was 'rather disgusted at the attitude of the Labour Party in this matter'. The Party, he maintained, was evoking 'racial and Communist bogeys' rather than helping the FAM arrive at 'some practical alliance with the Govt. and with the Labour Movement in the fight against Fascism'.[110] As for Gillies's own views – and Gillies was in any case well known for his anti-Communism – these are made apparent in a letter of 6 November 1942: 'I advise our friends to have nothing to do with "The Free Austrian Movement" [...] They are all under Communist influence, and even directly controlled by Continental Communists.'[111]

Efforts to discredit the Austrian Centre and Free Austrian Movement in this way continued unremittingly into the following year, such that by September 1943, in answer to a 'statement issued by an Austrian organization' claiming the Austrian Centre to be a Communist organization, the Committee of the Austrian Centre issued a joint declaration. While the signatories included committee members like Kolmer and West, who were known to be Communist functionaries, the former Socialist parliamentarian Marie Köstler also put her name to it, as did representatives of Austrian cultural life in exile like Oskar Kokoschka, Anna Mahler, the musician Paul Knepler and the actress Marianne Walla. The declaration claimed:

> We are proud to be able to assert that, within the ranks of our members, who hold a wide variety of political views and stem from a broad range of social class, a state of complete harmony prevails. Anyone who supports progress and democracy is welcome to join us as a fellow worker and comrade-in-arms.[112]

While such attacks on the Austrian Centre, though perhaps tedious, can be seen to have had some validity to them, the same can scarcely be said of the accusations levelled against both the Austrian Centre and the Free German League of Culture by one V.V. Millers in the right-wing *Catholic Herald* of 14 April 1944. Millers alleged that the members of these organizations – 'Jews mostly' – were encouraging strike action and carrying out sabotage against the British government. These charges were vigorously refuted by F.C. West, as President of the Austrian Centre, who maintained that, on the contrary, the Austrian Centre had encouraged hundreds of its members to enlist in the armed forces and to participate in war work and civil defence, moreover that the 'war effort of this country [...] is also our war effort'. The matter culminated in the *Catholic Herald* not merely tendering an apology but also making a donation to the Red Cross Prisoner of War Fund.[113]

The final attack of any significance mounted against members of the Austrian Centre and the other refugee organizations was of a rather different nature. An upsurge of xenophobia in Hampstead after the war was summed up in a headline of the *Hampstead and Highgate Express* of 12 October 1945: '2000 Residents Will Send Petition to Parliament: Aliens Should Quit to Make Room for Servicemen.' In the event, this petition, organized by two Hampstead women (one of them the daughter of Sir Edmund Gosse) and signed by the Mayor and Mayoress as well as by several Hampstead Borough Councillors, backfired on its initiators in that it generated forceful protest in the local area. Counter-petitions were organized by the Labour, Liberal and Communist Parties in Hampstead, the Hampstead Ethical Society and the Left Book Club, *inter alia*, and a mass protest meeting was arranged at which Eleanor Rathbone, H.N. Brailsford, Ernest Raymond and others elected to speak. A group of 'local professional people and artists' – of the eminence of the philosopher Dr C.E.M. Joad, the scientist Dr Julian Huxley and the composer Roger Quilter – formed themselves into a committee, 'which they hope will expand to national dimensions, to help solve the refugee problem in Britain'.[114]

A meeting was also held at the Austrian Centre, Hampstead, on 20 October 1945, with over 100 members present, where an overview of all these events was given and at which Georg Knepler, as the Secretary of the Austrian Centre, claimed:

> The most striking aspect of the xenophobia in Hampstead is not the fact that it has arisen. Something of this sort was only to be expected. The most striking thing about it is the huge storm of protest to which it has given rise in the English population of Hampstead.[115]

A resolution was passed, to be sent to the press and to all Hampstead Councillors and Aldermen, which concluded with a warm expression of gratitude to the British for their 'generosity and hospitality, understanding, sympathy and friendship towards us on countless occasions both during and after the war'.[116]

Helene Maimann has commented on the high degree of success of the propaganda that the FAM, of all the exiled Austrian groups, directed at their British hosts and on the number of individual Britons who were drawn into a direct involvement with the Free Austrian cause. She contrasts this with the, in her view, negligible effect that the FAM, like the other Austrian émigré groups, was able to have on official policy.[117] Nevertheless, the initial aims, at least, that were set out in the FAM's founding statement – British non-recognition of the Anschluss, alteration of the 'enemy alien' status, integration of Austrians into the British fighting forces, and so on – were largely met. It may be argued, of course, that such successes were due more to the course of the war in general and to the Moscow Declaration in particular than to the powers of persuasion of the exiled Austrians – though the work of influential British supporters on the FAM's behalf should not be underestimated here.

On the other hand, it is indisputable that the concerns close to the FAM's heart in the last eighteen months of the war, matters that were raised repeatedly with the British authorities, were less successfully resolved. These included the formation of an Austrian National Committee under its aegis, with a representative function; the recognition of the existence in Austria of a 'Freiheitsfront' or Freedom Front; the introduction of special Austrian platoons in British regiments or, failing that, of an 'Austria' shoulder flash for Austrians in HM Forces; FAM involvement in BBC broadcasting to Austria; the segregation of Austrian and German Prisoners of War; FAM involvement in Allied post-war planning for Austria and in reconstruction; and repatriation. Despite the intervention of their powerful friends, none of these matters was settled to the FAM's satisfaction: they were, in effect, excluded from Allied planning for Austria and, compared with their Socialist counterparts, allowed only a limited involvement in BBC broadcasting; the repatriation of Austrian exiles, with few exceptions, was delayed until 1946; the British authorities refused to the end to recognize any Austrian committee as representative and remained sceptical as to the Freedom Front's existence; Austrian platoons were not permitted (there had been a brief unsuccessful experiment of the kind in 1941, at Habsburg instigation) and even the 'Austria' shoulder flash was never officially permitted during wartime (although in practice tolerated in certain army units); and the segregation of Austrian and German prisoners, while some progress was made in this direction, had still not been completed by August 1945.[118]

However, the Austrians did have some successes, even in the later period, with British officialdom, as instanced by the deferment of the call-up both of Jenö Kostmann, as editor of *Zeitspiegel*, and of Fritz Walter, as the leading functionary in Young Austria, achieved by dogged persistence on the part of the Austrian Centre in 1943,[119] or by the way in which the Austrian Centre and the FAM managed, at least initially, to corner a University of London lecture programme on Austria in 1944, calling forth grudging admiration from Foreign Office official Denis Allen with his 'more smart work on the part of the Free Austrian Movement'.[120] In the manner of their post-war return to Vienna, too, carried out against the express wishes of the British authorities, the leading functionaries of the Austrian Centre and Free Austrian Movement can be said very much to have had the last word (see following chapter).

All these must be classed as small-scale satisfactions for the FAM, however, compared with that occasioned by the issuing of the Moscow

Declaration by the Allies back in November 1943. Since the establishment of an independent Austria after the war was one of the FAM's most fundamental tenets, the Declaration turning this into official Allied policy represented the fulfilment of a major political aim for the FAM and was greeted by them with jubilation. Maimann's doubts that Austrian exiles could have exerted any influence in this or in other areas of official policy-making were noted above.[121] It is, however, indisputable that, long before the Moscow Declaration, the FAM had been tireless in its lobbying of the Foreign Office on the independence of Austria; and it may perhaps be recalled that Geoffrey Harrison served not only as the chief point of contact between the Foreign Office and the FAM but was also the official responsible for drawing up the draft declaration. It is interesting to note in this connection that FAM members do appear, mistakenly or not, to have been under the impression that their careful fostering of relations with the Foreign Office did achieve some degree of success here. Jenö Kostmann, for instance, in a tribute to the work performed in this area by Eva Kolmer, maintained: 'Eva Kolmer must carry the chief credit for the softer line adopted by the Foreign Office; she carried out arduous negotiations that were finally successful in leading to the Moscow Declaration'[122] and elsewhere: 'We saw the Moscow Declaration as the culmination of all our efforts.'[123]

Against this, it should be noted that, well before the Moscow Declaration, Harrison had foreseen that the FAM would be sure to claim any sign of progress as its own doing. Indeed, with regard to the distinctly proprietorial attitude the FAM had adopted towards Eden's statement of 9 September 1942, Harrison had already seen fit to warn:

> These Austrians are slippery customers and we shall have to recognize that any forward step we may make as regards either the future of Austria or the status of Austrians in this country will be claimed by them to be the result of their pressure.[124]

It is, in fact, the commonly held view that it was pressure from the Soviet Union that caused the British Foreign Office to come round to the idea of an independent Austria, rather than any internal pressures:[125] Stalin had, after all, told Eden in Moscow in late 1941 that he supported the restoration of Austria as an independent state. Nevertheless, one has only to examine the Foreign Office files for 1942 and 1943 to appreciate the extent of the pressure being exerted at home, too, and from a variety of quarters.

The FAM campaign during the summer of 1942, urging the case for a government statement on the post-war independence of Austria, and culminating in Parliamentary Questions from Dugdale and Mander and in the statement by Anthony Eden of 9 September, has already been described. It is noteworthy that, despite the tributes usually paid to Kolmer on this score, it was in fact Emil Müller-Sturmheim who was coordinating FAM propaganda at the time, and that Müller-Sturmheim, as a leading figure in the Austrian Democratic Union, would certainly have presented the FAM to the British in a more generally acceptable manner than a known Communist might have done. Moreover, at the same time as the FAM's powerful British sponsors were agitating on the FAM's behalf, there was considerable pressure also from the Political Warfare Executive for a definite government commitment to the establishment of an independent Austria after the war since this could prove valuable in propaganda terms in appealing to the Austrians to contribute to the German defeat.[126] At this stage, however, the Foreign Office was still professing itself unwilling to commit itself on the future status of Austria and the PWE had to bow to Foreign Office opinion.[127]

Müller-Sturmheim, meanwhile, followed up an interview at the Foreign Office in late 1942 with a letter employing a line of argument very close to that of PWE: 'A declaration by the British Government [...] would paralyse this lying Nazi propaganda and stimulate the resistance of the Austrian people till it becomes a danger to Germany.'[128] On 13 January 1943, Allen, at the Foreign Office, entered a minute that, notably, indicated a degree of preparedness to entertain the demands not only of the PWE but also of the FAM:

> The question of a further statement on Austria has recently been raised by PWE and the question is under consideration [...] Although it is unlikely that we shall be able to go as far as the Free Austrian Movement would like, *the views expressed in their letter should perhaps be taken into account before a decision is made* [my italics].[129]

From around this point on, the idea of Austrian independence was very much a matter for public debate in Britain, particularly in what may loosely be termed 'progressive' circles. In the House of Lords debate on Austria, on 2 February 1943, Lord Strabolgi, as a FAM sympathizer, reminded the House that, at the previous Labour Party conference, 'we reiterated our view that Austria should receive her independence as one of the first objects of the war'.[130] Shortly after, on 8 March, the Amalgamated Engineering Union – a corporate FAM supporter – wrote to Eden with a resolution from its Paddington Branch, lending support to Strabolgi's statement.[131] When, on the following day, Müller-Sturmheim submitted a copy of his pamphlet *What to do about Austria?* (1943) to the Foreign Office, which pleaded the case for Austrian independence, Allen observed: 'We could agree with most of its conclusions.'[132]

In the meantime, on 24 February, a FAM deputation had again called on William Strang at the Foreign Office to request a Government statement to coincide with the fifth anniversary of the Anschluss.[133] At the same time, PWE, too, requested that the anniversary be taken as an opportunity to declare a British non-recognition of the Anschluss.[134] The Foreign Office continued to drag its feet on the issue, though Harrison, on 6 March, declared he could foresee a time when such a statement could be made (subject to Cabinet approval and in consultation with the US and Soviet Governments):

> Our own ideas are beginning to take shape and I do not think that it will be necessary to wait until the whole Central and East European jigsaw falls into place to make a statement in favour of a free and independent Austria.[135]

At the FAM's Kingsway Hall meeting to mark the Anschluss anniversary, messages of support from some of the most influential patrons, like Bishop Bell and Sir Walford Selby, were read out, and summaries promptly sent to the Foreign Office by Eva Kolmer. Selby, the former British Minister to Austria, who had already irritated the Foreign Office on more than one occasion by his support of the FAM, maintained: 'Today Austria stands at the head of the list of those countries whose liberty and independence the United Nations are committed to restore.' Likewise, Vansittart, that other Foreign Office luminary of independent mind, wished 'every success to every meeting held to further the cause of a really free Austria'.[136]

After the Anschluss anniversary, the FAM did not allow its propaganda efforts to slacken in any way. Meetings were organized, such as one at the Finsbury Park Austrian Centre that was presided over by the Mayor of Islington and 'attended by persons prominent in the social, religious and political life of the Borough'; at this, a resolution, moved by the Labour Member of Parliament W.S. Cluse, and carried unanimously, called on the Prime Minister and the Government, in view of the recent debate in the House of Lords, 'to make a declaration at an early date that the restoration of a free, independent, democratic Austria is one of the war aims of the United Nations'.[137] A few days later, Cluse followed this up in Parliament, asking of Eden

> whether he is aware of the resolutions passed at week-end meetings of the Free Austria movement [sic], asking for a firm statement by the United Nations as to the status of Austria after the war; and whether he is prepared to make that statement at the present time in order to reassure Austrian opinion in this country?[138]

Despite the non-committal nature of Eden's reply, matters were moving ahead by now in the Foreign Office. Research reports on Austria, commissioned by the Foreign Office, had arrived from the Foreign Research and Press Service (FRPS). On 4 April 1943, Geoffrey Harrison's first draft paper on the future of Austria, based largely on FRPS material, made the recreation of an independent Austria the first step (while allowing for the possibility of Austria's later association in some form of Central or South East European Confederation).[139] A revised version of Harrison's document was presented by Eden to the War Cabinet on 16 June 1943, with political warfare considerations – namely 'the possibility of causing embarrassment to Germany by encouraging resistance and sabotage in Austria' – as the paramount consideration.[140] Following agreement by the Cabinet, a further version of Harrison's document, dated 12 July 1943, was despatched to Washington and Moscow, with a 'Draft Declaration' attached to it that would later, after various amendments, be known as the Moscow Declaration on Austria.[141]

The question remains as to whether or not the FAM could have exerted any influence on the British decision-making process leading up to the Moscow Declaration. Clearly, the British political warfare considerations submitted by PWE were of the greatest importance in British policy-making but, as it happened, FAM interests regarding the future of Austria coincided with PWE interests, a state of affairs that worked to the advantage of both parties. Maimann's conclusion that the FAM failed to have an effect on British policy in this area appears too perfunctory: on the contrary, it seems likely that the intense pressure exerted by the FAM and, most importantly, by the prominent British supporters of the FAM played a part, by influencing the climate of public opinion, in the changing British policy on the future of Austria and, ultimately, in the Moscow Declaration. The economist and publicist Theodor Prager, a leading activist in exile in the FAM-affiliated National Union of Austrian Students in Great Britain, offers a more generalized and wide-ranging evaluation of the role of the FAM than Kostmann does, and probably a more apt one:

> The activity of the FAM was definitely extremely useful to the Austrian cause. Through the FAM's publications, its exhibitions, its lobbying of all possible authorities [...] Londoners, as well as a sizeable proportion of political opinion throughout the whole of England, were made aware to a quite remarkable degree of Austria and of the aim to restore Austrian independence. We were the best organized and most active of all the foreign groups, people were interested in us, and the fact that the Moscow Declaration came about

in 1943 was the result, not least, of the tenacious campaign that our people had been waging in London.[142]

As Geoffrey Harrison, in the Foreign Office, had noted of the FAM a year before the signing of the Moscow Declaration:

> The Movement have carried out during the past nine months some extremely able propaganda and have organized quite a body of public opinion in this country in favour of Austria and themselves. This body of opinion, which includes high local functionaries like the Mayor of Manchester and the Corporation of Glasgow, to say nothing of sentimentalists like Sir Walford Selby, Lady Violet Bonham-Carter and even Harold Nicolson cannot be ignored.[143]

It has already been observed that by the end of the war – and still more so in the immediate post-war period – the FAM was waning in influence, just as the fortunes of the rival Austrian Representative Committee were improving. Its close contacts with the Labour Party were obviously of particular benefit to the Representative Committee after Labour had taken power in 1945. Where the FAM was concerned, the shifting international situation and, in particular, the changing relations between the Western Allies and the Soviet Union inevitably also had an adverse effect on British official attitudes. Back in Vienna at the end of 1945, FAM functionaries F.C. West and Eva Kolmer attempted to lobby the British occupation authorities about fellow exiles wishing to return and received an unusually straight answer on the subject, as West reports:

> We had an experience there such as I had never had with the British authorities in all the preceding years. The British – it was part of their usual manner of going about things that they never made a direct statement unless it was on something very pleasant. Otherwise they would say: 'It's under discussion,' or 'We find your suggestions very interesting' or something like that. And in Vienna we said to them: 'Pollak is back, Czernetz is back, in the meantime other members of the Trades Union group have arrived back.' And to that, the official – I don't know his name – gave a very brief answer: 'Well you know, there are quite enough Communist emigrants arriving back from Moscow. We're therefore in no particular hurry to bring them back from London as well.' 'Thank you,' we said, and left.
> A clear answer, don't you think?[144]

On an unofficial level, however, the Free Austrians continued to enjoy a remarkable level of British support, as they had done throughout their years of exile. Indeed, when the Austrian Centre closed, the final issue of its *Bulletin* paid a heartfelt tribute to those British hosts through whose help, in the most difficult of circumstances, the Centre and the Free Austrian Movement were able to minister to the Austrian refugee population and serve the Austrian cause:

> In particular we must stress that our activity was only made possible by the exceptional hospitality of the English people. It was a hospitality that exceeded all our expectations and that we shall never forget. We would like to thank English friendsand organizations and the British authorities for all their help and for their extraordinary kindness towards us.[145]

Notes

1 See also, Charmian Brinson, 'Eva Kolmer and the Austrian emigration in Britain, 1938-1946', in Anthony Grenville, ed., *German-speaking Exiles in Great Britain: Yearbook of the Research Centre for German and Austrian Exile Studies*, vol. 2 (2000), pp. 143-69.

2 Eva Kolmer, 'Austrians in England', *The Spectator*, 3 February 1939, p. 181.

3 'Proposed Austrian Centre in London', n.d. [February/March 1939], Friedrich Otto Hertz Papers, Archive for the History of Sociology in Austria [AGSÖ], Graz, 28/5.15.

4 *First Annual Report of the Austrian Centre*, London 1940, p. 21. The author was almost certainly Eva Kolmer.

5 *Ibid.*, p. 3.

6 *Ibid.*, p. 6.

7 Eva Schmidt-Kolmer, 'Exil in England 1938 bis 1946', unpublished ms., n.d. [c. 1990], in private possession of Ruth Kolmer, Vienna, p. 8.

8 National Archives [NA], FO 371/23093.

9 In Friedrich Otto Hertz Papers, AGSÖ, 28/5.15.

10 'Austrian Refugees Dislike Being Classified as "Enemy Aliens"', *Evening Standard*, 24 October 1939, p. 7.

11 'Still "Enemy Aliens": Few of Austrians Escape Stigma', *Daily Herald*, 24 October 1939, p. 4.

12 Willi Scholz, 'Solidarität', *Zeitspiegel*, 14 September 1940, pp. 2 ff.

13 Interview with Prof. Dr Eva Schmidt-Kolmer, 22 June 1990, Documentation Archive of Austrian Resistance [DÖW], Vienna, Interview 719, p. 13.

14 Reproduced in Eva Kolmer, *Das Austrian Centre: 7 Jahre österreichische Gemeinschaftsarbeit*, London [1946], p. 6.

15 Schmidt-Kolmer interview, p. 12.

16 Interview with Jenö Kostmann, DÖW, Interview 044, p. 60.

17 Rev. J. Benson Harrison to Bishop Bell, 9 December 1940, Bell Papers, vol. 30, Lambeth Palace Library, London.

18 Cooper to Vansittart, 20 October 1939, NA, FO 371/23101.

19 See *First Annual Report of the Austrian Centre*, p. 20.

20 'Generalversammlung des Klubs Austrian Centre, London 26. Juni 1939', Friedrich Otto Hertz Papers, AGSÖ, 28/5.15, p. 2.

21 Kolmer to Foreign Office, 9 September 1939, NA, FO 371/23101.

22 Minute (Roberts), 16 September 1939, *ibid.*

23 See, for example, in Foreign Office files, 'Memorandum' of 5 November 1939 passed on by the (Labour) *Daily Herald* 'from a trustworthy source', NA, FO 371/24106.

24 Kolmer to Foreign Office, 30 July 1941, NA, FO 371/26538.

25 Cooper (HO) to Harrison (FO), 26 October 1942, NA, FO 371/30911.

26 On 30 May 1942, NA, FO 371/30910.

27 NA, FO 371/30911.

28 Held, for instance, in NA, FO 371/26539.

29 See Minute (Harrison), 14 December 1941, *ibid.*: 'I said that we had to start slowly and cautiously in such matters, but that I thought there would be no difficulty about being prepared to deal [handwritten insertion: informally] with the new organization as representing Austrians in this country.' But see also, Harrison (FO) to Brind (Ministry of Labour and National Service), 12 March 1942, NA, FO 371/30910: 'I think I told you on the telephone at the beginning of January that we may not after all go quite so far in dealing with the Movement.'

30 On 19 and 20 December 1941, NA, FO 371/26539.

31 Minute (Harrison), 9 December 1941, *ibid.*

32 Minutes of meeting, n.d. [c. 12 January 1942], *ibid.*

33 Maxwell (HO) to Strang (FO), 2 February 1942, NA, FO 371/30910.

34 Minute (Makins), 4 February 1942, *ibid.*

35 Eden to Lord Horder, 13 March 1942, *ibid.* The FAM had asked Horder, among others, for an expression of support on the occasion of the fourth anniversary of the Anschluss.

36 Harrison (FO) to Brind (Ministry of Labour and National Service), 1 January 1942, NA, FO 371/26539.

37 Harrison (FO) to Hutchinson (HO), 2 January 1942, *ibid.*

38 Minute (Harrison), 8 February 1944, NA, FO 371/38827.

39 Minute (Makins), 21 February 1942, NA, FO 371/30910.

40 Brind (Ministry of Labour and National Service) to Harrison (FO), 27 February 1942, *ibid.*

41 Letter of 12 March 1942, *ibid.*

42 Minute (Harrison), 19 December 1943, NA, FO 371/34421.

43 FAM to Foreign Office, 6 December 1943, *ibid.*

44 See confidential Foreign Office advice on dealing with the 'self-styled Free Austrian Movement' to Ministry of Labour, Ministry of Information, Dominions Office and Ministry of Supply, 11 March 1942, NA, FO 371/30910. Cf. 'the so-called Free Austrian Movement' in Eden to Churchill, 28 December 1942, NA, FO 371/30911.

45   Letter of 23 April 1943, NA, FO 371/34418.

46   Minute (Harrison) 24 July 1943, NA, FO 371/34419.

47   NA, FO 371/38831.

48   Minute (Grey), 31 August 1941, NA, FO 371/26539.

49   Minutes of meeting, n.d. [c. 12 January 1942], *ibid.*

50   *Hansard*, 5th Series, *Parliamentary Debates*, House of Commons, vol. 378, col. 620.

51   See *ibid.*, vol. 383, col. 1755; vol. 389, col. 778f.; and vol. 393, col. 1427.

52   *Ibid.*, vol. 399, col. 619.

53   For Bartlett's question on 13 June 1944, see *Hansard*, 5th Series, *Parliamentary Debates*, House of Commons, vol. 400, col. 1794; for Moore's questions on 21 December 1944 and 24 April 1945, see *ibid.*, vol. 406, col. 1995 and vol. 410, col. 678; for Hannon's question, see *ibid.*, vol. 414, col. 1815. The ability of the FAM to attract the broadest-based support is reflected in an observation of Con O'Neill's of 18 October 1945, in NA, FO 371/46659: 'Odd that Sir P. Hannon, an extreme right-wing Catholic, should champion the Communist FAM!'

54   *Hansard*, 5th Series, *Parliamentary Debates*, House of Lords, vol. CXXV, cols. 869, 875.

55   See Minute (Law), 29 January 1943, NA, FO 371/34464. For a similar incident involving Geoffrey Mander in July and August 1942, see NA, FO 371/30943.

56   'The Status of Austrians in the United Kingdom and the United States', NA, FO 371/30943.

57   See, for example, letter to R.K. Law, 6 July 1942, in NA, FO 371/30942. The postal initiative was backed up by a campaign in *Austrian News* (see issue of July 1942).

58   'Memo for a visit to the Foreign Office of a Delegation from the Free Austrian Movement, on 30th July 1942', NA, FO 371/30911.

59   *Ibid.*

60   Müller-Sturmheim to Bell, 16 September 1942, Bell Papers, vol. 41, Lambeth Palace Library.

61   Memorandum (Law), 30 July 1942, NA, FO 371/30943. On 18 February 1942, Churchill, on receiving a field canteen donated by exiled Austrians, had said: 'We can never forget here in this island that Austria was the first victim of Nazi aggression [...] The people of Britain will never desert the cause of the freedom of Austria from the Prussian yoke [...] In the victory of the Allies, free Austria, old Austria, shall find her honoured place.'

62   Parliamentary Questions were put by Dugdale and Mander on 9 September 1942 (see *Hansard*, 5th Series, *Parliamentary Debates*, House of Commons, vol. 383, col. 123); Sir Patrick Hannon, who was also considering submitting a Parliamentary Question at this time, wrote to Eden on 20 August 1942 to inform him of the great desire among promoters of the

FAM in Great Britain for Eden to make a statement on the future of Austria (NA, FO 371/30943).

63   *Hansard*, 5th Series, *Parliamentary Debates*, House of Commons, vol. 383, col. 124.

64   'Austrians for Britain', n.d. [1942], in NA, FO 371/30911.

65   A previous conference of this kind, the FAM's War Production Conference, had already been organized earlier in the year (31 January/1 February 1942).

66   '"Austrians for Britain" Campaign', *Austrian News*, November 1942, pp. 1ff.

67   Circular letter, n.d. [stamped as received 15 September 1941], in NA, FO 371/26538.

68   'Sprecher für Österreich', *Österreichische Kulturblätter*, January 1943, p. 15.

69   See 'Tätigkeitsbericht Austrian Centre 1944', DÖW 03016/23, p. 4.

70   'Laßt Zahlen sprechen', *Jung-Österreich*, 24 August 1946, pp. 4-5.

71   In *Rundbrief: Funktionär-Organ des Jungen Österreichs*, August 1944, p. 3.

72   *Ibid.*

73   'Memo for a visit to the Foreign Office of a Delegation from the Free Austrian Movement, on 30th July, 1942', NA, FO 371/30911.

74   Minute (Allen), 6 August 1942, *ibid.*

75   'British Friends of Austria', *Austrian News*, December 1942, pp. 3 f.

76   See '"Friends of Austria" to be formed in Northern Area' and 'Lord Mayor of Birmingham Patron of FoA', *Austrian News*, 19 February 1943, p. 5.

77   'Wir berichten: Friends of Austria in Hampstead', *Zeitspiegel*, 16 October 1943, p. 4.

78   Free Austrian Movement in Great Britain *Rundbrief*, November 1943, p. 1.

79   *Austria*, p. 32.

80   Compare 'Zweite Landeskonferenz "Friends of Austria"', *Zeitspiegel*, 5 August 1944, p. 4, and 'Jahreskonferenz "Friends of Austria"', *Zeitspiegel*, 11 August 1945, p. 2.

81   'Wir berichten: Londoner Konferenz "Friends of Austria"', *Zeitspiegel*, 26 February 1944, p. 4.

82   *Zeitspiegel*, 5 August 1944, p. 4.

83   Blackham to Dugdale, 4 June 1944, in NA, FO 371/38829.

84   See '"Friends of Austria": List of Distinguished Vice-Presidents', *Austrian News*, October 1944, [p. 5].

85   See 'Friends of Austria' notepaper (as in use on 29 October 1945), in NA, FO 371/46596.

86   'Why Friends of Austria Support the Free Austrian Movement', *Austrian News*, December 1944, p. 3. A copy of this article is also held in Foreign Office files, marked up in red and bearing exclamation marks against the names of Hannon and Pickthorn (NA, FO 371/46595).

87   'Diary: "Friends of Austria" – At Home', *Austrian Centre*, January 1944, p. 6.

88   Held at DÖW 0316/23, p. 10.

89   *Zeitspiegel*, 11 August 1945, p. 2.

90   Frederick Scheu, in *The Early Days of the Anglo-Austrian Society*, London 1969, recalls that Sir Stafford Cripps, then Minister of Aircraft Production, had addressed the Anglo Austrian Democratic Society's inaugural meeting in November 1944 and he observes: 'That a leading member of the British war cabinet was willing to speak at a public meeting sponsored by the democratic Austrian groups in Britain was itself a fact of great political significance' (p. 7).

91   See, for the FoA, H.J. Blackham, M. Corbett Ashby, W.D. Ross, Ernest Barker, 'Austrian Unity', *New Statesman and Nation*, 24 February 1945, p. 125; and, for the AADS, T.L. Horabin, G.R. Strauss, *ibid.*, 3 March 1945, p. 141.

92   '"Friends of Austria": List of Distinguished Vice-Presidents', *Austrian News*, October 1944, [p. 5].

93   Frederick Scheu, *Die Emigrationspresse der Sozialisten 1) 38-1) 45*, Vienna/ Frankfurt/Zürich 1968, p. 28.

94   '"Frends of Austria" – Empfang für den Gesandten', *Zeitspiegel*, 30 March 1946, p. 1.

95   Scheu, *The Early Days of the Anglo-Austrian Society*, pp. 19 ff.

96   *Ibid.*, p. 26.

97   See circular letter from Walter Citrine, 'Refugee Organizations: Communist Activities', 1 May 1941, National Museum of Labour History, Manchester, ID/CORR/AUS/2/1i.

98   'Refugee Groups are Suspect', *Daily Herald*, 3 May 1941, p. 3.

99   Kolmer, *Das Austrian Centre*, p. 13.

100   Hertz to Corbett Ashby, 15 May 1941, Friedrich Otto Hertz Papers, AGSÖ, 28/1.1. For an example of the bitter attacks on the Austrian Centre put about by the Austrian Socialists, see J. Svitanics' memorandum 'The Austrian Centre', n.d. [1941?], sent to William Gillies of the Labour Party, held at National Museum of Labour History, ID/CORR/AUS/1/6ii.

101   Corbett Ashby to Hertz, 22 May 1941, *ibid.*

102   Bell Papers, vol. 23, Lambeth Palace Library.

103   'Refugee Organizations', *New Statesman and Nation*, 31 May 1941, pp. 555-56.

104   On p. 556.

105   *Ibid.*

106   Private Wire, 'Our London Correspondence: Welfare and Politics', *Manchester Guardian*, 8 May 1941, p. 4.

107   See Bell to Citrine, 12 May 1941; Citrine to Bell, 15 May 1941; Bell to Citrine, 16 May 1941, Bell Papers, vol. 23, Lambeth Palace Library.

108   *Hansard*, 5th Series, *Parliamentary Debates*, House of Commons, vol. 372, col. 800 f.

109   Svitanics to Gillies, 28 November 1941, DÖW 8499.

110   National Museum of Labour History, ID/CORR/AUS/2/28.

111   Gillies to Eleanor Stewart (Transport House), 6 November 1942, *ibid.*, ID/CORR/AUS/2/22i.

112   'Erklärung des Vorstandes des Austrian Centre', *Zeitspiegel*, 18 September 1943, p. 4.

113   See V.V. Millers, 'The Background of the Strikes', *Catholic Herald*, 14 April 1944, p. 2; F.C. West, 'Background of Strikes', *ibid.*, 28 April 1944, p. 2; 'The Austrian Centre and the Free German League of Culture', *ibid.*, 26 May 1944, p. 2 (in which it is conceded that 'V.V. Millers' must be a fictitious name); and 'Zusammengebrochene Attacke gegen das Austrian Centre', *Zeitspiegel*, 3 June 1944, p. 3.

114   '"Eject Aliens" Petition Raises Storm of Protests', *Hampstead and Highgate Express*, 19 October 1945, p. 1.

115   'Fremdenhetze in Hampstead: "Der Sündenbock": Eine Versammlung im Austrian Centre Hampstead', *Austrian Centre*, November 1945, [p. 7].

116   *Ibid.*

117   Helene Maimann, *Politik im Wartesaal: Österreichische Exilpolitik in Großbritannien 1) 38-1) 45*, Vienna/Cologne/Graz 1975, p. 231.

118   On this, see Willi Scholz, 'Austrian POW's in British Camps', *Austrian News*, August 1945, p. 4.

119   See NA, FO 371/34424.

120   Minute (Allen), 9 August 1944, NA, FO 371/38829. The University had filled its programme with lecturers proposed by the Austrian Centre and FAM, at least until the Foreign Office, in an 'informal conversation', suggested it should also approach the Austrian Representative Committee.

121   Maimann, *Politik im Wartesaal*, p. 231.

122   Interview with Jenö Kostmann, DÖW, Interview 044, p. 56.

123   Jenö Kostmann, 'Zeitzeuge', in Friedrich Stadler (ed.), *Vertriebene Vernunft II: Emigration und Exil österreichischer Wissenschaft*, Vienna/Munich 1988, p. 841.

124   Minute (Harrison), 19 October 1942, NA, FO 371/30943. That month, under the heading 'Bericht über den Stand der österreichischen Freiheitsbewegung', *Austrian News* had proclaimed proudly: 'The declaration signifies the success of our endeavours and represents a milestone in the development of the FAM' (p. 2).

125   See, for example, Helene Maimann, 'Diskussion', in Dokumentations-archiv des österreichischen Widerstandes and Dokumentationsstelle für neuere österreichische Literatur, eds., *Österreicher im Exil 1) 34 bis 1) 45: Protokoll des internationalen Symposiums zur Erforschung des österreichischen Exils von 1) 34 bis 1) 45, abgehalten vom 3. bis 6. Juni 1) 75 in Wien*, Vienna 1977, p. 110.

126   See, for example, NA, FO 371/34464 which contains 'a first draft of a statement of His Majesty's Government's policy towards the future of Austria, on lines that would be helpful to Political Warfare Executive', dated 5 January 1942 [i.e. 1943].

127 See Minute (Scarlett), 20 January 1943, *ibid.* PWE frustration at the Foreign Office's official line on Austria is made clear in letters from Richard Crossman and others in FO 898/216.

128 Müller-Sturmheim to Strang, 7 January 1943, NA, FO 371/34464.

129 Minute (Allen), 13 January 1943, *ibid.*

130 Hansard *Parliamentary Debates*, House of Lords, 5th Series, vol. CXXV, col. 874.

131 Leo Teichmann (AEU) to Eden, 8 March 1943, NA, FO 371/34464.

132 Minute (Allen), 16 March 1943, *ibid.*

133 Minute (Allen), 5 March 1943, *ibid.*

134 Minute (Scarlett), 4 March 1943, *ibid.*

135 Minute (Harrison), 6 March 1943, *ibid.*

136 See Kolmer to Harrison, 24 March 1943, and enclosed FAM press release *World Message of Free Austrians*, n.d., *ibid.*

137 See Steffi Dinger (Secretary of the Finsbury Park Austrian Centre) to Anthony Eden, 2 April 1943, *ibid.*

138 Hansard *Parliamentary Debates*, House of Commons, 5th Series, vol. 388, col. 635 (7 April 1943).

139 See NA, FO 371/34464.

140 'Austria: Memorandum by the Secretary of State for Foreign Affairs', 25 May 1943, NA, FO 371/34465.

141 'The Future of Austria', NA, FO 371/34465.

142 Theodor Prager, *Zwischen London und Moskau: Bekenntnisse eines Revisionisten*, Vienna 1975, p. 65.

143 'Free Austrian Movement', 30 September 1942, NA, FO 371/3091.

144 Interview with Franz West (Weintraub), DÖW, Interview 92, p. 391.

145 J. Desser, 'An Unsere Freunde und Mitglieder', *Austrian Centre Bulletin* (Abschiedsnummer), [January 1947], [p. 1].

'AUSTRIA TOMORROW'? PLANNING FOR A POST-WAR AUSTRIA

MARIETTA BEARMAN

While the future of Austria was the question which increasingly dominated the political deliberations of Austrian exiles by 1943/44, the debate on the post-war political order in Austria had actually begun even before the war had broken out. As early as June 1939, a small working party and discussion group with the name 'Austria Tomorrow' or 'Das kommende Österreich' (also 'Kommendes Österreich') had been formed at the Austrian Centre. Three members of the Centre, or of the later Free Austrian Movement (FAM), played a particularly active role in this discussion forum: Alfred Reisenauer (originally Hrejsemenou) as Chairman, Ruth Zerner as Secretary and the journalist Bruno Heilig.[1]

The founding principles of this working party emphasized above all the necessity for all exile groups to cooperate in order to achieve the aim of liberating Austria from the Hitler regime and 'to keep alive the idea of a free and independent Austria'. Looking ahead to the situation after the end of the Hitler regime, it was further intended that this common task should, 'despite the different ideologies, survive the time of emigration for the benefit of the democratic and social reconstruction of Austria'.[2] The group 'Austria Tomorrow' organized discussion evenings at which leading members of the Austrian Centre such as Franz West and Walter Hollitscher, or Hans Winterberg, the Secretary of the Austrian Communist group in exile in Britain, appeared as speakers. In these lectures, political topics such as 'Stellung der österreichischen Kommunisten zur Einheit im Kampf gegen Hitler' ('The attitude of the Austrian Communists towards unity in the fight against Hitler') by Hans Winterberg or 'Rundfunkpropaganda – die österreichischen Sendungen des BBC' ('Radio propaganda – the Austrian broadcasts of the BBC') by Walter Hollitscher were discussed, as were topics focusing on the future shape of Europe such as 'Voraussetzungen einer mitteleuropäischen Föderation' ('Prerequisites for a Central European Federation') by F.

Bruegel. In the summer and autumn of 1941, in particular, a number of such events took place.

The working party is mentioned on various occasions in the Austrian Centre's correspondence of this time with the Socialist exile organization, the London Bureau, which objected to the fact that although 'Austria Tomorrow' purported to be non-party political, it was in fact controlled by the Communist Party. Similarly, a confidential report from the year 1943, held by the Foreign Office, concerning the Austrian refugee organizations in Great Britain emphasizes the group's Communist orientation and its links with the Austrian Centre:

> This organization was established before the German-Russian war at a time when the Centre was concerned to cover up its political intentions by using a front organization [...] After the start of the war against Russia the organization disappeared and the Centre openly supported Bolshevism.[3]

In the founding declaration of the Free Austrian Movement of December 1941, 'Austria Tomorrow' is listed as one of eleven signatories. After this, however, it virtually disappears from sight: apart from being mentioned as one of the organizations attending the first FAM mass meeting on 24 January 1942, no further references to 'Austria Tomorrow' have been found. However, discussions on the shaping of a future Austria continued to take place in all branches of the Austrian Centre. The following announcement of a lecture by Jenö Desser, for example, appeared in the 'Diary' section of the Austrian Centre's eponymous monthly publication in January 1944:

> How will one find deported or missing relatives after the war? What practical steps can already be taken towards this? How will repatriation be carried out? J. Desser, the foremost Austrian expert on refugee questions is speaking on these issues in all three clubs.[4]

In June 1944 a lecture entitled 'Wen wird man nach dem Krieg in Österreich brauchen?' ('Who will be needed in Austria after the War?') was held at the Austrian Centre Paddington in 'Das österreichische Forum' ('The Austrian Forum'), one of the regular Saturday events, while both at Paddington and at Swiss Cottage a public discussion, or 'brainstrust', was announced on the subject of 'Österreich heute und morgen' ('Austria Today and Tomorrow') with representatives of the various political groups within the FAM.[5]

* * *

Even if the real planning for a post-war Austria was mainly conducted from 1943 onwards, and by the FAM itself, the very name of the working party 'Austria Tomorrow' and its establishment shortly after the foundation of the Austrian Centre indicate the importance this task assumed from the very beginning. Their work focused on the re-establishment of an independent Austria after the end of the war and on the preparatory planning for this new state as well as on encouraging as many of their members as possible to return to Austria and participate in the political reconstruction of their country.

Jenö Kostmann, speaking years later, also emphasized that from the very beginning the Austrian Centre had played a significant role in the political work and organization of the Communist exiles, 'in order to accomplish our fundamental aim, the restoration of an independent Austria'. In this task the Austrian Centre, the place where so many of the Austrian exiles would gather, should itself be 'a great help for the activities that are now beginning'.[6]

Even before it was decided by the Allies in the Moscow Declaration of 1 November 1943 that an independent Austrian state should be re-established, the Austrian Centre saw it as an important propaganda aim to emphasize Austria's autonomy and viability. In fact, the propagation of an Austrian national and cultural identity quite separate from that of Germany runs like a leitmotiv through the activities and publications of the Austrian Centre up to and beyond the end of the war. However, there was widespread scepticism as to whether Austria, as the diminished heir to the former Habsburg Empire, crippled by political and social conflict during the inter-war years, could survive politically or economically as an independent unit. In addition, the diplomatic *de facto* recognition of the Anschluss had led British political and public opinion to doubt Austria's viability.[7] Concerted efforts had to be made to dispel these doubts.

A 26-page propaganda pamphlet published in English by the Austrian Centre at the end of 1942 with the title *This is Austria: The Story of a Beautiful County* was intended to be given to British sympathizers – the dedication read 'to all British Friends of Austria', as mentioned above – as a small Christmas gift in order to propagate a positive impression of Austria. The author of the booklet, Anna Hornik, writes of Austria in the inter-war years: 'Her enemies have always stressed that Austria could not exist as an economic unit, and even the well-meaning have repeated this fallacy.'[8] She argues against this view, citing statistics from agricultural and industrial production as well as from the Austrian balance of trade in the 1930s which indicate a strong upward trend in the economy. In her view, the picture of Austria as economically unviable was nothing but a lie spread by National Socialist propaganda: 'The argument of the (non) feasibility of Austrian existence served only as a cover for German propaganda. Austria was no less viable than other small states.'[9]

In contrast to Austrian Socialist exiles, who took a largely pan-German view up until the Moscow Declaration, the Communists regarded the independence of Austria as an incontrovertible political aim from the very beginning, and consequently their demand for the non-recognition of the Anschluss took pride of place in the FAM's founding declaration in 1941. Indeed, one of the first pamphlets bearing the Austrian Centre's imprint, *The Austrian Ally*, in October 1942, makes the case for Allied recognition of Austria as an occupied country. *Zeitspiegel* took the same line. In January 1943, an article by Hans Winterberg appeared entitled 'Warum Österreich unabhängig sein muß' ('Why Austria must be Independent') in which he stressed Austria's national autonomy and viability and repeated the FAM's demand for Austrian independence to be adopted as a war aim.[10]

Even after the Moscow Declaration, the question of Austrian viability was repeatedly debated. It was felt to be important to continue to present the case in a convincing fashion since plans for a Central European Confederation that were under discussion in British government circles differed markedly from the plans for a post-war Austria as drawn up by the exiled Austrian Communists. Equally the idea of continuing economic links with a post-Fascist Germany was roundly rejected. Ernst Fischer, the influential leader of the Austrian Communist Group in Moscow, which undoubtedly played a decisive role in Communist exile politics, warned against such ties. In a series of broadcasts, *The Rebirth of My Country*, transmitted by Radio Moscow and reproduced in 1944 by Free Austrian Books, Fischer called for a total separation of the Austrian and German economies after the end of the war. He condemned the idea of future economic links with post-war Germany as 'The German post-war trick for Austria', which would result in Austria's resources being drained by German finance and industry.[11] Against this, he recommended ties with Czechoslovakia and Yugoslavia, Austria's Slav neighbours to the East. Indeed, contacts between the Austrian exiles and the officially recognized Czech Government in Exile point to a close collaboration already in existence.[12] Similarly, support for Tito's partisan army in Yugoslavia played an important role in the politics of the Austrian Centre. It was with these states, therefore, that post-war Austria should ally itself economically and as an equal partner:

> She will be able to adapt herself to those neighbouring States [*sic*] for which a great expansion is in store, and to which our economy can far better adjust itself, above all, therefore, Czechoslovakia and

Yugoslavia. These countries offer us and we offer them a harmonious economic inter-action.[13]

A further vital propaganda task was to encourage as many Austrian exiles as possible to return home after the war. As we have seen, a lecture held at the Austrian Centre by its president F.C. West in spring 1942 was called 'Zurück oder nicht zurück – das ist keine Frage' ('To go back or not? There's no question'), the text being published as a pamphlet by Free Austrian Books. Although the lecture particularly exhorted the refugees to play an active part in the British war effort – Hitler's defeat being the prerequisite for the return of the exiles – the title of the lecture clearly indicates that the refugees' eventual return to Austria was one of the main goals of the Austrian Centre. However, the large majority of refugees in Britain were Jews, for whom a return to the former homeland was not merely a question of defeating Hitler and his regime. Long before the advent of National Socialism, Austria had provided a breeding-ground for anti-Semitism; and the idea of settling there again would certainly have seemed unattractive to many of the Jewish refugees. Austrian Zionists in England were also quick to stress the dangers for Jewish émigrés of returning to Austria. A lecture organized by the Zionist Jacob Ehrlich Gesellschaft in January 1943 declared, so it was reported, that 'for Austria's youth every path would be better than the one leading back to Austria'.[14] This was a problem the Austrian Centre had to contend with. Willi Scholz, one of the Centre's leading personalities, dealt thoroughly with this question in his pamphlet *Ein Weg ins Leben* (*A Way into Life*), which appeared in February 1943. Scholz himself was not Jewish and it may well have been for this reason that he was entrusted with compiling the pamphlet. He countered the Zionist argument 'that the return to Austria would be the way to certain death' with the assertion that a new Austria under a government of national unity would demonstrate a completely different character. There would be no place for anti-Semitism, presented here not as intrinsically Austrian but as a phenomenon of the Austrian pan-German movement. Moreover, the question of compensation and restitution is addressed in this pamphlet in an exceptionally positive manner.[15] Nothing should therefore hinder the return of the Austrian Jewish refugees:

The new Austria will compensate for the damages caused by German foreign rule. Austria's Jews have been robbed of everything. Austria will have a special duty of care towards them [...] To all questions and concerns about the fate of the Austrian refugees after the war we can reply: Austrian Jews, return to Austria!'[16]

Young Austria, for its part, took pains to show that this unambiguous endorsement of the aim of returning home was not only to be found among the refugee functionaries. In May 1943, a survey was carried out in two of Young Austria's London groups, Maida Vale and Finsbury Park, in which the question 'Where do our members want to go after the war?' resulted in 70% expressing their determination to return to Austria.[17]

It was particularly important that these young émigrés should be presented with the image of a viable state, of a country in which they would be able to build a good life for themselves. The leading Young Austrian Theodor Prager, for example, posed the question in *Young Austria* in March 1944: 'Why should not Austria be a going concern economically? If Denmark can build up a prosperous economy, why not Austria?'[18] As an argument for Austria's economic viability, Prager emphasized the wealth of raw materials and the strength of various Austrian industries, especially the hydroelectric industry, during the inter-war years. After the collapse of the Habsburg Monarchy, Austria, though greatly reduced in size and despite numerous other problems, had proved itself economically viable, and consequently it was to be expected that the country would develop successfully after the end of this war, too.

While the case for Austria's viability was made most emphatically, the article also stressed that the country would initially need to rely on some external aid; one may presume it was chiefly Soviet support that the writer had in mind. This, as well as references to Socialist-style economic pioneer work after the war, point, even while avoiding overt Communist propaganda, to the Austrian Centre's ideological programme for a future Austria.[19]

*   *   *

The Free Austrian Movement and Young Austria were the chief proponents both of detailed planning for Austria and the preparatory work for the return of the refugees. The youth organization, in particular, played an important part in preparing the young refugees for a future in which they were to assume leading positions in the youth organizations of the new Austria. These young people were seen as the torchbearers of the future: it was hoped that the political thinking they had imbibed through the Austrian Centre and Young Austria would serve to supplant Nazi ideology in Austria.

The main planning work was taken up by the FAM in 1943. In January, its English-language publication *Austrian News* reported that a Committee of Experts had been formed to consider the restoration of an independent Austria and initial post-war problems. To stress the FAM's broad political base, it was evidently important to indicate that the members of the committee represented a range of political viewpoints. In addition, the FAM wished to avoid any impression that the work of the committee might pre-empt decisions taken by the Austrian people after the end of hostilities. *Austrian News* aimed to inform an English readership, after all, and the FAM was only too conscious of the cautious attitude of the British authorities regarding Austrian affairs. Since they intended to work in step with the authorities, and indeed to seek their recognition, the FAM's aims in setting up the committee were expressed with great restraint:

> The Committee will limit itself strictly to drawing up an immediate programme, consisting solely of measures which must be put into operation without delay to complete the separation of Austria and make it independent [...] all the measures contemplated will have to be of a provisional nature to meet a state of emergency, and will not be intended as permanent institutions. It must be left to the Austrian people themselves, exercising the right to self-determination, to decide on the final setting of their house in order. The work of the committee must therefore be done so as not to prejudice in any way the future decisions of the Austrian people.[20]

Zeitspiegel, too, turned increasingly to post-war issues. An article entitled 'Probleme der Volksgesundheit nach dem Krieg' ('Problems of Public Health after the War'), signed Dr. L. B. – probably FAM member Paul Loew-Beer – refers to preparations in the USA and Britain for initial post-war aid in the newly liberated areas. The author considers that the major refugee organizations might find a new field of activity here through cooperation with international aid organizations and Allied aid programmes.[21] The pamphlet, *Das Free Austrian Movement in Großbritannien und der Wiederaufbau Österreichs* (*The Free Austrian Movement in Great Britain and the Reconstruction of Austria*) describes how the FAM, by compiling a master-plan for Austria, was hoping to engage the help of the Allies in rebuilding their country. This master-plan contained documentation prepared by the FAM on material requirements in Austria in the first six months after the war and in the year thereafter. It was to be presented via the Foreign Office to the Inter-Allied Post-War Requirements Bureau and from there to UNRRA.[22] A similar master-plan had already been drawn up by the Czech government in Exile in London and, since the Czechs enjoyed official recognition by the Allies, their plan had been accepted by the Bureau. The FAM hoped it would achieve important political successes if the suggestions it put forward in an Austrian master-plan were also to be accepted. A FAM information leaflet from October 1943 states:

The Free Austrian Movement is faced with the task, and for the first time has the opportunity, of taking practical and realistic steps to represent the interests of the Austrian Nation. It has therefore set up a number of committees to study the situation in Austria, the consequences of German rule and the problems of reconstruction. The committees have been instructed to present, on behalf of Austria, the necessary documentation to the various inter-allied organizations concerned with preparing for immediate post-war aid and the reconstruction of the occupied countries. This work was started some considerable time ago but only in the last three months have we been granted access to the inter-allied authorities and our work has found recognition [...] Incorporation into their master-plan would mean that in inter-allied negotiations Austria would for the first time be considered an equal partner to the other occupied countries. An important step has thus been taken towards integration into the framework of official inter-allied institutions and agreements.[23]

Although prior to the Moscow Declaration, of course, the Allies had not recognized Austria as an occupied country, the question of recognition was already being discussed in the Houses of Commons and Lords before then. As early as April 1943, Eva Kolmer had turned to the Foreign Office concerning a possible FAM involvement in the Allies' post-war work for Austria, requesting some information as well as a meeting with a representative of the Inter-Allied Post-War Requirements Bureau in order to discuss aspects of the re-education and treatment of war criminals. This met with the cool reception which the British authorities reserved for such overtures from the FAM or Austrian Centre. W.D. Allen at the Foreign Office advised that the FAM's request for its master-plan to be passed on to the Bureau and to UNRRA should be rejected, arguing 'that we anyhow do not consider that the technical can be divorced from the political side of these two matters mentioned' and furthermore 'that neither the FAM nor any other Austrian organization should be given any kind of standing officially or unofficially as regards the study of post-war Austrian problems'.[24]

The setting up of the FAM 'Kommission über Nachkriegsfragen' (Committee on Post-War Questions) represented an important step in its planning for Austria. To compile the master-plan, various committees were set up which dealt in astonishing detail with the topics within members' areas of expertise. In a lecture entitled 'Die Arbeiten des Free Austrian Movement über Nachkriegsfragen' ('The Work of the Free Austrian Movement on Post-War Questions') at the FAM's National Conference on 27-28 November 1943, Paul Loew-Beer gave a precise description of the work in hand (which scarcely matched the FAM's originally cautious wording as to the provisional nature of its plans).[25]

The document dealt with several subject areas. The first of these, legal and administrative questions, concerned the compilation of a list of 'German War Criminals and Austrian Quislings' – an interesting national distinction – and announced that it was planned to carry out a study on the reintroduction of the Austrian legal and administrative systems. Although the document does not indicate who was to lead this area of work, elsewhere the names of legal experts Dr Otto Hecht and Dr Georg Lelewer occur, the latter being responsible for legal affairs in the FAM's newly established Committee of Experts.

A further area, led by the former Social Democratic parliamentarian and Chair of the League of Austrian Socialists, Marie Köstler, dealt with social and health issues. In this field, work was to be undertaken in compiling a register of missing refugees which would be useful in the event of later repatriation. In addition, refugees were to be recruited, registered and trained for post-war relief work. With the help of Czech refugee groups, the Austrians attempted to make contact with international organizations such as the Red Cross, Bloomsbury House and the Technical Advisory Committee of UNRRA. The FAM Committee for Welfare also considered plans for the establishment of the social and health services in post-war Austria. These would be modelled on the highly progressive social institutions of the First Republic, for 'so impressive were the past achievements in this area that the best way forward would be to demand the restoration of what has been destroyed'.[26]

The committee dealing with questions of culture and education was led by Walter Hollitscher, Ernst Buschbeck and Richard F. Bayer. Since the FAM was particularly concerned to influence Austrians in this field, work here was already very advanced, *inter alia*, on plans to create an education authority immediately after the end of the war. The importance of this area to the Communists is also reflected in the KPÖ's appointment of Ernst Fischer to the post of Secretary of State for Education in the provisional government of 28 April 1945. However, none of the Austrian Communists from England would serve in the provisional government; they did not succeed in returning home until autumn 1945, and then only with the greatest difficulty.

The strengthening of Austrian national consciousness was an important aspect of the efforts to establish an independent Austria. Thus the FAM's 'Kulturkommission' (Committee for Cultural Issues) sought to erase National Socialist and pan-German attitudes by introducing new courses in history and literature with a specifically Austrian focus. It also drew up plans to establish a new broadcasting service and film industry, although the old adult education system that had operated successfully in the inter-war years was to be restored.

A further area of work, economic and transport issues, was the province of three separate committees, the 'Beschaffungskommission' (Procurement Committee) under Loew-Beer, the 'Finanzkommission' (Finance Committee) under Dr Victor Bloch and the 'Transportkommission' (Transport Committee) under Dr F. Rebl. In his lecture to the FAM National Conference, Loew-Beer particularly deplored the exploitation and destruction of the country's natural resources and pre-war industry by the Nazi regime. After the Anschluss, Austria's successful farming industry had been forced to supply other parts of the Reich, while German industry had swallowed up key Austrian industries that then had to gear their production to the interests of the Nazi regime. Loew-Beer, in commenting on this, was also counting upon active Austrian resistance and sabotage: 'All that will be left to us will be the ruins of the big war industries that were established in Austria by the Germans and that we expect to be destroyed by our own people as well as by the bombs of the Allies.' [27]

Despite the devastating effects of the war and of National Socialist rule on the Austrian economy, Loew-Beer nevertheless emphasized Austria's capacity to rebuild the country. Yet, while the Austrian Centre's and Free Austrian Movement's political aim of re-establishing an independent Austria remained of prime concern, the case was also made for the deployment of Allied aid in the immediate post-war period. Concrete plans had already been drawn up for emergency aid measures, particularly regarding the supply of provisions to the population for which cooperation with the Allied and Inter-Allied authorities would be especially important. However, so Loew-Beer conceded, the general FAM planning on economic questions was still very much at an early stage, and all FAM members were urged to play a part in the future work: '[We] ask each one of you to let us know your comments, your ideas, your plans in those areas that we have mentioned that you are particularly interested in.' [28]

In addition, the lecture pointed to the growth in Czech-Austrian collaboration which was particularly dear to the heart of Loew-Beer as Chairman of the Austrian Association for Cooperation with Czechoslovakia. Through this group, founded on the FAM's initiative in 1942, and a corresponding group set up by the Czechs under Vladimir Klecanda, London possessed an important forum 'for planning the closest future cooperation between the states'.[29]

In line with the work of the FAM, there were numerous articles in *Zeitspiegel* discussing detailed aspects of post-war planning. Walter Hollitscher, for example, described the preparation of new curricula and school textbooks, for which English publications might serve as a model. Educational planners might take their lead from the cheap Oxford Pamphlets or the 3/6*d.* books produced by the Oxford University Press. Furthermore, English publications on racism could be used in place of those promoting Nazi racial ideology. It was envisaged that British sponsors might negotiate the translation rights with authors and publishing houses and also assist with finance.[30]

Likewise, Dr. Georg Lelewer, in an Austrian Centre lecture on the punishment of war criminals, addressed an important post-war issue. He suggested that preparations for this should be initiated in exile: the names both of perpetrators and of eye witnesses should be collected and a law drafted on procedures for special war crimes courts. Lelewer who, as a leading Legitimist, was a FAM member representing the Monarchist camp, had held high office at the Supreme Court of Justice during the First Republic.[31]

Because of the expansion in its activities, in March 1944 the FAM underwent a re-organization, formalizing the loose arrangements that had existed up to then. The FAM was now headed by a new Committee which established a division of work at its first meeting. Areas such as refugee questions, social issues, legal affairs, cultural matters, the economy and the technical problems inherent in Austrian reconstruction were given their own departments which were led by FAM members with relevant specialist knowledge. However, even before this, the term 'FAM Department' had been used for some of these areas of work. The increase in planning was particularly evident in the specialist conferences held by the FAM during the year 1944. In March, for example, together with Young Austria, they put on a Welfare Conference while Young Austria organized its own Education Conference. A Teachers' Conference took place in April, in September there was a FAM Conference on Refugee Questions, in October the second Cultural Conference and in December a Conference on the Economy.

At the Welfare Conference, Emmi Walter, the Deputy Chair of Young Austria, gave a key speech entitled 'Die soziale und wirtschaftliche Lage der österreichischen Jugend unter der deutschen Fremdherrschaft' ('The Social and Economic Situation of Austria's Youth under German Occupation'). One of her sources for this was the pamphlet *Österreichs Jugend unter der deutschen Fremdherrschaft* (*Austria's Youth under German Occupation*) by Fritz Walter, but she extended the discussion to include measures that would be necessary after the end of the German occupation. No-one should be under any illusions about the extent of the work to be undertaken: 'We have to be prepared for the fact that welfare activities in Austria will have to start from square one.' She ended her lecture with a list in which emergency measures for youth welfare after the war were laid down in characteristic detail. These included such far-reaching tasks as repatriating and reintegrating young people who had been displaced or deported, the carrying out of medical examinations, the establishment of a provisional school system, as well as the provision of food through a school meals service. The necessity of winding up Fascist youth organizations, of confiscating the property of the German Hitler Youth and of punishing Hitler Youth leaders, as appropriate, was also emphasized. At the same time it would be necessary to support the setting up of new democratic youth organizations.[32] It was in this field that members of Young Austria saw a particularly important future role for themselves, and at least some of them were able to achieve their goal, notably Fritz Walter and also Herbert Steiner, the Secretary of Young Austria, who after his return served not only as National Secretary of the Freie Österreichische Jugend (Free Austrian Youth), but also on the youth advisory board to the Austrian Ministry of Education.

The FAM's Welfare Department organized a register of missing persons through which it was hoped to reunite those separated by the Nazi regime and the war. Forms were provided for this and a fee of 2/- was charged for enquiries. The department also organized a programme of courses on post-war problems, consisting of lectures by FAM experts, such as Dr Georg Lelewer on legal affairs, Dr F. Rabl on transport and Dr Oskar Strakosch on nutrition. There were British contributions, too, like a lecture that a Miss Keeling gave on the Citizens Advice Bureau's work on missing persons. While most of these lectures set out to provide the exiles with factual information, there was also a very comprehensive course – the printed material here came to 43 pages – that aimed to offer practical training to future welfare workers and thus was directly linked to the work likely to be undertaken upon return. On completion of the course, participants were issued with a certificate.

In the health field there existed an organization affiliated to the FAM, the Association of Austrian Doctors led by Dr Friedrich Silberstein, also a member of the Austrian Centre. In this area, too, there was a separate Committee for Post-War Medical Relief, which dealt with such issues as the planning of a health service as well as aid measures for the post-war period. In mid-1944 this committee submitted a memorandum to the FAM containing detailed plans of action. In particular, mention is made of the anticipated shortage of doctors, not only as a result of the war but also, an important factor, because a substantial number of doctors – the report cites a figure of around 40% of the former total – had been forced by the Nazis to leave Austria on racial grounds. In order to make up the shortfall, measures were to be taken to facilitate the return 'of the largest possible number of general practitioners and specialists, students and trained medical auxiliary staff'.

However, a survey carried out by the Association of Austrian Doctors in the autumn of 1945, in which only 45 doctors declared themselves prepared to resume work in Austria within the near future, indicates that the FAM's hope of persuading large numbers of doctors to return was unlikely to be fulfilled.[33] Further detailed suggestions contained in the Association's memorandum address the organization and administration of the health service, the supply of medicines and the setting up of emergency hospitals and mobile clinics.[34]

One of the most important fields as far as the FAM's planning activities were concerned was the future form of the Austrian economy. Since it was no longer necessary to defend the viability of the Austrian economy, discussion could now centre on emergency measures for the post-war period as well as the separation of the Austrian and German economies. A Committee for the Reconstruction of the Austrian Economy dealt in detail with topics like agriculture and forestry – of exceptional significance for Austria's existence – energy, trade, industry and banking. Study materials, 'which were kindly put at our disposal by acknowledged experts', were compiled on these topics. For example, the collected materials contained a 'memorandum on the wood industry by an Austrian expert', with exact statistics on production in the forestry industry in the inter-war years. With regard as to who might play a leading role in the future economy, the committee compiled a list of persons holding high positions in Austrian economic life at the time, with comments on their political views.[35]

In compiling its economic plans, the FAM was concerned to draw on a wide range of contributions. The Economic Committee also received input from highly qualified exiles in other countries, as exemplified by a 13-page report from Prof. Ing. Johann Grabscheid from Istanbul with the somewhat ponderous title 'Report Concerning the Guidelines for Initial Measures Aiming at and for Use during the Liberation of Austria with Particular Reference to the Energy Industry'.[36] While such reports and studies dealt largely with economic details, production statistics and balance of payments, or discussed the separation of Austrian and German industries, the FAM's ideological basis is clearly visible even here. Thus the report on forestry calls for 'the immediate deployment of agents of the Austrian Freedom Front' as well as the setting up of local agricultural production committees with equal representation of employers and employees.[37] And in an article in *Zeitspiegel*, the Chairman of the FAM Committee for Agriculture and Forestry addresses the subject of a new Austria free of the old class differences in unmistakably Marxist terms:

In conclusion, it should be stated that a fraternal alliance between the agricultural and industrial workforce will prove indispensible for the entire development of the new People's Republic of Austria. Prejudices and class differences must come to an end once and for all. Then a new Austria will arise in the future in which the peasant will find his rights and his freedom, and in which the friendship between the worker and the peasant will form a strong foundation for unity among the people as a whole.[38]

At the Economic Conference of 9 and 10 December 1944, the left-wing orientation of the FAM's economic planning was likewise made clear. The main topic here was the future administration of Austrian industry, thus the relationship between the state and the economy. While the draft prepared by the relevant FAM committee places some weight on promoting private enterprise, the principle of state control is also established, and not only in the industries targeted for nationalization. The draft has the following to say on state planning and control of the economy:

> The steering of the whole production in the direction indicated by the Representative Assembly of the people will be carried out by a Ministry of Production which will be the central economic organization of the state and divided into departments according to economic sectors. It will set priorities and determine the principles whereby the raw materials for the whole of industry (where these are under state control, owing to shortages), as well as credits, foreign currency and the workforce will be distributed among the different sections of industry by the appointed authorities. Furthermore, the departments will be able, if necessary, to take direct measures to control production, e.g. determining the kind of goods that are to be produced.[39]

It was envisaged that the Ministry of Production would carry out these tasks in the immediate post-war period, when shortages of raw materials and labour would largely justify vigorous state intervention in the economy. However, it was made clear that the Ministry's activity was not to be confined to this period alone. The idea of a centrally planned economy in post-war Austria was therefore clearly established.

The particular importance attached to the education of young people and the school system in post-war Austria is indicated by numerous conferences held in 1944 that were frequently reported in *Zeitspiegel*, *Young Austria* and *Austrian News*. As early as February 1944, the FAM was calling on refugee teachers to take part in the FAM 'Kommission für Erziehungsfragen' (Committee for Educational Matters).[40]

The Teachers' Conference of 8 and 9 April 1944 dealt extensively with plans for the post-war period. Here, too, it was not just a question of emergency measures such as the supply of teachers, auxiliary staff and teaching materials for schools, but also of fundamental principles involved in reshaping the whole curriculum. This would be particularly necessary in the subjects that had been most severely affected by Nazi ideology, that is to say History, German Literature and Biology. Although the idea of an independent Austrian state had been confirmed in the Moscow Declaration, the FAM was still painfully aware of the necessity of instilling a new Austrian national consciousness within the majority of the population in order to erase any remaining identification with National Socialism – or with the pan-German thinking of the Socialists. The school history curriculum, which was of particular relevance here, would place special emphasis on the country's cultural particularity throughout Austrian history.[41] To develop this concept of history still further, a special sub-committee was to be set up. Leading FAM members such as Ernst Buschbeck, the former curator of Vienna's Kunsthistorisches Museum, Georg Lelewer and Eva Priester were among those to volunteer for this task.

In literature, too, a shift in emphasis would be called for, with less attention being paid to German literary history and more to what was seen as specifically Austrian. At the same time, works of European literature, and Slavonic literature in particular, were certainly to be included, since they had to a large extent been excluded under National Socialism.

The future organization of the universities as well as the reconstruction of musical and theatrical life were discussed at the FAM's second Cultural Conference in October 1944, chaired by Ernst Buschbeck, and prepared and organized by Hermann Ullrich. Detailed planning even included a draft programme of performances at the Austrian national theatre, the Viennese Burgtheater. An express demand was made for the purging of all National Socialist elements from within Austrian theatrical life. However, the establishment of cultural relations between Austria and England, and obviously with the Soviet Union and Czechoslovakia, too, was seen as equally important. Several special committees then continued the work of this conference.[42]

Unquestionably, Young Austria also played an important role in preparing for the return to Austria. At Young Austria's fourth National Conference in December 1943, Fritz Walter looked ahead to the work to be undertaken by the younger generation in the post-war period: 'Our post-war period is already starting. We have the right to concern ourselves with these questions for it will be our generation who will give to the world of tomorrow a new and better face'.[43]

Important measures to be undertaken by the young functionaries were to include nurturing an Austrian national consciousness within the membership of Young Austria and also promoting the wish to return to Austria where Young Austrians would take up essential positions. It was within Young Austria, in particular – and it should be recalled that Young Austria's leadership was largely identical with that of the 'Kommunistischer Jugendverband' (Communist Youth Organization), the youth arm of the KPÖ – that political factors played a clearly visible role. To Young Austrians, the concept of a broad political base, determined by popular front policies and as promoted by the FAM and the Austrian Centre, was of lesser concern than was maintaining a clear political line.[44]

The fourth Young Austria National Conference in late 1943 had adopted the slogan 'Für Österreich und unsere Zukunft' ('For Austria and Our Future'), and members were spurred on with the optimistic words that the next conference would take place back in Vienna. By the fifth National Conference of December 1944, the Allies had of course come closer to victory, but the struggle was still not over. Thus the conference was called upon to make further efforts to bring about Austria's liberation; and the expected arrival of the Red Army on Austrian soil, an event joyfully anticipated, was used to inspire young exiles to even greater enthusiasm and activity. In his speech to the conference, Fritz Walter looked ahead with confidence: 'The Red Army, which will be the liberating army of Austria, is now on the frontiers of our homeland.'[45]

From 1944 on, Young Austria increasingly concerned itself with events and planning activities which ran largely parallel to those of the FAM. Thus a Post-War and Relief Committee of Young Austria was formed on the lines of the FAM Committee, working in close collaboration with them. The Young Austrian Committee was chaired by Emmi Walter and, as in the case of the FAM, set up numerous sub-committees responsible for specific areas of work. As well as participating in FAM conferences, Young Austria also organized conferences of its own. Following on from the FAM's Welfare Conference, Young Austria mounted an Education Conference in spring 1944 that was addressed by Richard Bayer, Xim Ungar and Fritz Walter, the last of these speaking on the education of young people in post-war Austria. Walter called on his audience to take part in the courses on post-war issues being organized by the FAM: 'What we are learning here under completely different conditions from those in our home country will help us a great deal back home in Austria. But for this we need, even more than before, to be totally focused on Austria.'[46] It was particularly important that Young Austrians should attend the courses for school support staff since the new Austria would need people trained in the right spirit: 'We have the opportunity to attend many good courses [...] Our Austrian history courses certainly won't turn us into history teachers but it will be possible for us to be of assistance when we are needed.'[47]

In the autumn of 1944, Young Austria started its own programme of preparatory courses, aimed at young functionaries who would be returning to Austria; these courses, carried out by and for the young exiles, dealt with practical as well as ideological issues. As mentioned above, the programme was given the perhaps unfortunate name 'Jugendführerschule des Jungen Österreich' (Young Austria School for Youth Leaders). Herbert Steiner, the Secretary of Young Austria, was later ruefully disparaging about the 'the grand name', adding: 'Today this sounds terrible but then they were all proud to attend such a "Jugendführerschule".'[48] On the other hand, he considered that these courses had had an importance that went beyond the exile situation, since the teaching materials, published in the Young Austria publishing series Jugend voran, were sent for use in Austria after the end of the war where they proved to be of real value. The leading Young Austria functionaries were involved in running the 'Jugendführerschule': Fritz Walter, Herbert Steiner, Xim Ungar, Paul Frischauer and Bertl Breuer, with overall responsibility being assigned to Emmi Walter.

The training courses were not intended for large numbers, participation being expressly restricted to those young exiles who wished to return to Austria: numbers of participants are variously given as between 200 and 300 Young Austria members.[49] Those wishing to be accepted on a course had to apply to the organizers and answer numerous questions, for example on their state of health, education, interests and even their favourite authors, as well as on the youth organizations they had belonged to back in Austria. This was a strict selection policy; after all, future Austrian youth leaders, who as time went on would become the party elite, had to be carefully chosen.

The training programme began on 19 October 1944, with individual courses lasting three to four months. They were held at weekends and on one evening per week; in addition the participants had to work through the course material themselves and take an examination in each subject. Successful candidates were issued with a diploma. The organizers demanded a great deal from their young participants:

> We demand serious commitment from each and every course participant. Our self-discipline at the 'Jugendführerschule' must be exemplary. We want to start punctually, and it goes without saying that every participant who has registered and has been accepted must attend the entire course. It may sometimes be difficult to concentrate on the lectures after eight or nine hours' work in a factory or in an office [...] Nevertheless, it is essential that every participant at the

school overcomes any difficulties that may arise in a disciplined fashion.[50]

The course topics, some extremely practical, others with a theoretical and ideological emphasis, were taught by FAM members who were experts in the fields in question. Doctors, for example, were in charge of courses on sex education and hygiene. The teacher Richard Bayer ran a course on 'Kinderbewegung und Kindergruppen' ('Children's Movement and Children's Groups') which stressed the particular importance of children being taught 'to become good Austrians' (p. 1). Courses such as 'How do I Read a Book and Give a Presentation?' as well as others on Austrian geography, history and citizenship were intended to raise the young people's general level of education. The course 'A Racial Theory?', run by the psychoanalyst and philosopher Walter Hollitscher, drew on teaching materials from the FAM's teacher training course. This set itself the important task of informing young exiles of the current thinking in human biology so that they would be equipped with the knowledge necessary to refute Nazi racial ideology (which had, of course, been adopted in Austria with considerable enthusiasm). As Hollitscher explained:

> Fascism has spread its particular 'theory of evolution' in all schools and with all available means of propaganda [...] Its intellectual poison has had its effect even on those most capable of resisting it; this racial myth may have lost all credibility, but it will still have left some traces.[51]

One of the crucial topics of the 'Jugendführerschule' was that covered in Herbert Steiner's course 'Die Organisation einer Jugendbewegung' ('The Organization of a Youth Movement'). In this he was able to draw on his own experience as Secretary of Young Austria. The establishment of youth groups, including their organization at local, regional and national levels, financial issues and political campaign work were discussed in great detail as was the role of a youth newspaper or publishing house in politicizing young people.

In setting up the 'Jugendführerschule', Young Austria, and of course also the FAM, were therefore pursuing a number of aims. One was that the young exiles should return home as conscious Austrians. It was intended to expand their knowledge of the country they had left seven years before, in most cases before the completion of their school education. The exiles would thus be returning not as strangers but as well educated anti-Fascist Austrians who would be able to influence their young compatriots by assuming leading roles in a new youth organization, having learned the practical organizational skills required of youth leaders. While the courses were intended to engender fresh enthusiasm in the participants for the tasks ahead, the organizers of the 'Jugend-führerschule' were certainly aware of the probable reception awaiting the returnees for, as Fritz Walter admitted with uncharacteristic bluntness: 'We should not be under any illusion, however, that back home people will be expecting us, that they will welcome us or indeed acclaim us as youth leaders.'[52]

In the event, it was precisely in the area of youth organizations – and in fact only there – that the returning exiles played any significant part in reconstruction. Their hopes for a meaningful political role in other areas were largely unfulfilled after the first post-war elections had produced such disappointing results for the Communists. The 'Jugendführerschule' ran for about a year. Certificates were still being issued to participants in September 1945 until, with the return of the leading activists – Fritz Walter, in particular, at the end of October and Emmi Walter a little later – the training programme came to an end.

In addition, Young Austria was involved in further planning work in connection with preparations for the London World Youth Conference of the Österreichische Weltjugendbewegung (Austrian World Youth Movement), held in October 1945. A youth programme for liberated Austria which was to be presented to the conference contained demands for a legal framework of working conditions for young people and their right to work, a central feature of constitutions in Communist states. Like Young Austria, the FAM also continued its training courses and its detailed planning activities in its various committees up until the end of the war and beyond. Several series of articles were published in *Zeitspiegel* focusing on such topics as the reconstruction of the school system and of the economy in post-war Austria, involving the nationalization of key industries.

Along with such preparatory work, the Austrian Centre and related organizations obviously continued to address the increasingly urgent issue of returning. The decision to return was an automatic one for the Centre's functionaries, indeed it may well be seen as the underlying motive for most of their activities. For the large majority of the refugees, however, this decision was by no means so clear-cut. The positive tone of the numerous articles appearing in the press of the Austrian Centre was therefore intended to have a decisive influence on the membership. An article in *Young Austria*, for example, 'Warum gehe ich nach Österreich zurück?' ('Why am I going back to Austria?'), presented its readers with the arguments firstly, that they were urgently needed for reconstruction and secondly, that the knowledge that they had played their part would be a source of pride and satisfaction to them. Above all, however, the article appealed to them as Austrians. They should decide to return, quite simply, 'because I am an Austrian [...] The sad thing is that it took exile to teach me to be an Austrian'.[53] While it was stressed that the organization should exert no pressure – 'It is essential that every individual should decide for himself. We stand by this'[54] – nevertheless Jenö Desser, the Austrian Centre's spokesman on such questions, was optimistic, writing early in 1944:

> In most cases, returning home will be the obvious solution. The overwhelming majority of exiles will wish for nothing better than to return home and to be reunited with their families.[55]

Desser took up the question of the return of the Jewish refugees (who after all made up the majority of the Austrian Centre's membership) in the pamphlet *Vom Ghetto zur Freiheit: Die Zukunft der Juden im befreiten Österreich* (*From the Ghetto to Freedom: The future of the Jews in Liberated Austria*), which appeared in April 1945. While demanding punishment for the crimes against Jews, and material restitution, he ended on a note of confidence which underscored the pamphlet's chief aim of encouraging exiles to return: 'The Austrian Jews will again take up their [rightful] place. They will have the opportunity as never before to play their part in the building of their future and that of their home country.'[56]

Despite this positive tone, the Free Austrians were under no illusions as to the extent of the logistical and organizational problems raised by repatriation. Throughout Europe, there were millions of displaced people who would have to be repatriated at the end of the war. Consequently, at the FAM Conference on Refugee Issues held in autumn 1944, this question was considered in a more realistic way. In a keynote lecture, 'Die österreichischen Flüchtlinge und ihre Zukunft' ('The Austrian Refugees and their Future'), Jenö Desser presented the three possibilities open to the exiles: return – as the preferred option this was the first to be discussed – settlement in Great Britain and onward emigration.[57]

The assumption was that the Allied authorities would give precedence, when it came to repatriation, to those would-be returners whose skills were particularly needed in the post-war period. For this purpose, the FAM had begun in June 1944 to set up a register of specialists in order to gain, for them at least, permission to return at the earliest possible date. Questionnaires in which exiles were asked to register details of their training and practical professional experience, as well as their desire to return, were compiled and sent out within the UK as well as to the overseas branches of the Free Austrian World Movement.[58] Eva Kolmer contacted the Foreign Office to inform them of this initiative and to obtain the British authorities' official support for the early return of

Austrian specialists in key areas.[59] The British reaction to this was muted, although the lists were certainly accepted, together with similar ones from other Austrian refugee organizations, and passed on to the War Ministry. In March 1945 the responses to the questionnaires, both from Britain and from other parts of the world, were evaluated by the FAM: around two thirds of the 1500 respondents had declared their intention to return to their former country.[60]

For those considering returning, the press of the Austrian Centre hardly constituted an objective source of information about the conditions prevailing in Austria, however. On 21 March 1945, *Zeitspiegel* greeted the arrival of the Red Army as the rebirth of Austria, and the liberation of Vienna as a new beginning, marked by an immediate return to normality: 'The shops are open [...] people are coming out of their cellars, starting to sort out their homes and to replace broken window panes with boards.'[61]

The reports soon reaching England about the excesses of the Red Army were not referred to in *Zeitspiegel*.[62] It was important to present the exiles with a positive picture of conditions in Austria in general, and of the Soviet occupation in particular, in order to encourage their resolve to return. Thus *Zeitspiegel* reported on Soviet generosity in the supply of food and the increase in food rations in their zone, on the friendly Russian soldiers who 'are not nearly as uneducated as certain Viennese like to claim' and on kindly female members of the Red Army who were not only speaking German within three months but also organizing truckloads of bread for the Austrian population.[63]

For the leading functionaries of the Austrian Centre and Young Austria, however, it was the political developments that were of primary concern, in particular the formation of the provisional government on 28 April 1945. Franz West would later recall his shock at the appointment of the Social Democrat Karl Renner as Chancellor – 'our stomachs turned over' – but as soon as key posts like the Ministries of the Interior and of Education were allocated to the Communists, 'everything was alright for us'.[64] Indeed, the Communists succeeded in gaining one third of all offices in the provisional government. In particular, the Political Council, made up of representatives from the three main parties, the Social Democrats, the conservative Austrian People's Party and the Communists, enjoyed the same composition as that proposed in emigration by the Austrian Centre and the FAM as part of their popular front policies. It seemed as if the new Austria would now fulfil all the aspirations the Free Austrians had fostered during the long years of planning and preparation.

Accordingly, the press of the Austrian Centre hailed the provisional government as a government of unity which would attract the wholehearted support of the exiles. Various declarations of loyalty during the following months, both in the exile press and also at the FAM National Conference in August, were also used to reiterate the desire to return and take part in the reconstruction of the country. At the same time, numerous reports from Austria itself stressed the urgent need for young workers and specialists in all areas.

Above all, it was necessary actually to bring about the return of the exiles. Between 1 July and 31 August 1945, the FAM carried out yet another campaign for the registration of Austrians throughout Great Britain, with the aim of providing the Austrian authorities with information concerning the numbers wishing to return and their qualifications, which could also be useful in compiling a repatriation plan. Like the register of specialists drawn up by the FAWM the previous year, the FAM's lists now revealed a total of around 1000 Austrians expressing their intention to return home.[65]

However, the decision as to *when* such a return might take place was initially not in their own hands. Austria was, after all, an occupied country. Allied permission was required for repatriation and, at the request of the military authorities, a ban on returning had been brought in which was officially attributed to transport difficulties and the poor state of food supplies in the country. Certainly refugees were permitted to apply for exit papers from Great Britain and several did so successfully, mostly to take part in international conferences; but, with few exceptions, entry into Austria was refused on principle. One of the exceptions was the leading member of the London Bureau, Oscar Pollak, who was permitted to return in September 1945. A British Foreign Office memorandum remarks on Pollak's application: 'It is in our interest to strengthen the Social Democrat and Christian Socialist elements in Austria against the Communists.' When the FAM enquired whether Pollak's return meant that the general ban had been lifted, however, the Foreign Office replied in the negative.[66]

Following the announcement in October that, earlier than expected, the first elections for the Austrian parliament would take place on 25 November, the return of the Austrian Centre's leading functionaries, in particular, became a matter of prime concern. How could they reap the benefits of their years of work in emigration if they were now to be prevented from taking part in the political activity of the new Austrian state? The prospects of a successful outcome to the elections seemed extremely favourable. In the Soviet Zone of Occupation, especially, the Communists had been able to establish themselves in the new local councils and in the works councils of key industries; in the new Austrian press, too, the influence of the KPÖ was initially very strong.

For the parliamentary elections, the Communist Party put up two candidates still in British exile: Willi Scholz, who originated from Graz, as their first candidate for Styria, and Fritz Walter, selected as youth candidate for a Vienna constituency. In view of the ban, however, both men felt that they had no option but to return against the wish of the British authorities (though with help from the Yugoslavs). Their reports on their journey home read like genuine adventure stories.

Willi Scholz and F.C. West were offered the opportunity of leaving Britain by air with a Yugoslav delegation who had been attending a conference in London. They were immediately prepared to leave their young families behind in order to follow their Party's instruction to return. They left, as Franz West later recalled, 'head over heals'.[67] After first managing to mislead the British authorities, and then experiencing a perilous landing on a small Russian military air base near Vienna, not to mention further complications, they reached the KPÖ Central Committee on 21 October. In the meantime, the British authorities had been informed of the arrival of 'two dangerous Communists who had left the country by means of deception'.[68] Scholz even received a visit from a British official who demanded that he return to England. This had little effect, however: 'I laughed at the British officer and said: "You can do what you like, I am an Austrian and I am staying in Austria and I remain an Austrian."'[69]

Fritz Walter had originally been supposed to act as delegation leader to the World Youth Conference that he had organized in London for the beginning of November. However, in October the party leadership decided that he should return to stand as a parliamentary candidate. *Zeitspiegel* printed several reports from the various stages of his return journey. With official British exit papers, he was able to reach Paris from where he, too, continued his journey with the help of the Yugoslavs. Though touching down in Vienna, he was not allowed to leave the plane, finally arriving back there by car from Belgrade.[70] Apart from his parliamentary candidature, he had also been chosen by the KPÖ to lead the Freie Österreichische Jugend (FÖJ) or Free Austrian Youth, founded in Austria in May 1945, a position in which he was to make use of his experience gained in emigration. The FÖJ was initially conceived as a broad, non-party political youth organization. This non-political basis was dropped a few months later, however, and replaced by a stronger Communist line after the Austrian elections had proved such a disappointment to the Party.[71]

Eva Kolmer – she too had received instructions from the Party to return to Austria – Marie Köstler and Steffi Heller likewise managed to return home illegally. After participating in the inaugural meeting of the International Democratic Women's Federation in Paris, the three women

were able to take the Arlberg Express to Austria, but were held in
Innsbruck for three days by the French Occupation Authorities before
finally arriving in Vienna at the start of 1946. Kolmer's delight at her
successful return was tempered by her first observations of the
entrenched Nazi mentality of the Austrian population:

> You see, the German soldiers were being transported back, and
> Tyrolian women were standing everywhere we looked, embracing
> them, crying etc. [...] And then we saw that there was no dislike of the
> Germans and there had been no resistance against them.[72]

A further group of leading functionaries, Jenö Kostmann, Herbert Steiner
and Theodor Prager, succeeded in returning to Austria via Prague which
they had been officially permitted to visit as delegates to a student
conference. It was a matter of extreme importance to them, however, to
be back in Austria by the forthcoming elections. Kostmann, who had
been appointed as editor of the *Österreichische Volksstimme*, had actually
obtained permission to return from the British Foreign Office, pending
security clearance; for, following Oscar Pollak's return, the British were
concerned not to appear unduly prejudiced against the Communists. This
clearance, however, took so long to come through that Kostmann finally
decided not to wait any longer but to join the other two functionaries on
their illegal journey from Prague to Austria. The official permit was only
sent on to him in Prague after he had already left for Vienna.[73] Thus
Kostmann, Steiner and Prager managed to arrive back in Austria just
before the general elections but were still unable to exercise their right to
vote as the deadline for inclusion in the electoral roll had by then
passed.[74]

The first post-war parliamentary election on 25 November 1945 was a
bitter disappointment to the functionaries of the Austrian Centre,
destroying their hopes of playing a leading role in the political
reconstruction of their country. The Communists had counted on
obtaining 20-25% of the vote. According to Kostmann they had been in
'extremely high spirits, everybody was convinced that the basic mandate
was as good as won'.[75] In the event, the KPÖ succeeded in gaining
merely 5.2% of the vote and only four seats in parliament. Both Willi
Scholz and Fritz Walter (the latter now using his former name Otto
Brichacek) proved unsuccessful in their parliamentary ambitions. The
Communists forfeited the strong position they had gained during the first
post-war months, being reduced to a mere minor party once again; and
despite the support of the Soviet Occupation Authority they were able to
exert little influence on future political developments. The electoral defeat
shattered their hopes of achieving parity with the major political parties in

Austria and of implementing their popular front policies. Jenö Kostmann has since spoken of the reaction within his party:

> Well, the comrades were bitterly disappointed and today I would say that this disappointment with the result of the first elections has affected the party like a lead weight, and even today it is still influenced by it somehow, although it was all a long time ago.[76]

It is not known exactly how many members of the Austrian Centre and related organizations actually settled in Austria again after the end of the war. While most of the leading functionaries did so, the great majority of the ordinary members chose not to. Jenö Desser, certainly, believed that, of the Austrian Centre's many members, 'a large number would have returned to Austria had the election results been different [...] Apart from the Party members, only very few returned to Vienna'.[77] What *is* clear is that the Second Republic was not the state that members of the Austrian Centre had hoped for. As things turned out, it was not the new Austria of which many had dreamed throughout the long years of exile, nor that for which the Free Austrian Movement and Young Austria had campaigned in their countless publications, conferences and committees.

Notes

1 'Memorandum by the Inter-Allied Group for the study of German and Satellite activities', Note de Bureau no. 50, 29 January 1943, National Archives [NA], FO 371/34474, p. 12.

2 'Leitsätze der Arbeitsgemeinschaft "Das kommende Österreich", angenommen im Juli 1939', Archive of the Society for the History of the Labour Movement, Vienna, File London Büro, Box 1, Folder 13A.

3 'Memorandum by the Inter-Allied Group for the study of German and Satellite activities.' The Foreign Office file describes this report (by a M. Kulski from the Polish Embassy) as 'highly coloured'.

4 *Austrian Centre*, January 1944, p. 6.

5 *Austrian Centre*, June 1944, p. 6.

6 Jenö Kostmann, in Documentation Archive of Austrian Resistance [DÖW], Vienna, Interview 044, 17 August 1983, p. 53.

7 Guy Stanley, 'British Policy and the Austrian Question', unpublished doctoral dissertation, London 1973, pp. 88 f.

8 Anna Hornik, *This is Austria: The Story of a Beautiful Country*, London 1942, p. 22.

9 *Ibid.*, p. 23.

10 *Zeitspiegel*, 2 January 1943, p. 5.

11 Ernst Fischer, *The Rebirth of my Country*, London [September 1944], pp. 19 f.

12 As early as 24 July 1943, *Zeitspiegel* reported on an address given by a member of the Czech Government in Exile, Franticek Nemec, entitled 'Ökonomischer und technischer Wiederaufbau in Zentraleuropa' ('Economic and Technical Reconstruction in Central Europe'). Nemec pointed out that the economies of the two countries ideally complemented each other and that therefore Austria would be 'a desired and sought after partner' (p. 3).

13 Ernst Fischer, *The Rebirth of My Country*, pp. 19 f.

14 'Memorandum by the Inter-Allied Group for the study of German and Satellite activities', p. 9.

15 The optimistic picture in this brochure regarding the reception of Jewish refugees was not borne out by the situation in post-war Austria. See Helga Embacher, 'Eine Heimkehr gibt es nicht? Remigration nach Österreich', in Claus-Dieter Krohn *et al.*, eds., *Exilforschung: Ein internationales Jahrbuch*, vol. 19: *Jüdische Emigration: Zwischen Assimilation und Verfolgung, Akkulturation und jüdischer Identität*, Munich 2001.

16 Wilhelm Scholz, *Ein Weg ins Leben: Das neue Österreich und die Judenfrage*, London 1943, p. 9. It is interesting to note that Scholz would later distance himself from this publication? 'That was the worst brochure' (Interview with Franz West und Willi Scholz, 27 June 1977, DÖW 13.00, p. 18).

17 *Rundbrief des Jungen Österreich*, June 1943, p. 11.

18 Theodor Prager, 'Can Austria Live?', *Young Austria*, 11 March 1944, pp. 1 f.

19 *Ibid.*

20 *Austrian News*, 28 January 1943, p. 4.

21 *Zeitspiegel*, 6 February 1943, p. 8.

22 Emil Müller-Sturmheim to Geoffrey Harrison, 27 April 1943, NA, FO 371/34464.

23 *Das Free Austrian Movement in Großbritannien und der Wiederaufbau Österreichs*, DÖW 3057/A/20c, p. 1.

24 W.D. Allen to J.H. Garvin, 12 April 1943, NA, FO 371/34464. See also previous chapter of this study.

25 'Free Austrian Movement in Great Britain? Landeskonferenz des Free Austrian Movement', [1943], DÖW 3057A/17b.

26 *Ibid.*, p. 5.

27 *Ibid.*

28 *Ibid.*, p. 8.

29 *Ibid.*

30 Walter Hollitscher, 'Volksaufklärung nach Hitlers Sturz', *Zeitspiegel*, 13 March 1943, p. 7.

31 Georg Lelewer, 'Bestrafung der Kriegsverbrecher', *Zeitspiegel*, 12 June 1943, p. 5.

32   Emmi Walter, *Die soziale und wirtschaftliche Lage der österreichischen Jugend unter der deutschen Fremdherrschaft*, London 1944, pp. 17-22.

33   *Austrian Medical Bulletin*, October 1945, p. 34.

34   *Ibid.*, pp. 16-20.

35   *Studienmaterialien der Kommission für den Wiederaufbau der österreichischen Wirtschaft, 3. Folge*, London, October 1944.

36   *Ibid.*

37   *Vorschläge des Free Austrian Movement für erste Maßnahmen zum Wiederaufbau der österreichischen Land- und Forstwirtschaft*, London [1944], p. 2.

38   *Zeitspiegel*, 18 November 1944, p. 4.

39   'Entwurf der Kommission für einen Wiederaufbau der österreichischen Wirtschaft über die Administration der österreichischen Industrie', DÖW 3016/29, p. 4.

40   *Zeitspiegel*, 5 February 1944, p. 7.

41   *Sofortprogramm für das Schulwesen im unabhängigen Österreich: Protokoll der Lehrerkonferenz des Free Austrian Movement am 8. und 9. April*, London [1944], p. 2.

42   *Zeitspiegel*, 28 November 1944, p. 8.

43   *Young Austria*, 18 December 1943, p. 2.

44   Jenö Kostmann, DÖW Interview 044, p. 54.

45   Fritz Walter, *Youth in the Reconstruction of Liberated Europe: Report on Youth Activities in France, Belgium, Holland, Italy, Yugoslavia, Poland, Greece, Bulgaria*, London, January 1945, p. 1.

46   Fritz Walter, *Probleme der Erziehung im neuen, demokratischen Österreich (Bericht über die Erziehungskonferenz des 'Jungen Österreich in Großbritannien')*, London 1944, p. 10.

47   *Ibid.*, p. 24.

48   Herbert Steiner, 'Workshop? Niederlassungsländer? Großbritannien', in Symposium 'Die Vertreibung des Geistigen', Vienna 1988 (transcript of cassette recording, p. 10), DÖW 16972.

49   In 'Tätigkeitsbericht des Jungen Österreich', [1945], DÖW 589(A), p. 11, the figures given are 60 functionaries from London and 50 from provincial branches, and a further 100 participants who had joined via correspondence courses. The final issue of *Jung-Österreich*, 24 August 1946, p. 4, cites 300 participants in all.

50   Fritz Walter, 'Unsere österreichische Jugendführerschule? Einleitung zu den Materialien der Jugendführerschule', in *Jugendführerschule des Jungen Österrreich*, London [1944], p. 4.

51   Walter Hollitscher, Preface to *Rassentheorie? 6 Lehrbriefe an österreichische Biologielehrer*, London 1944.

52   Fritz Walter, 'Unsere österreichische Jugendführerschule', p. 2.

53   *Young Austria*, 9 September 1944, p. 4.

54 *Austrian Centre*, August 1944, [p. 1].

55 Jenö Desser, 'Rücksiedlung und Weiterwanderung', *Zeitspiegel*, 5 February 1944, p. 8.

56 Jenö Desser, *Vom Ghetto zur Freiheit: Die Zukunft der Juden im befreiten Österreich*, London [1945], [p. 16].

57 In Jenö Desser, Eva Kolmer, Leopold Spira, *Bericht von der Konferenz über österreichische Flüchtlingsfragen der Free Austrian Movement*, London 1944, p. 4.

58 Free Austrian Movement, 'Spezialisten-Nachweis', in Friedrich Otto Hertz Papers, Archive for the History of Sociology in Austria, Graz, 19/2.1.

59 Eva Kolmer to Geoffrey Harrison, 17 July 1944, NA, FO 371/38834? 'This is the first of several lists we are going to send you. We have included all teachers and experienced doctors and nurses because we think there will be a considerable shortage of such personnel.'

60 *Österreichspiegel*, 7 March 1945, p. 3.

61 *Zeitspiegel*, 2 April 1945, p. 1.

62 Even much later on, Franz West would dismiss any criticism of the Red Army's behaviour as 'nichtige Verleumdung' ('pure slander') (Franz West, DÖW Interview 92, 1 December 1982, pp. 377 f.).

63 *Zeitspiegel*, 9 June 1945, p. 1, and 18 August 1945, p. 5.

64 Franz West, DÖW Interview 92, p. 376.

65 *Zeitspiegel*, 29 September 1945, p. 3.

66 NA, FO 371/46659.

67 Franz West, DÖW Interview 92, p. 383.

68 *Ibid.*, p. 389.

69 Willi Scholz, DÖW 8516, p. 54.

70 *Jung-Österreich*, 3 November 1945, p. 4.

71 *Jung-Österreich*, 16 February 1946, p. 3.

72 Eva Schmidt-Kolmer, DÖW Interview 719, 22 June 1990, p. 24.

73 NA, FO 371/46659 and 46660.

74 Jenö Kostmann, DÖW Interview 044, p. 71.

75 *Ibid.*, p. 72.

76 *Ibid.*, p. 73.

77 Jenö Desser, 'Mein Lebenslauf. 8. März 1904 – 8. März 1984', unpublished manuscript in the possession of Hans Desser, Vienna, p. 95.

'NO EASY MATTER'
CLOSURE – AND AFTER

MARIETTA BEARMAN AND
CHARMIAN BRINSON

When the Austrian Centre's chief activists returned to Vienna,[1] they left Jenö Desser in London, charging him with winding up the organization. This was, as he would later recall, 'no easy matter':

> It took us nearly a year before we had wound down everything, sold the contents, cleaned the houses, fulfilled all obligations and said goodbye everywhere etc. We then returned the four houses to the Church of England.[2]

The sale of the Centre's 'complete club, office and restaurant furniture' was announced in the 'Abschiedsnummer' or closing number of the *Austrian Centre Bulletin*, as was a valedictory celebration for employees and functionaries, scheduled for 16 January 1947, the day after the official closure. The *Bulletin* also briefly set out the arrangements for Austrian exiles remaining in Britain who could formerly have expected help from the Centre or associated Free Austrian organizations: since the Council of Austrians would cease to exist, assistance would have to be sought from the Austrian Representative, Dr Heinrich Schmid, newly arrived in London. Advice on repatriation must now be obtained from the Control Office for Germany and Austria while issues of a more local nature would have to be dealt with by the Citizens' Advice Bureau, so members were informed. 'We extend grateful thanks to all those Austrians,' the Council of Austrians concluded, 'who have put their trust in us during the past eight years and who, because of post-war developments, are now able to solve their problems without our help.'[3]

This coolness of tone is at distinct variance, however, with the mood that reportedly prevailed at the Austrian Centre's Extraordinary General Meeting, on 14 December 1946, at which the forthcoming closure was announced. Even the *Bulletin* admitted to the 'lively discussion' that took place 'in the overcrowded auditorium of the theatre',[4] while individual participants in the meeting have since recalled the strong feelings expressed from the floor by members who were both unprepared for and bitterly opposed to the loss of their Centre.[5]

Desser, as President, had announced the forthcoming liquidation on the grounds that 'the tasks and aims of the Austrian Centre have, in essence, been accomplished and the present situation no longer appears to justify the continuing existence of the Austrian Centre'. There were, he contended, also practical reasons for the closure: repatriation and onward emigration had resulted in 'a considerable reduction in membership', such that 'the Austrian Centre no longer enjoyed its previous level of income'.[6]

After winding up the whole organization on 15 January 1946, Desser and fellow functionary Walter Skrein reported on their actions to the Austrian Representative who in reply paid the Free Austrians a handsome official tribute:

> May I assure you on this occasion that I fully appreciate the activities your organization has been carrying out at such a difficult time for our country as well as for its people living here. You may now conclude these in the proud knowledge that you have done a great service to Austria and the Austrians and that you have made a valuable contribution to the reconstruction of our sorely tested homeland.

Schmid fully understood, he assured them, their reasons for closure[7] – it was, after all, part and parcel of the Communist agenda to persuade exiled Austrians to return to Austria, as Schmid would have known. Yet while closure of the Centre would have made sense to the activists who envisaged a future back in Austria, it constituted a cruel blow for those members – the majority – who had no wish to return but for whom the Centre had long provided a social and psychological lifeline in exile. There was, therefore, much discontent among the ordinary membership. One rumour of the time, as recalled even today by former members, was of the 'scorched earth' variety: it was said that the Communist activists, on leaving Britain, had not wished to allow any other group to benefit from their past efforts – including premises, organization and membership – but had chosen instead to put an end to the entire enterprise, regardless of those Austrian exiles remaining.[8]

Certainly it is reported that, on closure, all the former activities, including the very popular youth activities of the Centre, came to a halt, compelling members to seek out comparable British organizations if they could: a Jewish Youth Club in place of Young Austria,[9] for example, or – in the case of a keen Young Austria choir member – Alan Bush's Workers' Music Association.[10] There were, in addition, other Austrian exile organizations still in existence, of varying political persuasions, such as the Austria Office's British-Austrian Club and the Liberal/Social

Democratic Anglo-Austrian Democratic Society (after the closure of the Austrian Centre, significantly, given the more all-encompassing name of Anglo-Austrian Society) and it seems fair to assume such groups must have benefited in terms of membership from the Austrian Centre's demise.

There is, however, an interesting adjunct to all of this. The closing number of the *Austrian Centre Bulletin* which, as it happens, carries an advertisement for the above-mentioned British-Austrian Club, also features a small advertisement reading as follows:

FELLOW COUNTRYMEN

You are very welcome at the Austrian Friendship Club, 143, Seven Sisters Road, N. 7 [...] Events on Saturdays or Sundays. Open daily except Mondays. Viennese cooking.[11]

143, Seven Sisters Rd, notably, was the address of the Austrian Centre's Finsbury Park branch. This ties in neatly with a minute in a Home Office file from early 1947, referring to British security reports on the termination of the Austrian Centre's activities: according to this, the Finsbury Park branch had indeed become the 'Anglo-Austrian Friendship Club', with a membership of around 150. It was also reported, possibly erroneously, that the Council of Austrians in Great Britain was continuing to function as an advice bureau, still under the Chairmanship of Professor Walter Schiff.[12]

For the Austrian Centre's functionaries, at any rate, it was the developments back in Austria that now counted – to a greater or lesser extent, this had been the case since the end of hostilities. Within weeks of the Allied victory, Eva Kolmer, for the FAM, tried to re-establish contact with Viktor Matejka, the new Communist City Councillor for Culture and Education in Vienna, following up an initial letter with further communications in September and October 1945. Expressing the FAM's frustrations with the British authorities, who were delaying the Austrians' return home, Kolmer wrote to ask Matejka whether a call for a FAM delegation, 'to prepare for the return from Austria itself', might be issued directly from Vienna.[13] The twelve-person delegation, as she reported in a subsequent letter, would consist of representatives of various professional and political groups of Austrian exiles, including Hermann Ullrich for the Civil Service, Paul Loew-Beer for the scientists and technologists, Hans Winterberg, Marie Köstler and Kolmer herself.[14] At the same time, Kolmer continued to lobby for this in Britain, too, sending both the Intergovernmental Committee on Refugees and the Foreign Office a similar, if 14-strong, list;[15] the Foreign Office, though dragging its heels, finally granted permission for a delegation of six (only one of whom had figured on the original list) in January 1946.[16]

By this time, however, matters had moved on; as described in the previous chapter, several of the Free Austrian leaders had managed to find their way back to Austria, including Eva Kolmer who arrived in Vienna at the beginning of 1946. Together with Marie Köstler, another early returner, Kolmer involved herself there in matters of repatriation, foreign aid for Austria and the establishment of links between Austria and the 'Auslandsösterreicher' or exiled Austrians (about whom little was known in Austria). This last she had discussed with Matejka himself and it had been agreed, so she reported back to the FAM Executive in London

> that articles about the cultural activities of Austrians abroad should appear in various newspapers and magazines. For this I need material or articles about topics such as Austrian artists abroad, Austrian academics abroad etc. Also, we want to prepare to put on an exhibition about the Austrians and their organizations abroad.[17]

After returning to Britain in February 1946,[18] Kolmer continued to correspond with Matejka along these same lines, while Matejka used Kolmer as a means of establishing contact with cultural exiles of the reputation of Georg Ehrlich and Oskar Kokoschka[19] (Matejka was intent on persuading exiled Austrians of distinction to return to Austria).[20] Nor was, contrary to the accepted view, Matejka the only source of such invitations: in November 1945, for instance, Foreign Office documents record that Ernst Fischer, the Communist Minister for Education, was asking for the return of FAM member Ernst Buschbeck, the leading art expert, 'in order that his special knowledge can be used for the recovery of displaced objects of art and for the reorganization of the picture gallery'.[21] Another leading FAM member, Erich Schindel, was invited back in December 1945 by the Ministry of Social Welfare in Vienna 'in order to resume his medical work there';[22] and in March 1946 Hermann Ullrich, who had worked so hard to promote Austrian culture in exile, was offered employment as an Appeal Judge of the Ministry of Justice, as one of a number of Austrians returning 'at the urgent request of the Allied Commission and the Austrian Government, in order to strengthen the ranks of the Civil Service out there'.[23]

In fact, although this is not apparent from the Foreign Office documentation, Ullrich's recall, like that of others, may well have been set in motion by Viktor Matejka. For, when Kolmer had returned to London from Vienna, she had conveyed a letter from Matejka to Ullrich, expressing recognition of the latter's cultural work in exile and encouraging him, in addition to resuming his work in the judiciary, to play a role in post-war Austrian cultural life. Ullrich, while admitting to certain reservations concerning professional demands, his age and health, and the conditions currently prevailing in Austria, had nevertheless reacted positively:

> After my return – which I expect to take place in June or July – I'll certainly be happy to work in the field of culture, so long as my contribution is welcome and not regarded as a presumption on the part of a 'Zuagraster' [outsider] by those who remained in Austria; only a year ago, many of them may well have been members of the 'Reichsschrifttumkammer' [National Socialist Writers' Organization] or 'Kulturkammer' [National Socialist Artists' Organization]. What I would like best would be to work in my old field, that is as music critic of a big daily paper.[24]

Back in London, Kolmer convened a meeting of leading cultural figures within the FAM – including Ullrich, of course, the artist Georg Ehrlich, the publisher Kurt Maschler and so on – to discuss the plans for Anglo-Austrian interchange that she had brought back from her talks with Matejka. As immediate objectives, Kolmer had suggested the supplying of Austria with copies of post-Anschluss publications; the establishment of a two-way exchange programme of artists and scholars (with Benjamin Britten named as a possible cultural envoy to Vienna); and a number of larger scale projects that included inviting the Vienna Philharmonic Orchestra over to Britain.[25] Plans for achieving these aims were discussed and the desire was expressed by those present – exiled Austrians cut off from the Austrian mainstream – for information on the current state of cultural life in Austria as well as on its leading proponents and organizations.[26]

In a 1944 pamphlet, Jenö Desser had already anticipated that the Free Austrian Movement would need to work through a 'Rückwandererstelle' or remigration office in Vienna in order to organize the return of its membership.[27] Accordingly, when Franz West and Willi Scholz arrived back in Vienna, they took steps to establish the Free Austrian World Movement there and to represent, *inter alia*, the interests of the exiled Austrians. On 1 December 1945, *Zeitspiegel* reported that West, in his FAM capacity, had made a broadcast in which he delivered 'to the homeland regards from the 2500 Austrians abroad organized in the [Free Austrian] World Movement'. He had recalled the movement's origins – 'we were united by our fate, we had our suffering and our hopes in common, and increasingly also our programme for future action' – and had listed some of the achievements of the exiled Austrians, both in wartime in their support for the Allied war effort, and in peacetime in the organization of aid for Austria.[28] A month later Scholz, for his part, also published an article in *Zeitspiegel*, 'An meine Freunde in England' ('To my Friends in England'), in which he issued a direct appeal to the exiled

Austrians (including, notably, those with no intention of returning home) and assigned each of them their part to play in Austria's future:

> Support the cause of Austria's progress throughout the world, help all progressive elements abroad to support the new forces of Austria's democracy and fight against the old forces of the Austrian past which have once again emerged; for by doing this you can make your contribution to safeguarding the peace.[29]

The Freie Österreichische Weltbewegung (Free Austrian World Movement [FAWM]) had evidently succeeded in setting up its Viennese office by late 1945 – certainly Kolmer was using their address, Fleischmarkt 5, by 3 January 1946[30] – though its establishment was only announced in *Zeitspiegel* later in January 1946 in a letter from West. He had been making contacts, he wrote, with FAWM functionaries and members from some of the countries of emigration as well as with Austrians serving with the Allied forces, and he had found them unanimous in their view

> that every effort should be made from Vienna to support and guide the valuable activities of the FAWM's national organizations [in the respective countries of emigration] and their cooperation one with another so that we are now in the process of setting up a provisional office here in Viennna.

The FAWM would liaise with the Austrian government and the Allied occupation authorities on the issues it saw as its chief province, namely repatriation, demobilization of Austrians in the Allied armies and aid to Austria. These matters would be further promoted – and here West was certainly embellishing the facts somewhat – by the fact that Eva Kolmer and Marie Köstler had just arrived in Vienna, 'in order to negotiate on the spot, with the agreement of the British Foreign Office, about all questions concerning the Austrians abroad'.[31]

The following month, February 1946, Franz West held a Press Conference to announce the opening of the Vienna office, an event on which the Allied Commission for Austria reported back to London in some detail. The political aims of the FAM, namely to bring about a free, independent and democratic Austria, had been achieved, West had claimed, 'but it was considered that there was still some useful and necessary work which it can undertake'. The new office was being opened, therefore,

a) to organize relief and assistance for Austria
b) to facilitate the return to Austria of the emigrants

c) to maintain all possible contact with Austrian POWs abroad
d) to act as a channel of communication with those Austrians abroad who although they will not return to their country have its interests at heart.

West announced that the FAWM, whose 'world-wide nature [...] made it a particularly appropriate instrument to further these aims', planned to limit itself to the above agenda; once its aims had been achieved, it would be wound up. There would be no question of setting up a full-scale organization in Vienna but merely a committee, nor was there to be a political programme[32] (since, although this was naturally not made explicit, the programme to which West and Scholz were working was that of the KPÖ).

The Allied Commission's report led to a flurry of minutes and correspondence in Foreign Office circles, with M.F. Cullis recalling that 'West [...] was one of the two Austrian Communists who returned improperly to Austria last autumn'.[33] Further information on West and his Austrian Self-Aid, Austrian Centre and FAM activities while in London was then despatched to Vienna, including the interesting (if unverifiable) assertion, from a Legitimist source, that West had 'allowed himself to be acclaimed as the "future President of the Second Austrian Republic"'.[34] In the event, West, like other leading Austrian Centre functionaries, would have had to come to terms with his Party's, and therefore his own, progressive insignificance within the Austrian national arena. As for the FAWM, it seems unlikely that the Vienna office existed very much beyond the closure of the Free Austrian organizations in London.

There was, perhaps, a greater degree of continuity to be enjoyed by returning Young Austrians who could find a new but familiar home for themselves in the newly established Freie Österreichische Jugend (Free Austrian Youth [FÖJ]). On 1 December 1945, in *Jung-Österreich*, Franz Danimann, the FÖJ's Chairman, reported on discussions on the development of closer links between Young Austria and the FÖJ, wishing Young Austria every success in its future endeavours, yet at the same time promising the Young Austrians 'that we [...] will make every effort to bring you home'.[35] In the same issue, Fritz Walter himself, now back in Vienna, exhorted the Young Austrians to do their duty by Austria:

The FÖJ is sending you their very best regards and asking again and again: when are you finally coming? Each individual is needed. Every right thinking young Austrian is welcome here. And still more so, our well trained youth leaders. There is work for everyone.[36]

Theodor Prager, the Chairman of the FAM-affiliated National Union of Austrian Students in Great Britain, was instrumental in establishing a new student association on his return, the 'Vereinigung demokratischer Studenten' (Union of Democratic Students [VDS]), which, like the FÖJ, soon turned into a KPÖ-dominated organization.[37] In his memoirs, Prager also recalls the continuing existence, post-war, of the Anglo-Austrian Youth Friendship Association and a visit under its umbrella that a 14-strong English youth party managed to make to Austria in the summer of 1946, swelling the ranks of the FÖJ on a political march (though sporting their own Union Jack).[38]

Continuity is strongly suggested, moreover, by the appointment of Georg Breuer, former editor of *Young Austria* and *Jung-Österreich*, to the editorship of the FÖJ's weekly *Jugend Voran* (formerly also the title of the periodical of the Austrian World Youth Movement in British exile, as well as the imprint of the Young Austria publications series). It tended, in any case, to be the writers and journalists of the Austrian Centre and Free Austrian Movement who achieved a relatively smooth professional transition back to Austria. The Liberal Hermann Ullrich, while resuming his legal career, also served for years as music critic on Ernst Fischer's multi-party paper, *Neues Österreich*. Among the Communists who found a role for themselves in the Austrian Party press were Willi Scholz and Hans Winterberg, who both worked on the Graz paper *Die Wahrheit* (as editor and deputy editor). Similarly, as has already been mentioned, the three *Zeitspiegel* editors all continued as journalists in post-war Austria: Jenö Kostmann took over the Party mouthpiece, *Österreichische Volksstimme,* Hilde Mareiner became editor of the KPÖ's women's paper, *Stimme der Frau,* while Eva Priester edited the KPÖ weekly, *Die Woche.* As *Zeitspiegel* itself proclaimed in its closing number: '*Zeitspiegel* was a good school.'[39]

There were also clear links between the Austrian Centre's Free Austrian Books and the KPÖ's Globus Verlag, founded in Vienna soon after the end of the war. H.E. Goldschmidt, who played a significant role in Austrian exile journalism while in London, took charge of book production for a time within the Globus Verlag; Globus republished several booklets first published by Free Austrian Books or Jugend voran, like Ernst Fischer's *Grillparzer: Ein österreichischer Dichter* (*Grillparzer: An Austrian Writer*) or Hermynia Zur Mühlen's *Kleine Geschichten von großen Dichtern* (*Little Stories by Great Writers*). It also issued as new publications some of the fruits of research undertaken in British exile, such as Eva Priester's *Kurze Geschichte Österreichs* (*Short History of Austria*) (vol. I, 1946; vol. II, 1949) and Albert Fuchs's *Geistige Strömungen in Österreich 1867-1918* (*Intellectual Trends in Austria 1867-1918*) (1949).[40]

If the returning writers could to some degree take up from where they had left off, continuing their work within the German language, so too –

in theory at least – could the actors. Otto Tausig is a prime example here: while still a very young man, Tausig of course had made something of a name for himself in London exile circles with the amateur Young Austrian Players. Studying acting upon his return, Tausig then joined the politically radical Neues Theater in der Scala, which had the support of the Soviet occupying forces, remaining there until 1956 (and, despite being held back for a time in Austria by prominent anti-Communists like Friedrich Torberg and Hans Weigel, eventually becoming well known in all the German-speaking countries). Otto Stark of the Laterndl followed a different path: he also returned to Vienna and studied acting but left in 1949 for the German Democratic Republic. There he, too, made a successful theatrical career for himself.

Several of the Austrian Centre's leading functionaries succeeded in carving out a political career for themselves in post-war Austria – if not at a national level, as they had originally hoped, then certainly in one or other of the Party organizations: in the youth organizations, for instance, or, as in the case of Emmi Walter (who reverted to the name Berta Brichacek), in the Bund Demokratischer Frauen (Federation of Democratic Women). Marie Köstler, too, whose application to rejoin the SPÖ (i.e. Austrian Social Democrats) was rejected, found a role for herself in the Bund Demokratischer Frauen and indeed on the KPÖ's Central Committee. Other former Austrian Centre functionaries who were Central Committee members for varying periods of time were Fritz Walter (Otto Brichacek), Jenö Kostmann, Willi Scholz, Franz West and Leopold Hornik.

It should not be thought, however, that KPÖ membership conferred unalloyed benefits on the returning functionaries. On the contrary, Austrian Communists often experienced great difficulties in the Cold War period as a result of their political affiliation. Tausig's treatment at the hands of anti-Communists has already been mentioned; not until 1971 was he offered a contract at the Burgtheater. In a recent interview, Hilde Mareiner suggested that, as a direct result of her politics, Eva Priester had been 'terribly undervalued' as a lyric poet in post-war Austria.[41] And while Priester remained within the Party for the rest of her life, others took the decision to leave it, often at one of the crisis points in Communist history – 1956, 1968 and so on – or indeed were expelled from it, leading not infrequently to a state of semi-destitution: Willi Scholz's son Anthony has recalled the change in his family's material circumstances from the comfortable life they had led prior to Scholz's differences with the Party, to the loss of accommodation and employment that followed from 1957.[42]

Of course, many more Austrian Centre members decided, for a number of reasons, against going back to Austria after the war, even those who had initially intended otherwise. As mentioned previously, those Laterndl actors who wrote to Ernst Fischer in mid-1945 to express their readiness to play a part in the new Austria[43] chose in the end not to return. Martin Miller, moreover, who of all the Laterndl actors probably established himself most successfully in British theatre and film, appears never to have considered returning. Both he and his wife, the Laterndl actress Hanne Norbert, who had lost many members of her family in the Holocaust, felt 'very welcome and at home in this country [Britain]'.[44]

The losses experienced by Erich Fried, too, in the Holocaust probably influenced his decision not to return to Austria (which otherwise, for a poet deeply rooted in the German language, might have seemed a sensible course of action).[45] However, the politics of the Austrian Centre era played their part here as well: Fried, originally a keen Young Austria and Kommunistischer Jugendverband member, who had moved away from these organizations by 1944,[46] explained his thinking as follows:

> In England during the war, I intended to go back. But little by little I was so disturbed by some of the symptoms of the Stalin era displayed by *those* Austrians there [at the Austrian Centre] with whom I was most closely connected that I did not wish to return to Austria in order to work together *with* them. But I also didn't feel like returning in order to work *against* them. I empathized too strongly with many of them whose good intentions and tragic conflicts I knew from my own experience.[47]

Thus Fried remained in Britain.

There were, of course, also a number of prominent exiled Austrians who, despite the invitations issued by Matejka and others, were for one reason or another overlooked. Egon Wellesz was one of these; when asked by his biographer Franz Edler why he had not returned to Vienna before 1948, and then only as a visitor, Wellesz 'declared quite frankly that in fact nobody had invited him back before'. As Edler comments sharply: 'After 1945, the pupil and close friend of a man of the stature of Guido Adler was not even considered to succeed him at the University of Vienna where he was teaching before the war.[48]

Edler goes on to speculate whether, in some ways at least, Wellesz had not been better off remaining in England. For there were certainly many serious problems associated with returning, not least the desperate material conditions prevailing in Austria and, particularly for Jewish returners, the memories of the Holocaust and the continuing presence of anti-Semitism. Ernst Flesch, for instance, revisiting Vienna for the first time in 1948, took part in a FÖJ rally on the Rathausplatz, only to hear it dismissed afterwards in anti-Semitic terms by a fellow-passenger on the tram.[49] Moreover, as things turned out, the Moscow Declaration, which the Free Austrians had welcomed so joyfully back in 1943, was to prove positively damaging to the interests of the returning exiles: it was Austria's official position as a 'victim of Fascism' that made it possible to delay and indeed disregard issues of reparation and restitution.

It is therefore not surprising that even those former exiles most committed to the ideal of helping to build up a new democratic Austria should sometimes doubt the wisdom of their chosen course of action. Edith Rosenstrauch-Königsberg, for instance, a mainstay of the Austrian Centre and a committed Communist, for whom returning to Austria turned out to offer clear personal advantages in education and intellectual development, nevertheless asks herself whether she did right by her children who were obliged to grow up in Austria as 'children of Jewish émigrés', therefore as 'different'.[50] Similarly Hilde Mareiner, for whom returning was a matter of course, was asked by her British-born daughter why the family had not considered remaining in Britain.[51] Perhaps most telling of all here is the fact that Otto Brichacek, the leading figure in Young Austria, who was instrumental both in London and Vienna in persuading Young Austrians to return home, has since acknowledged the difficulties the returning youth faced in terms of anti-Semitism and anti-émigré feeling: 'Sometimes it was really heartbreaking to see how scandalously people behaved towards the émigrés.' In the light of these disappointments, he has even questioned the rightness of urging young exiles to return and of the tenor of the Young Austria/FÖJ message, conceding: 'We were probably too optimistic in what we told them.'[52]

On the other hand, it should also be recorded that at least two ex-Austrian Centre members, Alice Graber and Lisbeth Dichter, have claimed to have encountered no problems in integrating back into Austrian life and society, nor experiences of anti-Semitism in Austria. Contrary to others' accounts of anti-émigré feeling, Alice Graber was actually invited by the Austrian Ministry of Education to give talks on her emigration experiences to local Viennese schools.[53]

Looking back over 50 years at the Austrian emigration in Britain and its achievements, Walter J. Foster, the long-time General Secretary, later Director, of the Anglo-Austrian Society (former rival to the Austrian Centre and Free Austrian Movement), considered that, unlike his own organization, the Free Austrian Movement had left no lasting influence, while allowing for one notable exception:

> With the end of the war the influence of Free Austria and the Austrian Centre soon came to an end. Very few of them actually returned to Austria and for most the return was bitterly disappointing – they received little appreciation from the Austrian comrades, or from anybody else.

The only lasting effect of Free Austria that I am aware of remains the Documentation Archive of Austrian Resistance, a marvellous, very valuable and astonishingly objective collection.[54]

The Documentation Archive was founded by ex-Young Austria functionary Herbert Steiner in Vienna in 1963 to gather together materials relating to resistance and also to exile; proceeding from small beginnings, it has become a highly respected, indeed a unique research institute.

One further small point that Foster omits to mention is that the Anglo-Austrian Society's sister organization, the Anglo-Austrian Music Society – both groups are still in existence today – actually originated as an organization affiliated to the Free Austrian Movement, thus representing a trace, at least, of the FAM still to be found in Britain today. Moreover, in 1988, to mark the 50th anniversary of the Anschluss, a Young Austria reunion was held in Vienna, bringing together former members who had stayed in Britain with others who had returned. A commemorative booklet, published for the occasion, asserted that while members would undoubtedly have gone their different ways in the last 50 years and others would have died:

> There is one thing that we'll always have in common:
> The memory of our youth, of our Young Austria and of our determination to fight for the re-establishment of a free, independent and democratic Austria.[55]

Since then reunions have continued on a regular basis, both in Austria and in Britain.

This is, admittedly, an insubstantial legacy. But one must recognize that there is a close relationship between the Austrian Centre's lack of lasting influence, on the one hand, and, on the other, the progressive decline in support for the political ideals that inspired its leadership in the 1930s and 1940s.

In conclusion, the achievements of the Austrian Centre reside not in the vestiges of the past but rather in the organization at the height of its vigour and effectiveness in wartime Britain. The propaganda work, for instance, that the Free Austrians undertook in Britain was extraordinarily persuasive; as argued earlier in this study, we contend that the FAM succeeded in exerting an influence – indirect though this may have been – on British policy on Austria and, perhaps, even on the Moscow Declaration. However, the greatest achievements of Free Austria, even if short-term in nature, probably lay in the unrivalled support work carried out on behalf of beleaguered refugees, including the integration of young people, adrift in Britain, into the Austrian exile community, and the dedicated recreation and promotion of Austrian culture in exile. As Franz West would declare, on the first anniversary of the liberation of Vienna, of the work undertaken in exile in the name of Austria:

> One could talk endlessly about this time, about the odysseys, struggles and endeavours of thousands of expelled Austrians. It was a collective fate, a shared fight and a shared suffering [...] At the very time that Goebbels announced to the world that Austria had ceased to exist, the name and the idea of Austria were kept alive through the efforts of our organization [...] We never forgot our homeland and we felt a close affinity with it throughout all the years of enforced separation. We did everything that was in our power for Austria's freedom and independence.[56]

Notes

1 For the return of Austrian exiles, political and others, and their reception, see Helga Embacher's informative study 'Eine Heimkehr gibt es nicht? Remigration nach Österreich', in Claus-Dieter Krohn *et al.*, eds., *Exilforschung: Ein internationales Jahrbuch*, vol. 19: *Jüdische Emigration: Zwischen Assimilation und Verfolgung, Akkulturation und jüdischer Identität*, Munich 2001, pp. 187-209, which draws on a combination of published, unpublished and oral history materials.

2 Jenö Desser, 'Mein Lebenslauf. 8. März 1904 – 8. März 1984', pp. 95-96, unpublished manuscript in private possession of Hans Desser, Vienna.

3 *Austrian Centre Bulletin*, 'Abschiedsnummer', [January 1947], [p. 7].

4 'Bericht über die außerordentliche Generalversammlung des Austrian Centre', *ibid.*

5 See, for example, Brinson interview with Ernst Flesch, London, 9 March 1996, transcript held at the Institute of Germanic & Romance Studies, London.

6 *Austrian Centre Bulletin*, 'Abschiedsnummer', [p. 7].

7 Letter dated 19 January 1947, in private possession of Hans Desser, Vienna.

8 Oral communication from Ernst Flesch, 15 February 2002.

9 Interview with Ernst Flesch, 9 March 1996.

10 Brinson interview with Schlomo Kesten, London, 2 January 2001.

11 On [p. 8].

12 Undated minute, on inside cover, National Archives [NA], HO 213/2088. The security reports are no longer extant.

13 Eva Kolmer to Viktor Matejka, 26 September 1945, Documentation Archive of Austrian Resistance, Vienna [DÖW], 18861/72. Kolmer's initial letter has not been preserved.

14 Kolmer to Matejka, 24 October 1945, *ibid.*

15 See NA, FO 371/46660.

16 See NA, FO 371/55103. The revised list included the names of Georg Knepler and Walter Hollitscher; only Max Schacherl, representing the doctors, appeared on both the original and the revised lists.

17 Kolmer to FAM Executive, 3 January 1946, DÖW 3269/1.

18 By returning to Britain where she had formed a relationship with the leading German Communist Heinz Schmidt, Kolmer was also relinquishing her future prospects in the KPÖ (she had been selected for the post of Secretary to the KPÖ's parliamentary party). She subsequently accompanied Schmidt back to the Soviet Zone of Germany. On this, see Charmian Brinson, 'Eva Kolmer and the Austrian Emigration in Britain', in Anthony Grenville, ed., *German-speaking Exiles in Great Britain: Yearbook of the Research Centre for German and Austrian Exile Studies*, vol. 2 (2000), pp. 162 ff.

19 See, for example, Matejka to Kolmer, 13 February 1946, DÖW 18861/72.

20 Though not always successfully, as the Kokoschka case illustrates (see Viktor Matejka, 'How Arnold Schönberg came to be honored', in Friedrich Stadler and Peter Weibel, eds., *Vertreibung der Vernunft: The Cultural Exodus from Austria*, Vienna/New York 1995, p. 343).

21 See Allied Commission for Austria (British Element) to Foreign Office, 7 November 1945, NA, FO 371/46660.

22 Foreign Office to Allied Commission for Austria, 27 December 1945, NA, FO 371/46661. (In fact, official British permission for Schindel's return was not forthcoming, leading Schindel to return illegally to Austria in March 1946.)

23 War Office (C.A. (D.P.)) for Control Office to Foreign Office, 18 March 1946, NA, FO 371/55105.

24 Ullrich to Matejka, 21 February 1946, DÖW 18861/147.

25 In fact the Vienna Philharmonic did not visit Britain until September 1947, i.e. after the dissolution of the FAM, when it gave concerts in Oxford and London under the auspices of the Anglo-Austrian Music Society.

26 See Kolmer to Matejka, 4 March 1946, DÖW 18861/72.

27 See Jenö Desser, 'Die österreichischen Flüchtlinge und ihre Zukunft', in Jenö Desser, Eva Kolmer, Leopold Spira, *Bericht von der Konferenz über österreichische Flüchtlingsfragen der Free Austrian Movement*, London [1944], p. 2.

28 See 'F.C. West im Radio Wien: Die patriotische Leistung der Weltbewegung', *Zeitspiegel,* 1 December 1945, p. 2.

29 *Zeitspiegel,* 5 January 1946, p. 5.

30 In her letter to the FAM Executive, 3 January 1946, DÖW 3269/1.

31 'Ein Büro der Oesterr. Weltbewegung in Wien', *Zeitspiegel,* 26 January 1946, p. 3.

32 Political Division, Allied Commission for Austria (British Element), Vienna, to German Department, Foreign Office, 25 February 1946, NA, FO 371/55251.

33 Minute (Cullis), 5 March 1946, *ibid.*

34 'F.C. West', Memorandum (R.D.F.O. German & Austrian Section), 11 March 1946, *ibid.*

35 'Auf Wiedersehen in der Heimat', *Jung-Österreich*, 1 December 1945, p. 1.

36 'Fritz Walter schreibt', *ibid*, p. 3.

37 Theodor Prager, *Zwischen London und Moskau: Bekenntnisse eines Revisionisten*, Vienna 1975, p. 77.

38 *Ibid.* pp. 80 f.

39 See F.C. West, 'Abschied vom *Zeitspiegel*', *Zeitspiegel*, 24 August 1946, p. 1.

40 For a complete list of early Globus publications, see *Zehn Jahre Globus Verlag Wien 1945-1955*, Vienna 1955.

41 Brinson interview with Hilde Nürnberger-Mareiner, Vienna, 20 September 2001.

42 Bearman interview with Anthony Scholz, Graz, 7 August 1998.

43 See 'Kunst und Kultur', *Zeitspiegel*, 25 August 1945, p. 6.

44 Brinson interview with Hanne Norbert-Miller, London, 10 December 1995, transcript held at the Institute of Germanic & Romance Studies, London.

45 On this, see Steven W. Lawrie, *Erich Fried: A Writer Without a Country*, New York 1996, pp. 101 ff.

46 Matters came to a head for Fried in October 1943 with the suicide of his friend Hans Schmeier who had suffered as a result of the KJV's dogmatic ideological approach.

47 Erich Fried, 'Die Freiheit, zu sehen, wo man bleibt', lecture held on 6 March 1981 in Vienna at Erster Österreichischer Schriftstellerkongress, reproduced in Volker Kaukoreit and Heinz Lunzer, eds., *Erich Fried und Österreich: Bausteine zu einer Beziehung: Eine Ausstellung der Dokumentationsstelle für neuere österreichische Literatur und der Internationalen Erich Fried-Gesellschaft für Literatur und Sprache im Literaturhaus* (*Zirkular*, Sondernummer 33, November 1992), p. 87.

48 Franz Edler, ed., *Egon Wellesz: Leben und Werk*, Vienna/Hamburg 1981, p. 266.

49 Interview with Ernst Flesch, 9 March 1996.

50 Edith Rosenstrauch-Königsberg, 'Die Gegenwart ist die Vergangenheit von morgen', in Walter Hinderer *et al.*, eds., *Altes Land, neues Land: Verfolgung, Exil, biografisches Schreiben: Texte zum Erich Fried Symposium 1999* (*Zirkular*, Sondernummer 56, October 1999), pp. 83-84.

51 Interview with Hilde Nürnberger-Mareiner, 20 September 2001.

52 Bearman interview with Otto Brichacek, Vienna, 10 August 1999.

53 Bearman interviews with Alice Graber and Lisbeth Dichter, Vienna, 11 August 1998 and 12 August 1998.

54 Walter J. Foster, London, to Reinhard Müller, Graz, 15 October 1997 (in the private possession of the recipient). .

55 *Young Austria in Großbritannien: Wiedersehenstreffen anläßlich des 50. Jahrestages der Besetzung Österreichs, Wien, im Mai 1988*, [p. i].

56 West, speaking on Radio Wien, as given in Eva Kolmer, *Das Austrian Centre: 7 Jahre österreichische Gemeinschaftsarbeit*, London [1946], p. 36.

NOTES ON THE AUTHORS

Marietta Bearman, born in Austria, living in England since 1970. Studied History and English in Vienna. PhD on 'Austria and its History in the Works and Policies of Winston Churchill'. 1983-2006 Lecturer in German at Imperial College London. Member of the Research Centre for German and Austrian Exile Studies, University of London.

Charmian Brinson, studied German in London, now Professor of German at Imperial College London. Founder member of the Research Centre for German and Austrian Exile Studies. Publications, largely on political exile and women in exile, include *The Strange Case of Dora Fabian and Mathilde Wurm: A Study of German Political Exiles in London during the 1930s* (1997).

Richard Dove, studied Modern Languages at Oxford, now Emeritus Professor of German at the University of Greenwich. Founder member of the Research Centre for German and Austrian Exile Studies. Publications, largely on literary exile, include *He was a German: A Biography of Ernst Toller* (1990) and *Journey of No Return: Five German-Speaking Literary Exiles in London 1933-45* (2000).

Anthony Grenville, son of Austrian refugees, studied Modern Languages at Oxford. Lectured in German at Reading, Bristol and Westminster Universities, now editor of the journal of the Association of Jewish Refugees. Secretary of the Research Centre for German and Austrian Exile Studies. Publications include *Continental Britons: Jewish Refugees from Nazi Europe* (2002).

Jennifer Taylor, studied German in Bristol and Berlin. PhD on 'The Depiction of the Third Reich in German Drama'. Freelance researcher specializing in German-speaking exiles in Great Britain. Publications include articles on BBC radio propaganda, exile organizations (for instance, Club 1943) and the exile press. Founder member of the Research Centre for German and Austrian Exile Studies.

BIBLIOGRAPHY

BOOKS AND PAMPHLETS

Altner, Manfred, *Hermynia zur Mühlen: Eine Biographie*, Berne 1997

Amann, Klaus, *PEN: Politik, Emigration, Nationalsozialismus: Ein österreichischer Schriftstellerklub*, Vienna 1982

Austrians in Great Britain, London: Austrian Centre, 1943

Bauer, Stefan, *Ein böhmischer Jude im Exil*, Munich 1995

Bearman, Marietta/Brinson, Charmian, "'Jugend voran'': Sieben Jahre Junges Österreich in Großbritannien', in Crohn, Claus-Dieter, *et al.*, (eds.), *Exilforschung: Ein internationales Jahrbuch*, vol. 24: *Kindheit und Jugend im Exil – ein Generationenthema*, Munich 2006, pp. 150-67

Berghaus, Günter (ed.), *Theatre and Film in Exile: German Artists in Britain 1933-1945*, Oxford/New York/Munich 1989

Bolbecher, Siglinde *et al.*, eds., *Zwischenwelt 4: Literatur und Kultur des Exils in Großbritannien*, Vienna 1995

Breuer, Georg, *Rückblende: Ein Leben für eine Welt mit menschlichem Antlitz*, Vienna 2003

Brinson, Charmian, 'Eva Kolmer and the Austrian emigration in Britain, 1938-1946', in Grenville, Anthony (ed.), *German-speaking Exiles in Great Britain: Yearbook of the Research Centre for German and Austrian Exile Studies* (vol. 2), Amsterdam/Atlanta GA 2000, pp. 143-69

Brinson, Charmian/Dove, Richard/Malet, Marian/Tayor, Jennifer (eds.), *England? Aber wo liegt es? Deutsche und österreichische Emigranten in Großbritannien 1933-1945*, Munich 1996

Brinson, Charmian/Dove, Richard/Taylor, Jennifer (eds.), *Immortal Austria? Austrians in Exile in Britain: Yearbook of the Research Centre for German and Austrian Exile Studies* (vol. 8), Amsterdam/Atlanta GA 2006

Das Free Austrian Movement in Großbritannien und der Wiederaufbau Österreichs, London: Free Austrian Movement in Great Britain, 1943

Desser, Jenö/Kolmer, Eva/Spira, Leopold, *Bericht von der Konferenz über österreichische Flüchtlingsfragen des Free Austrian Movement*, London: [Free Austrian Movement], [1944]

Desser, Jenö, 'Mein Lebenslauf 8. März 1904–8. März 1984, unpublished ms. [1984]

Desser, Jenö, *Vom Ghetto zur Freiheit: Die Zukunft der Juden im befreiten Österreich*, London 1945

Dokumentationsarchiv des österreichischen Widerstandes/ Dokumentationsstelle für neuere österreichische Literatur (eds.), *Österreicher im Exil 1934 bis 1945: Protokoll des internationalen Symposiums zur Erforschung des österreichischen Exils von 1934 bis 1945, abgehalten vom 3. bis 6. Juni 1945 in Wien*, Vienna 1977

Dove, Richard, *Journey of No Return: Five German-speaking Literary Exiles in Britain 1933-1945*, London 2000

Edler, Franz, *Egon Wellesz: Leben und Werk*, Vienna/Hamburg 1981

Eicher, Thomas, *et al.*, (eds.), *Kontinuitäten und Brüche: Österreichs literarischer Wiederaufbau nach 1945*, Oberhausen 2006

Embacher, Helga, 'Eine Heimkehr gibt es nicht? Remigration nach Österreich', in Krohn, Claus-Dieter *et al.*, (eds.), *Exilforschung: Ein internationales Jahrbuch,* vol. 19: *Jüdische Emigration: Zwischen Assimilation und Verfolgung, Akkulturation und jüdischer Identität*, Munich 2001

Feinberg, Anat, 'Das Laterndl in London 1939-1945' in *German Life and Letters*, 37/3 (1984), pp. 211-17

First Annual Report of the Austrian Centre, London: Council of Austrians in Great Britain at the Austrian Centre, 1940

Fischer, Ernst, *The Rebirth of My Country*, London: Free Austrian Books [1944]

Five Years Hitler Over Austria (Special Edition *Austrian News*), London: Free Austrian Movement in Great Britain, 1943

Landeskonferenz des Free Austrian Movement, London: Free Austrian Movement in Great Britain, [1943]

[Fried, Erich], *They Fight in the Dark: The Story of Austria's Youth*, London: Young Austria in Great Britain, [1944]

Fried, Erich, 'Ring-Rund', in *Kunst und Wissen: Eine Materialsammlung für Veranstaltungen*, no. 20, London [1941], pp. 20-24

Fuchs, Albert, *Ein Sohn aus gutem Hause*, London: Free Austrian Books, 1943 (republished Vienna 2004)

Fuchs, Albert, *Über österreichische Kultur: Vortrag gehalten auf der Kulturkonferenz des PEN, London, 1942*, London: Austrian Centre, [1942]

Fuchs, Albert (ed.), *Die Vertriebenen: Dichtung der Emigration*, London: Free German League of Culture/Austrian Centre/Young Czechoslovakia, 1941

Fuchs, Albert, *Geistige Strömungen in Österreich*, Vienna 1949

Hansard, 5th Series, *Parliamentary Debates*, House of Commons/House of Lords, 1938-1946

Hausjell, Fritz/Langenbucher, Wolfgang, *Vertriebene Wahrheit: Journalismus aus dem Exil*, Vienna 1995

Heilig, Bruno, *Men Crucified*, London 1941

Heimat Österreich, London: Free Austrian Movement, [1945]

Herman, Jury, *Viel Glück: Aus dem Tagebuch einer Soviet WAAF*, trans. Eva Priester, London: Free Austrian Books, 1943

Herz, Peter, *Gestern war ein schöner Tag*, Vienna 1987

Hinderer, Walter, et al. (eds.), *Altes Land, neues Land: Verfolgung, Exil, biografisches Schreiben: Texte zum Erich Fried Symposium 1999* (*Zirkular*, Sondernummer 56), Vienna October 1999

Hippen, Reinhard, *Satire gegen Hitler: Kabarett im Exil*, Zurich 1986

Hirschfeld, Gerhard (ed.), *Exile in Great Britain: Refugees from Hitler's Germany*, Leamington Spa 1984

Hornik, Anna, *This is Austria: The Story of a Beautiful Country*, London: Austrian Centre/Young Austria, 1942

Hollitscher, Walter, *Rassentheorie? 6 Lehrbriefe an österreichische Biologielehrer*, London: Jugend voran (Jugendführerschule des Jungen Österreich), 1944

Kaukoreit, Volker, *Vom Exil bis zum Protest gegen den Krieg in Vietnam: Frühe Stationen des Lyrikers Erich Fried: Werk und Biographie 1938-1966*, Darmstadt 1991

Kaukoreit, Volker/Lunzer, Heinz (eds.), *Erich Fried und Österreich: Bausteine zu einer Beziehung: Eine Ausstellung der Dokumentationsstelle für neuere österreichische Literatur und der Internationalen Erich Fried-Gesellschaft für Literatur und Sprache im Literaturhaus* (*Zirkular*, Sondernummer 33), Vienna November 1992

Kaukoreit, Volker/Thunecke, Jörg, *126 Westbourne Terrace: Erich Fried im Londoner Exil (1938-1945)*, Vienna 2001

Klahr, Alfred, 'Zur nationalen Frage in Österreich' in Klahr, Alfred, *Zur österreichischen Nation*, Vienna 1997

Knepler, Georg, *Five Years of the Austrian Centre*, London: Free Austrian Books, [1944]

Kolmer, Eva, *Das Austrian Centre: 7 Jahre österreichische Gemeinschaftsarbeit*, London: Austrian Centre, [1946]

Kostmann, Jenö, *Restive Austria*, London: Austrian Centre/Young Austria, [1942]

Lafitte, François, *The Internment of Aliens*, Harmondsworth 1940 (republished London 1988)

Lawrie, Steven W., *Erich Fried: A Writer Without a Country*, New York 1996

Maimann, Helene, *Politik im Wartesaal: Österreichische Exilpolitik in Großbritannien 1938-1945*, Vienna/Cologne/Graz 1975

Mareiner, Hilde, '*Zeitspiegel*': *Eine österreichische Stimme gegen Hitler*, Vienna / Frankfurt a. M./Zurich, 1967

Muchitsch, Wolfgang (ed.), *Österreicher im Exil. Großbritannien 1938-1945: Eine Dokumentation*, Vienna 1992

Muchitsch, Wolfgang, *Mit Spaten, Waffen und Worten: Die Einbindung österreichischer Flüchtlinge in die britischen Kriegsanstrengungen 1939-1949*, Vienna 1992

Muchitsch, Wolfgang, 'The Cultural Policy of Austrian Refugee Organizations in Great Britain', in Timms, Edward/Robertson, Ritchie (eds.), *Austrian Exodus: The Creative Achievements of Refugees from National Socialism* (*Austrian Studies*, vol. 6), Edinburgh 1995, pp. 22-40

Müller, Reinhard (ed.), *Destination England: Austrian Exile in Britain 1938-45*, transl. J.M. Ritchie, London: Austrian Cultural Institute, 1999

Mut: Gedichte junger Österreicher, London: Jugend voran, 1943

Pass, Walter/Scheit, Gerhard/Svoboda, Wilhelm, *Orpheus im Exil: Die Vertreibung der österreichischen Musik von 1938 bis 1945*, Vienna 1995

Patsch, Sylvia, *Österreichische Schriftsteller im Exil in Großbritannien: Ein Kapitel vergessene österreichische Literatur*, Vienna/Munich 1985

Prager, Theodor, *Zwischen London und Moskau: Bekenntnisse eines Revisionisten*, Vienna 1975

Priester, Eva, *Austria – Gateway to Germany*, London: Free Austrian Books, [1943]

Pross, Stefan, *In London treffen wir uns wieder: Vier Spaziergänge durch ein vergessenes Kapitel deutscher Kulturgeschichte*, Berlin 2000

Raab Hansen, Jutta, *NS-verfolgte Musiker in England: Spuren deutscher und österreichischer Flüchtlinge in der britischen Musikkultur*, Hamburg 1996

Rösler, Walter, 'Aspekte des deutschsprachigen Exilkabaretts 1933-45', in *Exiltheater und Exildramatik 1933-1945*, Maintal 1991, pp. 283-93

Scheit, Gerhard, 'Zwei Arten, das Verhältnis von Musik und Politik zu beschreiben', in *Aufrisse*, vol. 5, 2 (1984), pp. 44-47

Scheu, Frederick [Friederich], *Die Emigrationspresse der Sozialisten 1938-1945*, Vienna/Frankfurt a. M./Zurich 1968

Scheu, Frederick [Friederich], *The early days of the Anglo-Austrian Society*, London 1969

Scholz, Wilhelm, *Ein Weg ins Leben: Das neue Österreich und die Judenfrage*, London: Free Austrian Books, 1943

Seeber-Weyrer, Ursula, '"Ergötze dich am längst nicht mehr Vorhandenen": Österreich-Bilder des Exils', in Prutsch, Ursula/ Lechner, Manfred (eds.), *Das ist Österreich: Innensichten und Außensichten*, Vienna 1997, pp. 123-40

Seyfert, Michael, *Im Niemandsland: Deutsche Exilliteratur in britischer Internierung: Ein unbekanntes Kapitel der Kulturgeschichte des Zweiten Weltkriegs*, Berlin 1984

Soyfer, Jura, *Vom Paradies zum Weltuntergang*, ed. by Otto Tausig, Vienna 1947

Spiel, Hilde, *Die hellen und die finsteren Zeiten: Erinnerungen 1911-1946*, Munich/ Leipzig 1989

Spitz, Rudolf, 'Das Laterndl in London', in *Theater im Exil 1933-45*, exhibition catalogue, Berlin 1973, pp. 28-30

Stadler, Friedrich/Weibel, Peter (eds.), *Vertreibung der Vernunft: The Cultural Exodus from Austria*, Vienna/New York 1995

Stadler, Friedrich, *Vertriebene Vernunft*, vol. II: *Emigration und Exil österreichischer Wissenschaft*, Vienna/Munich 1988

Stanley, G.D.D., 'British Policy and the Austrian Question 1938-1948', unpublished doctoral dissertation, London 1974

Steiner, Herbert, *Die Organisation einer Jugendbewegung: Organisationsformen und Erfahrungen des 'Jungen Österreich in Großbritannien'*, London: Jugend voran (Jugendführerschule des Jungen Österreich), [1945]

Tausig, Otto, *Kasperl, Kummerl, Jud: Eine Lebensgeschichte*, Vienna 2005

Thunecke, Jörg, '"Doch wer den Mut verliert ist besser tot!"': Young Austria and the Problem of Political Poetry', in Timms, Edward/Robertson, Ritchie (eds.), *Austrian Exodus: The Creative Achievements of Refugees from National Socialism (Austrian Studies*, vol. 6), Edinburgh 1995, pp. 41-58

Vogelmann, Karl, 'Die Propaganda der österreichischen Emigration in der Sowjetunion für einen selbständigen Nationalstaat (1938-1945)', unpublished doctoral dissertation, Vienna 1973

Wallace, Ian (ed.), *Aliens – Uneingebürgerte: German and Austrian Writers in Exile*, Amsterdam/Atlanta GA, 1994

Walter, Emmi, *Die soziale und wirtschaftliche Lage der österreichischen Jugend unter der deutschen Fremdherrschaft*, London: Jugend voran, 1944

Walter, Fritz, 'Die Erziehung der Jugend im neuen Österreich', in *Probleme der Erziehung im neuen demokratischen Österreich: Bericht über die Erziehungskonferenz des Jungen Österreich in Großbritannien'*, London: Jugend voran, 1944

Walter, Fritz, *Youth in the Reconstruction of Liberated Europe: Report on Youth Activities in France, Belgium, Holland, Italy, Yugoslavia, Poland, Greece, Bulgaria*, London: Jugend voran, 1945

Weidle, Barbara/Seeber, Ursula (eds.), *Anna Mahler: Ich bin in mir selbst zu Hause*, Bonn 2004

Weigl, Hans (ed.), *Weit von Wo: Kabarett im Exil*, Vienna 1994

Weinert, Willi, 'Zum Leben von Albert Fuchs', in *Die Alfred Klahr Gesellschaft und ihr Archiv: Beiträge zur österreichischen Geschichte des 20. Jahrhunderts*, Vienna 2000, pp. 259-76

West, F.C., *Zurück oder nicht zurück?*, London: Free Austrian Books, [1942]

Wipplinger, Erna, 'Österreichisches Exiltheater in Großbritannien (1938 bis 1945)', unpublished doctoral dissertation, Vienna 1984

Wipplinger, Erna, 'Zünden soll d'Latern': Österreichisches Exiltheater in Großbritannien', in *Wespennest*, 56 (1984), pp. 29-38

Young Austria in Großbritannien: Wiedersehenstreffen anläßlich des 50. Jahrestages der Besetzung Österreichs, Wien im Mai 1988, Vienna 1988.

Zwischen gestern und morgen: Neue österreichische Gedichte, London: Austrian Centre/Young Austria, 1942

NEWSPAPERS AND JOURNALS

Austrian Medical Bulletin
Austrian News/Austrian Centre News/Austrian Centre/Austrian Centre Bulletin
Austrian News
Daily Herald
Evening Standard
Frau in Arbeit: Periodical of the Working Refugee Woman
Jugend voran
Kulturblätter des FAM/Kulturelle Schriftenreihe des Free Austrian Movement
London Information

Manchester Guardian
New Statesman and Nation
News Chronicle
Österreichische Jugend/Junges Österreich/Young Austria/Jung-Österreich
Österreichische Kulturblätter
Österreichische Nachrichten
Österreichspiegel
PEN News
Picture Post
Rundbrief: Funktionär-Organ des Jungen Österreich
The Music Review
The Spectator
The Times
Zeitspiegel
Die Zeitung

INDEX